*Praise for Simon Critchley's*

# THE BOOK OF
# DEAD PHILOSOPHERS

"A provocative and engrossing invitation to think about the human condition and what philosophy can and can't do to illuminate it." —*Financial Times*

"Concise, witty and oddly heartening."
　　　　　—*New Statesman* (A 2008 Book of the Year)

"Full of wonderful absurdities. . . . Extremely enjoyable."
　　　　　—*The Independent* (London)

"Simon Critchley is probably the sharpest and most lucid philosopher writing in English today."
　　　　　—Tom McCarthy, author of *Remainder*

"Ingenious. . . . Packed with great stories."
　　　　　—*Time Out London*

"A tremendous addition to an all too sparse literature. . . . Brilliant, entertaining, informative."
　　　　　—*New Humanist* (UK)

"A fabulous concept. . . . [Critchley writes] with dash, humour and an eye for scandalous detail."
　　　　　—*The Vancouver Sun*

"[Critchley is] among the hippest of (living) British philosophers." —The Book Bench, *newyorker.com*

"Surprisingly good fun. . . . Worthy of the prose writings of Woody Allen. . . . Not the least of the pleasures of this odd book, lighthearted and occasionally facetious as it is, is that in surveying a chronological history of philosophers it provides a sweep through the entire history of philosophy itself." —*The Irish Times*

"Critchley has a lightness of touch, a nimbleness of thought, and a mocking graveyard humour that puts you in mind of Hamlet with a skull." —*The Independent on Sunday* (London)

"*The Book of Dead Philosophers* is something of a magic trick: on the surface an amusing and bemused series of blackout sketches of philosophers' often rather humble and/or brutal deaths, it actually is an utterly serious, deeply moving, cant-free attempt to return us to the gorgeousness of material existence, to our creatureliness, to our clownish bodies, to the only immortality available to us (immersion in the moment). I absolutely love this book." —David Shields, author of *The Thing About Life Is That One Day You'll Be Dead*

"[Critchley] brings the deaths of his predecessors to life in 190 or so energetic bursts." —*The Sunday Herald* (UK)

"Critchley gives the nonspecialist, the reader for pleasure, a point of access into complex material." —*The Sydney Morning Herald* (Australia)

"Simon Critchley's book looks death in the face and draws from the encounter the breath of life. No philosopher can pull a more welcome rabbit out of a more forbidding hat and Mr. Critchley does so in a prose style that is as deft as his intelligence." —Lewis Lapham, editor of *Lapham's Quarterly*

*Simon Critchley*

# THE BOOK OF
# DEAD PHILOSOPHERS

Simon Critchley is Professor and Chair of Philosophy at the New School for Social Research in New York. He is the author of many books, most recently, *On Heidegger's* Being and Time and *Infinitely Demanding: Ethics of Commitment, Politics of Resistance*. *The Book of Dead Philosophers* was written on a hill overlooking Los Angeles, where he was a scholar at the Getty Research Institute. He lives in Brooklyn.

# THE BOOK OF
# DEAD PHILOSOPHERS

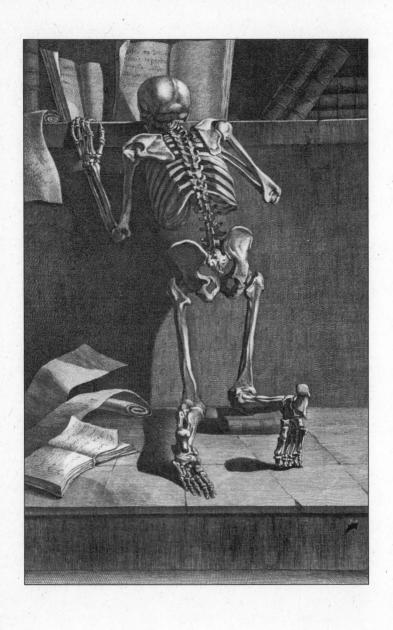

*The*

# BOOK

*of*

# DEAD

# PHILOSOPHERS

*Simon Critchley*

**VINTAGE BOOKS**

*A Division of Random House, Inc.*

*New York*

FIRST VINTAGE BOOKS EDITION, FEBRUARY 2009

*Copyright © 2008 by Simon Critchley*

All rights reserved. Published in the United States
by Vintage Books, a division of Random House, Inc.,
New York, and in Canada by Random House of Canada
Limited, Toronto. Originally published in hardcover in
Great Britain by Granta Books, London, in 2008.

Vintage and colophon are registered trademarks of
Random House, Inc.

Illustration credits appear on page 266.

Library of Congress Cataloging-in-Publication Data:
Critchley, Simon, 1960–
The book of dead philosophers / Simon Critchley.
p.   cm.
Includes bibliographical references.
ISBN 978-0-307-39043-1
1. Philosophers—Death.   2. Philosophers—Anecdotes.
I. Title.
B72.C68 2009
190—DC22
[B] 2008047719

*Author photograph © John Simmons*
*Book design by Rebecca Aidlin*

www.vintagebooks.com

Printed in the United States of America
10  9  8  7  6  5  4  3  2

*If I were a maker of books, I would make a register, with comments, of various deaths. He who would teach men to die would teach them to live.*

MONTAIGNE,
"That to Philosophize Is to Learn How to Die"

# CONTENTS

*xi*

# INTRODUCTION

This book begins from a simple assumption: what defines human life in our corner of the planet at the present time is not just a fear of death, but an overwhelming *terror* of annihilation. This is a terror both of the inevitability of our demise with its future prospect of pain and possibly meaningless suffering, and the horror of what lies in the grave other than our body nailed into a box and lowered into the earth to become wormfood.

We are led, on the one hand, to deny the fact of death and to run headlong into the watery pleasures of forgetfulness, intoxication and the mindless accumulation of money and possessions. On the other hand, the terror of annihilation leads us blindly into a belief in the magical forms of salvation and promises of immortality offered by certain varieties of traditional religion and many New Age (and some rather older age) sophistries. What we seem to seek is either the transitory consolation of momentary oblivion or a miraculous redemption in the afterlife.

It is in stark contrast to our drunken desire for evasion and escape that the ideal of the philosophical death has such sobering power. As Cicero writes, and this sentiment was axiomatic for most ancient philosophy and echoes down the ages, "To philosophize is to learn how to die." The main task of philosophy, in this view, is to prepare us for death, to provide a kind of training for death, the cultivation of an attitude towards our finitude that faces—and faces down—the terror of annihilation without offering promises of an afterlife. Montaigne writes of the custom of the Egyptians who, during their elaborate feasts, caused a great image of death—often a human skeleton—to be brought into the banquet hall accompanied by a man who called out to them, "Drink and be merry, for when you are dead you will be like this."

Montaigne derives the following moral from his Egyptian anecdote: "So I have formed the habit of having death continually present, not merely in my imagination, but in my mouth."

To philosophize, then, is to learn to have death in your mouth, in the words you speak, the food you eat and the drink that you imbibe. It is in this way that we might begin to confront the terror of annihilation, for it is, finally, the fear of death that enslaves us and leads us towards either temporary oblivion or the longing for immortality. As Montaigne writes, "He who has learned how to die has unlearned how to be a slave." This is an astonishing conclusion: the premeditation of death is nothing less than the forethinking of freedom. Seeking to escape death, then, is to remain unfree and run away from ourselves. The denial of death is self-hatred.

It was a commonplace in antiquity that philosophy provides the wisdom necessary to confront death. That is, the philosopher looks death in the face and has the strength to say that it is nothing. The original exemplar for such a philosophical death is Socrates, to whom I will return in detail below. In the *Phaedo* he insists that the philosopher should be cheerful in the face of death. Indeed, he goes further and says that "true philosophers make dying their profession." If one has learnt to die philosophically, then the fact of our demise can be faced with self-control, serenity and courage.

This Socratic wisdom finds even more radical expression several centuries later in the Stoicism of Seneca, who writes that "He will live badly who does not know how to die well." The philosopher, for him, enjoys a long life because he doesn't worry over its shortness. What Stoicism tries to teach is "something great and supreme and nearly divine," namely a tranquillity and calm in the face of death.

Seneca knew whereof he spoke, having been all but condemned to death by Caligula in AD 39 and banished by Claudius on a charge of adultery with the emperor's niece in 41. Eventually, when he was the most important intellectual figure in the Roman world and one of its most powerful administrators, he was forced to commit suicide by Nero in 65. He writes, prophetically,

> I did know in what riotous company Nature had enclosed me. Often has the crash of a falling building echoed beside me. Many who were linked to me through the forum and the senate and everyday conversation have been carried off in a night, which has severed the hands once joined in friendship. Should it surprise me if the perils which have always roamed around me should some day reach me?

Now, although the actual manner of philosophers' deaths is not always as noble as Socrates, and the vile circumstances of Seneca's botched suicide will be described below, I want to defend the ideal of the philosophical death. In a world where the only metaphysics in which people believe is either money or medical science and where longevity is prized as an unquestioned good, I do not deny that this is a difficult ideal to defend. Yet, it is my belief that philosophy can teach a readiness for death without which any conception of contentment, let alone happiness, is illusory. Strange as it might sound, my constant concern in these seemingly morbid pages is the meaning and possibility of happiness.

Very simply stated, this is a book about how philosophers have died and what we can learn from philosophy about the appropriate attitude to death and dying. My hope, to echo the epigraph from Montaigne, is "to make a register, with comments, of various deaths." My wager is that in learning how to die we might also be taught how to live.

Allow me a caveat and a word on the form of *The Book of Dead Philosophers*. The book comprises short, sometimes very short,

entries on various philosophers, cataloguing the manner of
their demise and often linking this to their central ideas. The
entries run from a sentence or two up to a short essay in the
case of philosophers of great importance or whom I particularly value. For example, the reader will find more extensive
and recurring discussions of figures like Socrates, Diogenes,
Epicurus, Lucretius, Zhuangzi, Seneca, Augustine, Aquinas,
Montaigne, Descartes, Locke, Spinoza, Hume, Rousseau,
Hegel, Schopenhauer and Nietzsche. I have also given a lot
of attention to twentieth-century thinkers like Wittgenstein,
Heidegger, Ayer, Foucault and Derrida. The entries are listed
chronologically from Thales in the sixth century BC up to the
present. They are divided into a series of chapters that reflect
the major epochs in the history of philosophy. However, my
chronology will not be exact and the philosophers will not be
treated in a strict temporal succession, particularly when it
suits my purposes to do otherwise.

I have not attempted to describe how *every* significant
philosopher died. The learned eye will see some gaps and will
doubtless disagree with many of my choices. Some philosophers have been omitted either because I could find nothing
particularly interesting to say about their deaths—such as
Frege, Gilbert Ryle or J. L. Austin—or because their deaths felt
too close—such as Richard Rorty, who died on 8 June, 2007, as
I was finishing this book. Simply stated, I have focused on the
philosophers who appeal to me. But that's already quite a few,
around 190.

As well as trying to cover many major and minor figures
in the history of Western philosophy, including a hopefully
surprising number of women philosophers, the reader will
find a smattering of saints, classical Chinese philosophers and
medieval Islamic and Jewish philosophers, some of whom
held fascinating views on death (and a few of whom died spec-
tacularly).

The entries can be read either from beginning to end or
by dipping in and out. I have no objection to the book being
used as a miscellany, but my hope is that, if read from beginning to end, a cumulative series of themes will emerge that

add up to a specific argument about how philosophy might teach one how to die and, by implication, how to live.

Matisse was once asked if he believed in God. He answered, "I do when I'm working." Let's just say that this book has been a lot of work. Although my research has involved marshalling a vast array of literary sources, I have decided not to clutter the text with footnotes. The reader will have to trust me. Those who want to follow up my sources and discover more for themselves can use the annotated bibliography at the end. Those seeking a little more context and a few more signposts on the history of philosophy and philosophers are encouraged to look at the final pages of this introduction.

# Learning How to Die—Socrates

Philosophy is conventionally considered to begin with the trial and death of Socrates, who was condemned to death on the trumped-up charges of Meletus, Anytus and Lycon. There were two charges levelled against him: corrupting the youth of Athens and failing to revere the city's gods. In Plato's account, there is also a third charge, namely that Socrates introduced his own "new" gods. Whatever the truth of the latter accusation, Socrates always claimed to follow his own *daimon*, what Cicero called a "divine something": a personal god or spirit, what we might be inclined to think of as conscience. However, Socrates' *daimon* was not some "inner voice," but an external sign or command that would suddenly cause him to stop in his tracks.

Socrates' death is sometimes seen as the political show trial and execution of an innocent dissident at the hands of a tyrannical state. However, it should not be forgotten that Socrates counted some pretty reactionary characters among his followers. Socrates' pupil Critias was leader of the Thirty Tyrants' anti-democratic reign of terror in 404–3 BC. It should also be remembered that, according to Xenophon, the only time that Socrates advised one of his disciples to enter politics, the recipient was a reluctant Charmides, another of the Thirty Tyrants who died on the battlefield alongside Critias. Finally, Alcibiades, the handsome, charismatic and dissolute aristocrat who bursts drunk into Plato's *Symposium*, defected from Athens to the enemy on two occasions: once to the Spartans and once again to the Persians. Socrates, especially in the version given by Plato in *The Republic*, is hardly a fan of democracy, and his teaching could justifiably be seen as fomenting disillusion with democracy among right-wing aristocrats.

Socrates' death is a tragedy in many acts. Indeed, Hegel writes that Socrates' trial is the moment when tragedy leaves the stage and fully enters political life, becoming the tragedy of the decay and collapse of Athens itself.

Plato devotes no fewer than four dialogues to the events surrounding Socrates' trial and death (*Euthypho, Apology, Crito* and *Phaedo*), and in addition we have the *Memorabilia* and *Apology* of Xenophon. In the *Phaedo*, which is commonly seen as the latest of Plato's four dialogues, Socrates' words become suffused with Plato's Pythagorean belief in the immortality of the soul. But the earlier *Apology* gives a rather different view of the matter. Socrates says that death is not at all an evil, but on the contrary a good thing. That said, death is one of two possibilities:

Either it is annihilation, and the dead have no consciousness of anything; or, as we are told, it is really a change: a migration of the soul from this place to another.

But Socrates insists that, regardless of which of these possibilities is true, death is not something to be feared. If it is annihilation, then it is a long, dreamless sleep, and what could be more pleasant than that? If it is a passage to another place, namely Hades, then that is also something to be wished as we will meet old friends and Greek heroes and be able to converse with Homer, Hesiod and the rest of the immortal company.

There is another story told of Socrates, that when a man told him, "The Thirty Tyrants have condemned you to death," he replied, "And nature them." Socrates likewise turns the table on his accusers and jury, asserting that they should face death with confidence. Having been condemned to death, Socrates concludes his speech with the following extraordinary words:

Now it is time that we were going, I to die and you to live;
but which of us has the happier prospect is unknown to
anyone but God.

These words encapsulate the classical philosophical attitude towards death: it is nothing to be feared. On the contrary, it is that in relation to which life must be lived.
Socrates' enigmatic last words—"Crito, we ought to offer a
cock to Asclepius"—articulate the view that death is the cure
for life. Asclepius was the god of healing, and the offering of
a sacrifice was something that people suffering from an ailment would offer before sleep in the hope of waking up
cured. Thus, death is a curative slumber.

What must be emphasized in Socrates' attitude towards
death in the *Apology* is that although death might be either
of the two possibilities discussed, we do not *know* which one
is right. That is, philosophy is learning how to die, but that
which is learnt is not *knowledge*. This is an essential point.
What philosophy teaches is not some quantifiable sum of
knowledge that can be bought or sold like a commodity in
the marketplace. Such is the business of the Sophists—
Gorgias, Prodicus, Protagoras, Hippias and the rest—whose
views Socrates relentlessly dismantles in Plato's dialogues.
Although Socrates is himself described as a Sophist by the
lampooning Aristophanes in *The Clouds*, the Sophists were a
class of professional educators that appeared in the fifth century BC and who offered instruction to young men and
public displays of eloquence in return for a fee. The
Sophists were masters of eloquence, "honey-tongued," as
Philostratus writes, who travelled from city to city, offering
knowledge in exchange for money.

In opposition to the charismatic and often colourfully
dressed Sophists who come promising knowledge, the poorly
attired and rather ugly Socrates only seems to embody a
weak paradox. On the one hand, Socrates is declared the
wisest man in Greece by the Oracle at Delphi. On the other
hand, Socrates always insists that he knows nothing. How
therefore can the wisest man in the world know nothing?

This seeming paradox evaporates when we learn to distinguish wisdom from knowledge and become lovers of wisdom, in other words, philosophers.

For example, in *The Republic*, the object of inquiry is justice. "What is justice?" asks Socrates and various more or less conventional views of justice are discussed, dismantled and dismissed. But in the central books of *The Republic*, Socrates does not give his interlocutors an answer to the question of justice or some theory of justice. Instead, we are given a series of stories — most famously the myth of the cave — that indicate to us *indirectly* the matter at hand. The path to justice, we are told, is only to be followed by orienting the soul towards the Good, which is precisely not a matter of knowledge but a work of love. Philosophy begins, then, with the questioning of certainties in the realm of knowledge and the cultivation of a love of wisdom. Philosophy is erotic, not just epistemic.

There has never been a more important time to emphasize this distinction between philosophy and sophistry. We are surrounded by countless new sophistries. Televangelists offer authoritative knowledge of the true word of God and perform miraculous cures in exchange for appropriate donations to the cause. An entire New Age industry has arisen where Knowledge (capital K) of something called Self (capital S) is traded in expensive, brightly coloured wrappings. I am writing these lines on West Sunset Boulevard, Los Angeles, not far from the palatial "Self-Realization Center," complete with lavish gardens, a lake shrine, Hindu kitsch architecture and expensive programmes for improving spiritual self-knowledge and communion with God.

I think it is fair to say that Western societies, and not just Western societies, are experiencing a deep meaning gap that risks broadening into an abyss. This gap is being filled by various forms of obscurantism that conspire to promote the belief that, first, such a thing as self-knowledge is attainable; second, it comes with a price tag; and third, it is completely consistent with the pursuit of wealth, pleasure and personal salvation. By contrast, Socrates never claimed to know, never promised knowledge to others and, crucially, never accepted a fee.

What this desire for certainty betrays is a profound terror of death and an overwhelming anxiety to be quite sure that death is not the end, but the passage to the afterlife. True, if eternal life has an admission price, then who wouldn't be prepared to pay it? By way of contrast, it is striking to go back to Socrates and his scepticism. He does not simply give voice to an uncertainty with regard to life after death, but also raises the question of which is preferable: life or death. The philosopher is the lover of wisdom who does not claim to know, but who expresses a radical doubt with regard to all things, even with regard to whether life or death is the better state. "Only God knoweth," as a slightly more antique translation of Socrates' final words at his trial runs. Indeed, Diogenes Laertius, author of the hugely influential *Lives of Eminent Philosophers* from the third century AD, tells a fascinating story of Thales, usually considered the first philosopher.

> He held there was no difference between life and death. "Why then," said one, "do you not die?" "Because," said he, "there is no difference."

To be a philosopher, then, is to learn how to die; it is to begin to cultivate the appropriate attitude towards death. As Marcus Aurelius writes, it is one of "the noblest functions of reason to know whether it is time to walk out of the world or not." Unknowing and uncertain, the philosopher walks.

# To Die Laughing

*The Book of Dead Philosophers* is not a "Book of the Dead," whether Egyptian or Tibetan. These exquisite ancient writings carefully describe the rituals necessary to prepare with certainty for the afterlife. *The Egyptian Book of the Dead* comprises 189 spells to ensure that the soul passes to an astral or solar afterlife. *The Tibetan Book of the Dead* describes the death rituals necessary to break the illusory cycles of existence and achieve the Enlightenment (capital E) that allegedly comes with the realization of Nirvana.

The influence of such approaches is vast, from the "Secret Doctrine" of Madame Blavatsky's Theosophical Society in the late nineteenth century, through Timothy Leary's psychedelic 1960s version of *The Tibetan Book of the Dead* achieved with the help of LSD, to the contemporary obsession with "near-death" or "out-of-the-body" experiences spawned by Raymond Moody's *Life after Life*, from 1976.

Such is the position that Nietzsche called "European Buddhism," although there is a good deal of American Buddhism around as well. The crucial point is that in both the Egyptian and Tibetan Books of the Dead and their contemporary epigones, *death is an illusion*. Existence is a cycle of rebirth that is only broken by a final passage to Enlightenment. It is thus a question of gaining access to the right Knowledge (capital K, once again) that will strip away what Schopenhauer saw as the illusory veils of Maya and allow the soul to free itself.

This approach to death is encapsulated in the words of the

influential Bengali poet Rabindranath Tagore, "Death is not extinguishing the light; it is putting out the lamp because the dawn has come." One can detect the influence of such approaches to death and dying in the still extremely widely read writings of Elisabeth Kübler-Ross. She fostered a deep psychological approach to dying patients based on the famous five stages of dying (denial, anger, bargaining, depression and acceptance) which has been extremely influential in palliative care. In *On Death and Dying* (1969), each chapter begins with a citation from Tagore, and the revealingly entitled *Death: The Final Stage of Growth* (1974) pays a rather hyperbolic tribute to *The Tibetan Book of the Dead*.

I do not want to deny the undoubtedly beneficial therapeutic effects of such approaches. My worry is that they cultivate the belief that death is an illusion to be overcome with the right spiritual preparations. However, it is not an illusion, it is a *reality* that has to be accepted. I would go further and argue that it is in relation to the reality of death that one's existence should be structured. Possibly the most pernicious feature of contemporary society is the unwillingness to accept this reality and willingness to flee the fact of death.

*The Book of Dead Philosophers* is, rather, a series of reminders of death or memento mori. Rather than being the clarion call of a new esoteric dogma, it is a book of 190 or so question marks that might begin to enable us to face the reality of our death.

So much for the good news. For the history of philosophers' deaths is also a tale of weirdness, madness, suicide, murder, bad luck, pathos, bathos and some dark humour. You will die laughing, I promise. Let me enumerate some examples to be discussed at greater leisure below:

Pythagoras allowed himself to be slaughtered rather than
   cross a field of beans;
Heracleitus suffocated in cow dung;
Plato allegedly died of a lice infestation;

Aristotle is reported to have killed himself with aconite;

Empedocles plunged into Mount Etna in the hope of
   becoming a god, but one of his bronze slippers was
   spat out by the flames in confirmation of his mortality;

Diogenes died by holding his breath;

So did the great radical Zeno of Citium;

Zeno of Elea died heroically by biting a tyrant's ear until
   he was stabbed to death;

Lucretius is alleged to have killed himself after being
   driven mad by taking a love potion;

Hypatia was killed by a mob of angry Christians and her
   skin was peeled off with oyster shells;

Boethius was cruelly tortured before being bludgeoned
   to death on the orders of the Ostrogoth king
   Theodoric;

John Scottus Eriugena, the great Irish philosopher, was
   allegedly stabbed to death by his English students;

Avicenna died of an opium overdose after engaging much
   too vigorously in sexual activity;

Aquinas died twenty-five miles from his birthplace after
   banging his head against the bough of a tree;

Pico della Mirandola was poisoned by his secretary; Siger
   of Brabant was stabbed by his;

William of Ockham died of the Black Death;

Thomas More was beheaded and his head was stuck on a
   pike on London Bridge;

Giordano Bruno was gagged and burnt alive at the stake
   by the Inquisition;

Galileo narrowly escaped the same fate, but got away with
   life imprisonment;

Bacon died after stuffing a chicken with snow in the
   streets of London to assess the effects of refrigeration;

Descartes died of pneumonia as a consequence of giving
   early-morning tutorials in the Stockholm winter to the
   prodigious and cross-dressing Queen Christina of
   Sweden;

Spinoza died in his rented rooms at The Hague while
   everyone else was at church;

Leibniz, discredited as an atheist and forgotten as a public figure, died alone and was buried at night with only one friend in attendance;

The handsome and brilliant John Toland died in such dire poverty in London that no marker was placed at his burial spot;

Berkeley, a fervent critic of Toland and other so-called "freethinkers," died one Sunday evening on a visit to Oxford while his wife read him a sermon;

Montesquieu died in the arms of his lover, leaving unfinished an essay on taste;

The atheist, materialist La Mettrie died of indigestion caused by eating a huge amount of truffle pâté;

Rousseau died of massive cerebral bleeding which was possibly caused by a violent collision with a Great Dane on the streets of Paris two years earlier;

Diderot choked to death on an apricot, presumably to show that pleasure could be had until the very last breath;

Condorcet was murdered by the Jacobins during the bloodiest years of the French Revolution;

Hume died peacefully in his bed after fending off the inquiries of Boswell as to the atheist's attitude to death;

Kant's last word was *"Sufficit,"* "it is enough";

Hegel died in a cholera epidemic and his last words were "Only one man ever understood me . . . and he didn't understand me" (presumably he was referring to himself);

Bentham had himself stuffed and sits on public view in a glass box at University College London in order to maximize the utility of his person;

Max Stirner was stung on the neck by a flying insect and died of the resulting fever;

Kierkegaard's gravestone rests against that of his father;

Nietzsche made a long, soft-brained and dribbling descent into oblivion after kissing a horse in Turin;

Moritz Schlick was murdered by a disturbed student who went on to join the Nazi Party;

Wittgenstein died the day after his birthday, for which his
   friend Mrs. Bevan gave him an electric blanket saying
   "Many happy returns"; Wittgenstein replied, staring at
   her, "There will be no returns";

Simone Weil starved herself to death for the sake of
   solidarity with occupied France in the Second World
   War;

Edith Stein died in Auschwitz;

Giovanni Gentile was executed by anti-Fascist Italian
   partisans;

Sartre said, "Death? I don't think about it. It has no place
   in my life"; 50,000 people attended his funeral;

Merleau-Ponty was allegedly discovered dead in his office
   with his face in a book by Descartes;

Roland Barthes was hit by a dry cleaning van after a
   meeting with the future French minister for culture;

Freddie Ayer had a near-death experience where he
   reportedly met the masters of the universe after
   choking on a piece of salmon;

Gilles Deleuze defenestrated himself from his Paris
   apartment in order to escape the sufferings of
   emphysema;

Derrida died of pancreatic cancer at the same age as his
   father, who died of the same disease;

My teacher Dominique Janicaud died alone on a beach
   in August 2002 close to the foot of *le chemin Nietzsche*
   outside Nice in France after suffering a heart attack
   while swimming.

Death is close and getting closer all the time. Funny, isn't it?

My own view of death is closer to that of Epicurus and what
is known as the four-part cure: don't fear God, don't worry
about death, what is good is easy to get and what is terrible is
easy to endure. He writes in the final of the four extant letters
attributed to him,

Get used to believing that death is nothing to us. For all good and bad consists in sense-experience, and death is the privation of sense-experience. Hence a correct knowledge of the fact of death makes the mortality of life a matter for contentment, not by adding a limitless time to life but by removing the longing for immortality.

The Epicurean view of death was hugely influential in antiquity, as can be seen in Lucretius, and was rediscovered by philosophers like Pierre Gassendi in the seventeenth century. It represents a distinct and powerful sub-tradition in Western thought to which insufficient attention has been given: when death is, I am not; when I am, death is not. Therefore, it is useless to worry about death and the only way to attain tranquillity of soul is by removing the anxious longing for an afterlife.

Highly tempting as it is, the obvious problem with this position is that it fails to provide a cure for the aspect of death that is hardest to endure: not our own death, but the deaths of those we love. It is the deaths of those we are bound to in love that undo us, that unstitch our carefully tailored suit of the self, that unmake whatever meaning we have made. In my view, odd as it may sound, it is only in grief that we become most truly ourselves. That is, what it means to be a self does not consist in some delusory self-knowledge, but in the acknowledgement of that part of ourselves that we have irretrievably lost. The entire difficulty here is imagining what sort of contentment or tranquillity might be possible in relation to the deaths of those we love. I cannot promise to resolve this issue, but the reader will find it taken up and developed in various of the entries below.

# Writing about Dead Philosophers

Writing a book about how philosophers die is admittedly an odd way to spend one's time. Reading such a book is, perhaps, even odder. However, it does raise a couple of searching questions about how the history of philosophy is to be written and how the activity of philosophy is to be understood.

The initial and finally intractable difficulty with writing about the history of philosophy consists in knowing exactly where to begin. The earliest versions of the history of philosophy still extant are by a teacher and his student: Book Alpha of Aristotle's *Metaphysics* and Theophrastus' *On Sensation*. In both texts, the philosophers develop their own views in relation to previous doctrines. On the one hand, Aristotle brilliantly reviews the doctrines of the pre-Socratic physical philosophers whom he calls the *physiologi*, like Thales, Anaxagoras and Empedocles, and their views on the material cause of nature. On the other hand, he then turns a critical eye to his teacher, Plato, and the views of the Pythagoreans on the ideal cause of nature. In a way that becomes a standard pattern of philosophical argument, Aristotle dispatches and integrates both the materialist and idealist approaches before introducing his own notion of substance, which is the core of what a later tradition called "metaphysics."

The case of Theophrastus gives a particularly poignant example of the poverty of our situation with regard to philosophical antiquity. Theophrastus' "On the Opinions of the Physical Philosophers" ran to eighteen books and was the major source in antiquity for pre-Socratic thought. All that remains is a fragment, *On Sensation*, which gives but a tantalizing taste of the whole through discussions of the nature of the senses in Empedocles, Anaxagoras, Democritus and Plato.

Our situation with regard to the literary remains of antiquity is tragic. As we know, the archive of ancient texts was largely lost, for example when an angry mob of Christians destroyed the greatest library of the classical world at Alexandria at the end of the third century AD. All we are left with are fragments of a rich totality the scale of which we can barely imagine. It is like trying to guess at the holdings of the British Library with a hundred or so Penguin Classics in one's hands.

My concern in this book is with what scholars of ancient philosophy call "doxography," that is, an account of the lives, opinions and tenets of philosophers, and sometimes their deaths. The word "doxa" can mean "opinion" in the common sense of the word, but it can also mean "reputation," i.e., the opinion entertained about one by others. Because of the huge importance of reputation, especially posthumous reputation, in Greek culture, "doxa" develops the meaning of "great reputation" or even "glory." The latter is a key concept for the Greeks and there was a widespread belief that one's immortality consisted in the glory of one's reputation, that is, in the stories recounted after one's death.

Understood in this expanded sense—which I confess is somewhat idiosyncratic—doxography can be seen as an account of the glorious reputations of philosophers, and doxographers were those who wrote the biographies of these exemplary figures. As such, the concept of doxography is a kissing cousin of hagiography. From Socrates to Spinoza and from Hume to Wittgenstein, it is interesting to see how closely the accounts of the lives of the philosophers resemble those of the saints. The crucial difference is that philosophers are exemplary not by their holiness, but by the way in which they show their weaknesses as well as their strengths. The lives of philosophers are often rather less than saintly and this is often what attracts us to them. It is in the odd details of philosophers' lives that they become accessible to us: Hobbes's predilection for playing tennis and singing in his bedroom, Kant's fondness for English cheese and horror of perspiration, and Marx's carbuncles.

My point in this book is to show that the history of philosophy can be approached as a history of philosophers that proceeds by examples remembered, often noble and virtuous, but sometimes base and comical. As we will see, the manner of the death of philosophers humanizes them and shows that, despite the lofty reach of their intellect, they have to cope with the hand life deals them like the rest of us.

"Doxography" is the neologism of the German scholar Hermann Diels, whose monumental synthesis of Greek philosophical biography was published in Latin in 1879 as *Doxographi Graeci, The Greek Doxographers*. However, for entirely contingent historical reasons, our major guide to the "doxographical" approach to the history of philosophy, particularly with regard to philosophers' deaths, is Diogenes Laertius from the third century.

Sadly, however likeable and readable one may find his *Lives of Eminent Philosophers*, it can hardly be described as accurate, complete or philosophically acute. Diogenes gives us a rather chatty, anecdotal and highly syncretic ramble through antiquity. At times, it is terrific fun. His translator, Herbert Richards, rightly says "the man was foolish enough," and Jonathan Barnes and Julia Annas describe his *Lives* as "chatty and unintelligent." It is also true that he peppered his book with the most awful verses, as we will see. However, Richards goes on to say "the book is of extreme value for the history, especially the literary history, of Greek philosophy." I find Diogenes Laertius very amenable company and I rather like the way in which he collates facts uncritically, particularly unreliable and scandalous ones. My approach has also tended towards the scandalous in places. He also has some unsurpassed stories about philosophers' deaths.

Diogenes Laertius begins by considering the possibility that philosophy first arose amongst the "barbarians," such as the Chaldeans of Babylon and Assyria, the Gymnosophists of India, the Druids who lived among the Celts and Gauls, the Thracians like Orpheus, the Zoroastrians in Persia and the Egyptians. However, he quickly moves on to assert that it was from the Greeks that philosophy took its rise and "its very name refuses to be translated into foreign or barbaric speech." Philosophy speaks Greek, then, and its history begins with Greece and therefore with Europe. Such is what has become the standard account of the history of philosophy which reduces the non-Greek, non-European, "barbaric" sources to so-called "wisdom traditions," but not philosophy proper. On this view, the idea of comparative philosophy is a non-starter, as there is nothing with which to compare Greek philosophy.

Diogenes Laertius' approach is entirely emulated by the itinerant Englishman Walter Burley or Gualteri Burlaei in his *Liber de vita et moribus philosophorum* (*The Book of Philosophers' Lives and Opinions or Habits*). The latter was possibly written in Italy or southern France in the 1340s and remained the standard history of philosophy for the next few centuries. John Passmore rightly describes Burley's account of the history of philosophy as "free and unreliable," although it does include some curiosities. For example, one finds entries not only on figures like Hermes Trismegistus, Aesop and Zoroaster, but also on Euripides, Sophocles, Hippocrates, and later Roman writers like Plautus, Virgil and even Ovid. Also, Burley rather curiously notes the ethnic origin of most philosophers — "*Thales, asianus*" ("Thales, Asian"), "*Hermes, egipcius*" ("Hermes, Egyptian") — and which Hebrew king was on the throne during their lifetime.

The writing of the history of philosophy is continued by Thomas Stanley in 1687 in the impressively printed three-volume *History of Philosophy, containing the lives, opinions, actions and discourses of the philosophers of every sect, illustrated with effigies of divers of them*. Indeed, the "effigies" are particularly handsome and the volumes are littered with large and heroic engravings of the dead ancients. Although Stanley's model for the history of philosophy is still very much based on

Diogenes Laertius—he only deals with antiquity—there is much that is new. In particular, there is a long closing chapter on the "Chaldaick" philosophy, complete with text and commentary on the Oracles of Zoroaster, plus various remarks on Persian and Sabean philosophers.

As Stanley makes clear in the dedicatory epistle of his *History*, "The Learned *Gassendus* was my precedent." This refers to Pierre Gassendi's *De Vita et Moribus Epicuri* (*The Lives and Opinions or Habits of Epicurus*, 1647), which is a compelling and extended (it comprises eight books) defence of Epicurean philosophy against the infamies and distortions to which it had been submitted since Zeno, the Stoics, Cicero, Plutarch and right through to the Church Fathers. The question for Gassendi which I would like to echo is not so much "what is philosophy?" as "what is a philosopher?," which is indistinguishable from the question "how does a philosopher die?"

According to one William Enfield of Norwich, Stanley's *History* is written in "an uncouth and obscure style." Whatever the truth of the matter, there is no doubt that Stanley's work is totally eclipsed by the publication of Jakob Brucker's *Historia Critica Philosophiae* (*The Critical History of Philosophy*), published in Leipzig between 1742 and 1767, which was the principal authority on the history of philosophy in the eighteenth century. It was freely adapted into English by the aforementioned Enfield in 1791.

What is astonishing about this compendious work is its treatment of the diversity of philosophical traditions, with extensive initial discussions of the philosophy of not only the Chaldeans, Persians, Indians and Egyptians, but also the Hebrews, Arabians, Phoenicians, Egyptians, Ethiopians, Etrurians, the "northern nations" like the Scythians and Thracians, and the Celts (even including the Britons). (Incidentally, the great virtue of the Celts was their dismissal of death; Brucker writes, "We find no people superior to them in the magnanimous contempt of death.")

The idea that philosophy has a uniquely Greek source and that everything prior to the Greeks is simply not philos-

ophy finds its most powerful modern expression in Dietrich
Tiedemann's six-volume *Geist der spekulativen Philosophie* (*The
Spirit of Speculative Philosophy*, 1791–7). This is a work that
deeply influenced much subsequent writing of the history of
philosophy, and John Passmore describes it as "the first history of philosophy in the modern manner." Tiedemann
makes crystal clear in his Preface that he is not going to deal
with "Chaldeans, Persians and Indians," and he judges these
traditions to be either poetic or religious, but not philosophical in the strict sense. What also happens in Tiedemann's
approach is that the doxographical elements in the history of
philosophy are minimized and emphasis is placed, as his
title suggests, on the speculative *spirit* of philosophy that can
be expressed systematically, rather than the individual flesh
and bones of a philosopher's life.

This disregard for individual life goes together with the
belief that the history of philosophy makes progress of a scientific kind, or at least that the various philosophies can
be expressed in a scientific form where they exhibit logical development. This idea finds expression in Gottlieb
Tenneman's *Geschichte der Philosophie* (*History of Philosophy*,
1789–1819), where philosophy is the passage of the scientific
spirit towards truth. Let me say that I am highly dubious as to
whether the spirit of philosophy can be separated from the
body of the philosopher and deeply sceptical about the belief
that philosophy makes progress of a scientific kind.

Crucially, both Tiedemann and Tenneman deeply influenced Hegel in his *Lectures on the History of Philosophy* (1833–6).
For Hegel, nothing could be less philosophically significant
than knowing how a philosopher lived and died and the
nature of his opinions, habits or reputation. Philosophy is
defined as "its own time comprehended in thought." What is
therefore being articulated in a philosophy is the entire world
of the Greeks, the Medievals or whoever. Furthermore, on
Hegel's account, the previous history of philosophy is not so
much a history of errors as a progressive unveiling of the truth,
a truth that finds complete expression—surprise, surprise—in
the work of Hegel.

Although Hegel's conception of history has been the frequent recipient of attacks, from Marx and Kierkegaard onwards, it is still the way in which the history of philosophy continues to be written. Philosophy is a magisterial procession of ideas from east to west, from the Greeks to "us Europeans" or "us Americans." This is what Geoffrey Hartman famously called "the westering of spirit." But this "westering" is also a "bestering," as it were. We are akin to the Greeks, but somehow even smarter, possessing intellectual jewels like self-consciousness, proper logic and empirical science. Philosophy doesn't begin with a ragbag of multiple traditions, but with a pristine and unique Greek—and therefore European—source.

To say that this version of the history of philosophy has justified and continues to justify forms of Eurocentrism is an understatement. To what extent such a Eurocentrism is or is not justified with regard to philosophy is a vast debate that I do want to enter into directly in this book. Let me say, however, that I am sceptical of both Eurocentric approaches to philosophy and of attempts to criticize the privilege of Greek philosophy by saying that the true source of philosophy lies in Persia, India or China, and therefore in Asia, or in Egypt, and therefore in Africa. Philosophy has no true source and to a great extent the virtue of focusing on philosophers' lives and deaths consists in realizing that it is a messy, plural and geographically spread-out affair.

*The Book of Dead Philosophers* is a history of philosophers rather than a history of philosophy. It is a history of how a long line of mortal, material, limited creatures faced their last moments, whether with dignity or delirium, with nobility or night-sweats. My approach is therefore deeply at odds with that of Hegel. I do not see the history of philosophy as the progressive logical unfolding of "Spirit," which culminates in showing that it has its destiny in the Western philosophy of the present. This is "westering" as "bestering," which judges the facts of philosophers' lives as irrelevant. Indeed, there is something intensely narcissistic about such a conception of philosophy, where the sole function of history is to hold up a mirror so that we may see the reflection of ourselves and our own world.

On the contrary, I hope to show how the material quality of the many lives and deaths that we will review disrupts the move to something like "Spirit" and places a certain way of doing philosophy in question. To that extent, there is something intensely arrogant, even hubristic, about a philosopher's disregard for the lives and deaths of other philosophers. In a lecture course on Aristotle from 1924, Heidegger said,

> The personality of a philosopher is of interest only to this extent: he was born at such and such a time, he worked, and died.

What this reveals is an Olympian, godlike stance towards philosophy and life. Such a stance is unwilling and perhaps incapable of considering the philosopher as a creature who is subject to "all the ills that flesh is heir to." In my view, the philosopher who disregards the lives and deaths of philosophers is hostile to their and his or her own individuality, embodiment and mortality. It also leads—as is the case with Hegel and Heidegger—to a triumphalist and self-aggrandizing version of the history of philosophy that utterly disfigures the past.

What I have presented here is a messy and plural ragbag of lives and deaths that cannot simply be ordered into a coherent conceptual schema. It is my hope that what we see when we look into these many deaths is not just our own reflection striding forth to meet us, but something quite unlike us, remote and removed, something from which we might learn. It is high time we made a start.

# 190 OR SO
# DEAD PHILOSOPHERS

# Pre-Socratics, Physiologists, Sages and Sophists

Philosophical thought emerged in the Greek-speaking world two and a half millennia ago. First we encounter the various sages and so-called "physiologists," like Thales and Anaxagoras, who attempted to explain the origins of the universe and the causes of nature. We will then turn to the sometimes shadowy figures, like Pythagoras, Heracleitus and Empedocles, who define the world of thought prior to the birth of Socrates and the struggle between philosophy and sophistry in Athens during the Classical period of the fifth and fourth centuries BC.

Of course, one might with some justice claim that the Sphinx was the first philosopher and Oedipus the second. This would also have the merit of making philosophy begin with a woman and continuing with an incestuous parricide. The Sphinx asks her visitors a question, which is also a riddle, and perhaps even a joke: what goes on four legs in the morning, on two legs at noon, and on three legs in the evening? If they get the answer wrong, she kills them. Furthermore, when Oedipus guesses the right answer to the riddle — man crawls on all fours as a baby, walks on two legs as an adult and with a cane in old age—the Sphinx commits philosophical suicide by throwing herself to the ground from her high rock.

## Thales

### (FLOURISHED IN THE SIXTH CENTURY BC)

Thales came from the once mighty port of Miletus, close to the present Turkish coast, whose harbour long ago dried up thanks to the unending attention of silt.

Thales was the possible originator of the saying "know thyself," who famously predicted the solar eclipse of May 585 BC. He believed that water was the universal substance and once fell into a ditch when he was taken outdoors by a Thracian girl to look at the stars. On hearing his cry, she said, "How can you expect to know about all the heavens, Thales, when you cannot even see what is just beneath your feet?" Some feel—perhaps rightly—that this is a charge that philosophy never entirely escaped in the following two and a half millennia.

Thales died at an advanced age of heat, thirst and weakness while watching an athletic contest. This inspired Diogenes Laertius to the following execrable verse:

*As Thales watched the games one festal day*
*The fierce sun smote him and he passed away.*

## Solon

### (630–560 BC)

Solon was a famed Athenian legislator who repealed the bloody laws of Dracon (although it was Dracon whose name was turned into an adjective). Plutarch remarks that Solon suggested that brides should nibble a quince before getting into bed. The reason for this is unclear. When Solon was asked why he had not framed a law against parricide, he replied that he hoped it was unnecessary. He died in Cyprus at the age of eighty.

## Chilon
(FLOURISHED IN THE SIXTH CENTURY BC)

A Spartan to whom the saying "know thyself" is also sometimes attributed. He died after congratulating his son on an Olympic victory in boxing.

## Periander
(628–588 BC)

Like Thales, Solon and Chilon, Periander of Corinth was considered one of the Seven Sages of Greece. To others, like Aristotle, he was simply a tyrant. However, there is a bizarre story about the lengths to which Periander went in order to conceal his place of burial: he instructed two young men to meet a third man at a predetermined place and kill and bury him. Then he arranged for four men to pursue the first two and kill and bury them. Then he arranged for a larger group of men to hunt down the four. Having made all these preparations, he went out to meet the two young men for he, Periander, was the third man.

## Epimenides
(POSSIBLY FLOURISHED IN THE SIXTH CENTURY, POSSIBLY A MYTHICAL FIGURE)

A native of Crete, the setting for Epimenides' famous paradox. Epimenides' original statement was "Cretans, always liars." He appears to have intended this literally, as the great Cretan lie is the belief that Zeus is mortal, whereas every sensible person knows that he is really immortal. However, in logic, this paradox takes on a more acute form. Consider the sentence "This statement is not true." Now, is this statement true? If it is, then it is not; if it is not, then it is. This is a perfect example of a paradox. That is, it is a proposition whose truth leads to a contradiction and the denial of its truth also leads to a contradiction.

Legend has it that Epimenides was sent into the countryside by his father to look after some sheep. But instead of tending to the sheep, he fell asleep in a cave for fifty-seven years. Upon waking, he went in search of the sheep, believing that he had only taken a short nap. When he returned home, everything (unsurprisingly) had changed and a new owner had taken possession of his father's farm. Eventually, he found his younger brother, by now an elderly man, and learnt the truth.

Epimenides' fame spread and it was believed thereafter that he possessed the gift of prophecy. Diogenes tells of how the Athenians sent for him when the city was suffering from the plague. He again took some sheep and went to the Areopagus, the high rock in the centre of Athens. He commanded that a sacrifice be made at each spot where a sheep decided to lie down. In this way, apparently, Athens was freed from the plague.

According to Phlegon in his work *On Longevity*, Epimenides lived to be 157 years old. This makes him a centurion, excluding his long nap in the cave. The Cretans claim that he lived to be 259 years old. But, as we all know, Cretans are always liars.

## Anaximander
(610–546/545 BC)

Anaximander somewhat obscurely claimed that the Unlimited or that which is without boundaries (*apeiron*) is the original material of all existing things. He discovered his own limit at the age of sixty-four.

# Pythagoras
(580–500 BC)

Sadly, it is now almost universally assumed by classical scholars that Pythagoras never existed. It seems that there was a group of people in southern Italy called Pythagoreans who invented a "Founder" for their beliefs who, accordingly, lived and died in a manner consistent with those beliefs. But let's not allow Pythagoras' mere non-existence to deter us, as the stories that surround him are so compelling. They are also illustrative of the wider point that disciples of a thinker will often simply invent stories and anecdotes that illustrate the life of the master in whom they want to believe. Perhaps we should be suspicious of this desire for a master.

Be that as it may, Pythagorean doctrines were bound by an oath of secrecy, so we know very little prior to the version of them that appears in Plato. These include a belief in the immortality and transmigration of the soul and the view that the ultimate reality of the universe consists in number. Pythagoreans regarded even numbers as female and odd numbers as male. The number 5 was called "marriage" because it was the product of the first even (2) and odd (3) numbers (the ancient Greeks considered the number 1 a unit and not a proper number, which had to express a multiplicity). Pythagoreans also believed that their master had established the ratios that underlie music. This had huge influence in the notion of *musica universalis* or music of the spheres, where the entire cosmos was the expression of a musical harmony whose key was given in mathematics.

However, the Pythagoreans also observed a number of other, more worldly doctrines, involving food in particular.

They abstained from meat and fish. For some reason red mullet is singled out for especial prohibition, and Plutarch notes that they considered the egg taboo, too. Pythagoras and his followers also inherited from the Egyptians a strong revulsion to beans, because of their apparent resemblance to the genitalia. Apparently, "bean" may have been a slang term for "testicle." But there are many other possible reasons for this dislike of beans.

There are some fascinating remarks in the *Philosophumena* [*Philosophizings*] *or the Refutation of All Heresies* by the Christian Bishop Hippolytus written around AD 220. According to him, if beans are chewed and left in the sun, they emit the smell of semen. Even worse, if one takes the bean in flower and buries it in the earth and in a few days digs it up, then, "We shall see it at first having the form of a woman's pudenda and afterwards on close examination a child's head growing with it." Of course, as many of us know to our cost, beans should be avoided, as they produce terrible flatulence. Oddly, it was because of beans that Pythagoras is alleged to have met his end. But I am getting ahead of myself.

So the legend goes, Pythagoras left his native Samos, an island off the Ionian coast, because of a dislike of the policies of the tyrant Polycrates. He fled with his followers to Croton in southern Italy and extended considerable influence and power in the region of present-day Calabria. Porphyry, in his *Life of Pythagoras*, relates how a certain Cylo, a rich and powerful local figure, felt slighted by the haughtiness with which Pythagoras treated him. As a consequence, Cylo and his retinue burnt down the house in which Pythagoras and his followers were gathered. The master only escaped because his followers bridged the fire with their own bodies. He got as far as a field of beans, where he stopped and declared that he would rather be killed than cross it. This enabled his pursuers to catch up with him and cut his throat.

Yet, there is another story, related by Hermippus, that when the cities of Agrigentum and Syracuse were at war, the Pythagoreans sided with the Agrigentines. Unbelievably, Pythagoras was killed by the Syracusans as he was trying to avoid a beanfield. Thirty-five of his followers were subsequently burnt at the stake for treachery.

Diogenes Laertius devotes possibly the worst of his verses to this incident, which begins thus: "Woe! Woe! Whence, Pythagoras, this deep reverence for beans?" The wonderful second-century satirist Lucian depicts Pythagoras in Hades in dialogue with the cynic Menippus, in which Pythagoras is pestering Menippus for food.

PYTHAGORAS: Let me see if there's anything to eat in
  your wallet.
MENIPPUS: Beans, my good fellow—something you
  mustn't eat.
PYTHAGORAS: Just give me some. Doctrines are different
  among the dead.

## Timycha
### (DATES UNKNOWN, FOURTH CENTURY BC)

One would be forgiven for thinking that the history of philosophy is something of a boys' club. In this book, where I can, I will seek to rectify this view. It might be noted that in 1690, the French classical scholar Gilles Ménage wrote *Historia Mulierum Philosopharum* (*The History of Women Philosophers*). Ménage—somewhat opportunistically it is true—identifies sixty-five women philosophers. In the ancient world, the philosophical school that attracted the most women was without doubt the Pythagoreans. These include Themistoclea, Theano and Myia, Pythagoras' sister, wife and daughter respectively.

However, I'd like to get back to the topic of beans. This brings us to Timycha and a story told in Iamblichus' *Life of Pythagoras*. After the persecution of the Pythagorean community by the Sicilian tyrant Dionysius, Timycha and her husband, Myllias, were captured and tortured. The purpose of the interrogation was to find an answer to the following question: why do Pythagoreans prefer to die rather than tread upon beans? Timycha was pregnant and Dionysius threatened her with torture. Before she was killed, Timycha bit off her own tongue and spat it in the tyrant's face for fear that she might betray the secrets of the Pythagorean sect.

## Heracleitus
(540–480 BC)

Traditionally Heracleitus was known as the "weeping philosopher" or "the obscure." He was, according to Plutarch, afflicted with terrible diseases. All that remains of his work are 139 fragments. Some of these are as obscure as his moniker would suggest: "Souls have a sense of smell in Hades." Others are colourful illustrations of his views on the relativity of judgement, such as "Donkeys prefer chaff to gold," and "Pigs wash themselves in mud, birds in dust and ashes."

The cause of Heracleitus' tears was human behaviour, in particular that of his fellow citizens of Ephesus. As the first of his extant fragments insists, everyone should follow *logos*, a term meaning something like the law, principle or reason for the existence of the universe. However, the vast majority of people do not follow *logos*, but act instead as if they were asleep and have as much awareness of what they do as chaff-munching donkeys.

Heracleitus became such a hater of humanity that he wandered in the mountains and lived on a diet of grass and herbs (no beans are mentioned). Sadly, his malnutrition gave him dropsy and he returned to the city to seek a cure. It was through this cure that he met his end, for he asked to be covered in cow dung. Now, there are two stories of Heracleitus dying in cow dung. He apparently believed that its action would draw the bad humours out of his body and dry up his dropsy. In the first story, the cow dung is wet and the weeping philosopher drowns; in the second, it is dry and he is baked to death in the Ionian sun.

(There is a third story told by Diogenes Laertius, which relates that Heracleitus' friends were unable to remove the dried cow dung from his body and, being unrecognizable, he was devoured by dogs. This confirms fragment 97, "Dogs bark at those whom they do not recognize." Sadly, they also bite.)

## Aeschylus
(525/524–456/455 BC)

Aeschylus is not usually seen as a philosopher, although the handful of his plays that survive are full of deep wisdom about how mortals must, in the repeated refrain of *The Oresteia*, suffer into truth. In the surviving fragment of the *Niobe*, Aeschylus writes,

> *Alone of gods Death has no love for gifts,*
> *Libation helps you not, nor sacrifice.*
> *He has no altar, and hears no hymns;*
> *From him alone Persuasion stands apart.*

Aeschylus fought with great distinction in the battles against the Persians at Marathon and Salamis, and his military prowess was proudly mentioned in the epitaph on his tombstone. It is Aeschylus' tombstone, however, that is apparently the origin of the amusing, but apocryphal, story of his death.

It was widely believed that Aeschylus was killed when an eagle dropped a live tortoise on his bald head, apparently mistaking his head for a stone. Apparently, the great tragedian was represented on his tombstone slumped over, while an eagle— the bird of Apollo—carried off his soul to heaven in the form of a lyre. However, a lyre looks like, and perhaps was originally, a tortoise shell strung with a few strings. Presumably, someone ignorant of the iconography mistook "eagle-taking-the-soul-of-dead-poet-to-heaven-in-the-form-of-lyre" to mean "eagle-drops-tortoise-on-head-of-sleeping-poet-killing-both."

## Anaxagoras
(500–428 BC)

A student of Anaximenes, Anaxagoras held that air was the universal, unlimited substance through which we come into existence.

He suggested that *nous* (mind or intellect) was the moving principle of the universe and counselled his fellow citizens of Miletus to study the moon, sun and stars. When someone asked him, "Have you no concern with your native land?," he replied, "I am greatly concerned with my native land" and pointed to the stars.

Anaxagoras was banished from Miletus after a trial at which he was charged with claiming the sun to be a mass of red-hot metal. He died in exile and, according to Plutarch, asked that children be given a holiday on the day of his death.

## Parmenides
(515–? BC)

He was apparently a Pythagorean in his youth, and originator of the Eleatic School, but there is no record of Parmenides' death and precious few facts about his life, although he plays a very important role in Plato's eponymous dialogue with a very young Socrates. Yet, we do not even know for sure if Socrates and Parmenides ever met. The core of his novel metaphysics is the distinction between being, which is described as "round like a ball," and non-being, which is presumably not like a ball at all. We have no account of how Parmenides passed from one state to the other.

## Zeno of Elea
(495–430 BC)

Zeno was the author of the now lost *Epicheirêmata* (*Attacks*), written in defence of his master Parmenides. He defended Parmenides' doctrines in a unique manner by taking up the

opposite view and showing how it leads to irresolvable paradoxes. For example, Zeno argues against motion by saying
that if anything moves, then it must either move in the place
where it is or in the place where it is not. Given that the latter
is impossible because no thing can be or be acted upon at the
place where it is not, a thing must be at the place at which it
is. Therefore, things are at rest and motion is an illusion.

This argument against motion finds further expression in the
famous paradoxes of the arrow and of Achilles and the tortoise.
An arrow that appears to be in flight is really at rest because
everything that occupies a space equal to itself must be at rest in
that space. Given that an arrow can only occupy a space equal
to itself at each instant of its flight, the arrow is motionless.

Similarly, if speedy Achilles gives the slow-footed tortoise
a head start in their race, then he will never overtake it.
Why? For the simple reason that by the time that Achilles
has reached the point from which the tortoise started, the latter will have moved on. And when he has covered that distance, the tortoise will have moved on again, and so on ad
infinitum. Aristotle takes some pleasure unpicking these
paradoxes in his *Physics*. There is also a story that when Diogenes the Cynic heard someone declare that there was no
such thing as motion, he got up and walked about.

The manner of Zeno's death is heroic and dramatic. He
was involved in a plot to overthrow the tyrant Nearchus, but
the plot was discovered and Zeno was arrested. During his
interrogation, Zeno said that he had something to tell the
tyrant about certain people but only in his private ear, as it
were. When Nearchus was summoned, Zeno laid hold of
the tyrant's ear with his teeth and would not let go until he
was stabbed to death. (Demetrius, in his *Men of the Same
Name*, claims that he attacked not the ear but the nose.)

## Empedocles
(490–430 BC)

There is perhaps no more curious and yet attractive figure
amongst the Pre-Socratics than Empedocles. Certainly none

met a more spectacular end. As Plutarch relates, he left philosophy in a state of wild excitement. Stories abound about Empedocles' transformation into a god. He wrote two long and no longer extant poems, "On Nature" and "Purifications," and described himself as a "deathless god, no longer a mortal." Diogenes describes him as wearing the purple robes of royalty, a golden girdle, slippers of bronze and a Delphic laurel wreath. He had thick hair, always carried a staff and had a train of boy attendants. There is something of the magician and magus about Empedocles, as well as something of the charlatan. Yet he is also always seen as a political radical and identified with democracy. There is a story that he persuaded his fellow citizens of Agrigentum in Sicily to end their factionalism and cultivate equality in politics.

In one of Empedocles' extant fragments, he refers to death as "the great avenger" and there is a legend that he kept a woman alive for thirty days without breath or pulse. According to Aëtius, Empedocles believed that sleep results from a cooling of the blood and that death ensues when the heat has left it entirely. Now, if heat is the vehicle of life, then it is through the heat of volcanic fire that Empedocles meets his end in a quest for immortality. So the story goes, he threw himself into Mount Etna in all his finery to confirm reports that he had become divine. But the truth was discovered when one of his bronze slippers, thrown up by the flames, was found on the slope of the volcano.

There are other, less ecstatic stories of Empedocles' death: he left Sicily for Greece and never returned, he broke his thigh on the way to a festival and died from the ensuing malady, he slipped into the sea and drowned because of his great age.

Some twenty-two centuries later, in the wake of both the enthusiasm and disappointment that followed the French Revolution, it was this combination of mystical hubris and political radicalism that attracted the great German philosopher-poet Friedrich Hölderlin to write his verse drama, *The Death of Empedocles*. This quite stunning modern tragedy was left unfinished and unappreciated in three versions from the late 1790s. Hölderlin calls Empedocles "the god-drunken man" and he clearly identifies with him as a religious reformer and a political revolutionary. His death in what Hölderlin calls "the highest fire" is seen as a sacrifice to nature and the acceptance of a power greater than human freedom: destiny.

Empedocles is always described as grave and stately and this is reason enough for the ridicule that is heaped upon him by Lucian in *Dialogues of the Dead*, who depicts him in Hades coming "half-boiled from Etna." When asked by the cynic Menippus as to the reason why he jumped into the crater, he responds, "A fit of mad depression, Menippus." To which the latter quips,

> No, but a fit of vanity and pride and a dose of driveling folly; that was what burnt you to ashes, boots and all — and well you deserved it.

(Unrelatedly, but continuing our Pythagorean bean theme, Empedocles' fragment 141 reads, "Wretches, utter wretches, keep your hands off beans!")

## Archelaus
### (DATES UNKNOWN, PROBABLY BORN EARLY FIFTH CENTURY BC)

Archelaus was the pupil of Anaxagoras and the teacher of Socrates. He is usually seen as the bridge between Ionian natural philosophy and Athenian ethical thinking. The cause of his death is unknown and his writings are lost apart from the following enigmatic words: "The cold is a bond."

## Protagoras
### (485–410 BC)

Protagoras was the first and greatest of the Sophists, whom we met in the introduction, although one might make the case that the cunning and smooth-talking Odysseus was the real father of sophistry. Plato devotes a dialogue to Protagoras in which he is

presented in a more favourable light than many other adver-
saries of Socrates. He famously said that "Man is the measure of
all things," and professed agnosticism about the nature of the
gods: "About the gods, I am not able to know whether they
exist or do not exist." Protagoras was also the first to charge a
fee for teaching honey-tongued eloquence and the gentle arts
of persuasion.

In *Lives of the Sophists*, from the early third century, Philostratus asserts that we should not criticize Protagoras for
charging a fee, "since the pursuits on which we spend
money we prize more than those for which no money is
charged." Philostratus knew whereof he spoke, for he came
from a long line of Sophists and enjoyed considerable
material luxury at the court of the highly intellectual Syr-
ian empress Julia Domna. (Incidentally, she was herself a
very interesting figure, the wife of the Roman emperor Sep-
timus Severus; Philostratus calls her "Julia the philosopher." After the death of Severus on a military campaign in
Britain, Julia remained a hugely influential figure through
her sons, the joint emperors Caracalla and Geta. It is said
that Caracalla murdered Geta in his mother's arms and
that Julia starved herself to death after Caracalla was, in
turn, murdered in 217.)

Protagoras is credited with many works, including *Of
Forensic Speech for a Fee, two books of opposing arguments*. A vivid
example of the monetary use of opposing arguments can be
seen in the following anecdote: when Protagoras asked his
disciple Euathlus for his fee, the latter replied, "But I have
not won a case yet." To which Protagoras riposted,

> If I win this case against you I must have the fee for win-
> ning; if you win, I must have it, because *you* win it.

Protagoras apparently drowned in a shipwreck after he
had been tried and banished (or in some stories condemned
to death) for his agnostic religious views. He also wrote a
treatise on wrestling.

# Democritus
(460–370 BC)

For some, "the prince of philosophers." Yet, Plato never mentions him and there is a rumour that has circulated down the ages that he wanted to burn Democritus' books. Very sadly, Plato's wish was unwittingly fulfilled by the disasters of history and very little of Democritus' work survives.

From Cicero and Horace onwards, Democritus was known by the sobriquet of the "laughing philosopher" (as opposed to "weeping" Heracleitus), and they are often depicted in this way in medieval iconography. Robert Burton, in his mountainous book *The Anatomy of Melancholy* (1621), playfully signs himself "Democritus Junior." Democritus was the pupil of the shadowy Leucippus, none of whose works survive, and co-originator of Greek atomism. The latter is an entirely materialist explanation of the physical world in terms of the organization of atoms in space. Dogs, cats, rats and ziggurats are simply different arrangements of atoms, a theory that powerfully prefigures the modern scientific worldview.

Democritus writes, "Fools want to live to be old because they fear death." Though he was no fool, Democritus lived to be very old, dying in his 109th year, and the manner of his death shows no fear. When it was clear that he was approaching his end, his sister grew vexed because she feared that her brother would die during the festival of Thesmophora and she would be prevented from paying due respect to the goddess. In a seemingly odd gesture, Democritus ordered many hot loaves of bread to be brought to his house. By applying these to his nostrils he somehow managed to postpone his death.

Lucretius tells a different story, namely that when Democritus reached a ripe old age and was aware that "the mindful motions of his intellect were running down," he cheerfully committed suicide.

## Prodicus
(PRECISE DATES UNKNOWN, BORN BEFORE 460 BC)

There was a standing joke in antiquity that Prodicus, an apparently money-hungry Sophist, used to offer a one-drachma or fifty-drachma lecture on semantics. Socrates quips in *Cratylus* that if he had been able to afford the fifty-drachma lecture he would have understood everything about "the correctness of names," but he had to make do with the one-drachma discount version. Although we do not know the date of Prodicus' death, he was alive at the time of Socrates' trial and execution and met an eerily similar end: there is a story that Prodicus was put to death by the Athenians on the charge of corrupting their youth. His final extant fragment reads, "Milk is best if one draws it actually from the female."

# Platonists, Cyrenaics,
# Aristotelians and Cynics

### Plato
(428/427–348/347 BC)

Like Pythagoras, Anaxagoras, Christ and the Virgin Mary, it is said that Plato was never seen to laugh outright. That said, Nietzsche insists that Plato used to sleep on a copy of the works of Aristophanes, the great comic poet. The truth is that considering Plato's overwhelming philosophical importance, we have relatively little information about his life and know nothing reliable about his death.

Plato only mentions himself twice in his two dozen or so dialogues, where he is named as having been present at the trial of Socrates, but absent at the moment of Socrates' death. Xenophon, who wrote much about Socrates, mentions Plato only once, and Demosthenes mentions him twice in passing. However, there is a questionable story told by Apuleius that Socrates dreamt he saw a fledgling cygnet on his knee. All at once, it grew feathers, spread its wings and flew into the sky singing the sweetest songs. The next day, the newborn Plato was presented by his father to Socrates, who said, "This is the swan I saw."

In his famous Seventh Letter, Plato gives us the few autobiographical insights that we possess. Sadly, the letter is widely considered inauthentic among classical scholars. Plato writes of his early career and his first two visits to Sicily at the invitation of Dionysius the Elder. In fact, it might be the case that he made three visits to Sicily before becoming entirely disillusioned with politics. There is a story told in the centuries after Plato's death that such was Dionysius' appreciation of Plato's efforts that he sold him into slavery and Plato was only saved by being ransomed by the Cyrenaic philosopher Anniceris. St. Jerome claims that Plato was captured by pirates and sold into slavery, but, "because a philosopher, he was greater than the man buying him."

What else do we know? Plato was thirty-one years old when Socrates was executed. He never married. According to Plutarch, who did much to popularize Plato, he was a lover of figs. In fact, we don't even know why he was called "Plato," which means "broad" in Greek and perhaps alludes to a muscular physique and can be connected with stories of prowess in wrestling.

According to Cicero, Plato died at his writing desk. But according to Hermippus, he died at a wedding feast at the age of eighty-one and was buried in the grounds of the Academy. The Renaissance Platonist Marsilio Ficino adds that Plato died on his birthday and that the number 81 is of huge significance, since it is the most perfect number, the sum of 9 times 9. But there is another story that he died of a lice infestation. Although, as the learned Thomas Stanley points out in his 1687 *History of Philosophy*, those that spread such a nasty story about Plato "do him much injury."

## Speusippus
(DATE OF BIRTH UNKNOWN, DIED 339/338 BC)

Plato's nephew and successor as head of the Academy (originally an olive grove outside the old city of Athens, where Plato
offered instruction in philosophy to those who were interested). Speusippus committed suicide because of a painful,
paralysing disease.

## Xenocrates
(DATE OF BIRTH UNKNOWN, DIED 314 BC)

A pupil of Plato and successor to Speusippus, he died at the
age of eighty-two after falling over some unidentified bronze
utensil in the night.

## Arcesilaus
(316/315–241 BC)

Founder of what became known as "the Middle Academy,"
who introduced scepticism into the school but wrote nothing.
Arcesilaus refused to either accept or deny the possibility of
certainty, but advocated a suspension of judgement or *epoché* in
all things. He died through drinking too freely of unmixed
wine.

## Carneades
(214?–129? BC)

Carneades was the founder of "the New Academy" and a follower of Arcesilaus. He, too, was a sceptic who wrote nothing.
Plutarch notes that he spoke in a very loud voice. There is a
story of Carneades giving two (presumably quite noisy) orations in Rome in 155 BC. In the first, he argued in favour of
justice, while in the second, he argued against it. By showing
that one could consistently argue for or against a thesis, he

demonstrated that the proper philosophical attitude is a sceptical suspension of judgement.

According to Victor Brochard in *Les Sceptiques grecs* (1887 — which was incidentally one of the last books that Nietzsche seems to have read before his mental collapse), old age did not treat Carneades well. He became blind and suffered from cruel infirmities and an all-consuming languor. He was criticized for not having the courage to commit suicide, although it seems he came close. He said, "Nature which formed me will also destroy me," and died at the age of eighty-five.

## Hegesias
### (DATES UNKNOWN, THIRD CENTURY BC)

A little-known follower of the Cyrenaic school of philosophy, named after Cyrene in present-day Libya, which was also Carneades' home town. The Cyrenaics held that pleasure experienced in the present moment is the only criterion of goodness. However, Hegesias was too gloomy to entertain this form of hedonism. In his view, as reported in Brucker's *Historia Critica Philosophiae*, pleasure was impossible and the only concern of human beings was the avoidance of pain. He was so thoroughly dissatisfied with life that he wrote a book to prove that death, as the cure for all evil, was the greatest good. He became known as *peisithanatos*, "death's persuader." He positively advocated suicide although it is unclear whether he followed his own prescription.

## Aristotle
### (384–322 BC)

The Medievals called him simply "The Philosopher." We know some curious facts about Aristotle: he had small eyes, his calves were slender and he spoke with a lisp, which according to Plutarch was mimicked by some. He wore rings and had a distinctive style of dress. Tradition relates that, like Aeschlyus, Aristotle was bald, which gives an ironic twist to the discussion of mutilation in the *Meta-physics*. Aristotle argues that a cup is not mutilated if a hole is made in it, but only if the handle or some other part is broken. Similarly, a human being is not muti-lated if he loses some flesh or his spleen, but only if some extremity is missing. Now, Aristotle immediately qualifies this by adding that this is not true of *every* ex-

tremity, "but only such as cannot grow again when completely removed." He concludes that "bald people are not mutilated." Presumably this is because one's hair can, at least in principle, grow back. (For reasons that I would prefer not to reveal, I find this a reassuring conclusion.)

As is well known, Aristotle was tutor to Alexander before he was Great, between the ages of thirteen and sixteen. However, Alexander seems to have been more impressed by Diogenes the Cynic and said, with mixed humility, that if he were not himself, the person he would most like to be was Diogenes. When Alexander visited Diogenes, he stood over him as the latter was sitting in his tub and said he could have anything he wanted, to which Diogenes replied, "Get out of my light." There is a story that Diogenes offered Aristotle some dried figs, which the latter accepted and lifted aloft exclaiming, "Great is Diogenes."

After news of Alexander's death in 323 BC spread to Athens, there was an uprising against Macedonian rule which eventually led to the defeat and subjugation of Athens in the Lamian War. Because of Aristotle's association with Alexander, the Athenians brought their now familiar charge of impiety against him. He left the city saying, "I will not allow the Athenians to sin twice against philosophy." Aristotle withdrew to his late mother's estate at Chalcis on the island of Euboea and died there the following year.

According to Eumelus, Aristotle died by drinking aconite at the age of seventy, but Apollodorus says that he was sixty-three when he died a natural death, and there is a story of Aristotle dying from a stomach disease from which he apparently had long suffered.

Thanks to Diogenes Laertius, we have a record of his will, although this is very probably a later invention. Aristotle makes generous provision for Herpyllis, his concubine, a status that was not at all discreditable in the ancient world, saying that she "has been good to me." But Aristotle instructs his executors that the bones of his wife, Pythias, who died ten years after their marriage, should be buried together with his remains.

## Theophrastus
### (372–287 BC)

Pupil of Aristotle, successor as head of the Peripatetic school (so called because Aristotle liked to walk and talk), executor of his will, and possible editor of his teacher's works.

Diogenes Laertius lists over 200 works, amounting to some 232,808 lines, including treatises on honey, hair, fruit and frenzy. According to Plutarch, Theophrastus said that the soul pays a high rental to the body. All that survives of this vast corpus are two botanical works and the ninety-one-page fragment *On Sensation* (see pp. xxxi–xxxii).

Theophrastus died at the age of eighty-five and his final words typify the philosophical death. When his disciples asked if he had any final words of wisdom, Theophrastus said,

> Nothing else but this, that many of the pleasures which life boasts are but in the seeming. For when we are just beginning to live, lo! We die. Nothing then is so unprofitable as the love of glory. Farewell and may you be happy. Life holds more disappointment than advantage. But as I can no longer discuss what we ought to do, please go on with the inquiry into right conduct.

With those words, Theophrastus breathed his last. Later heads of the Peripatetic school did not come to so noble an end.

## Strato
(DATE OF BIRTH UNKNOWN, DIED 270 BC)

Strato became so thin that it is said that he felt nothing when he died.

## Lyco
(DATES UNKNOWN)

Immaculately dressed and of athletic disposition. He died at seventy-four after suffering greatly from gout.

## Demetrius
(DATES UNKNOWN)

Fatally bitten by an asp.

## Antisthenes
(445–365 BC)

An intimate of Socrates of whom almost nothing survives. He is sometimes seen as the founder of the Stoics, as this provides them with a direct line of descent from Socrates. More truly, he is best seen as the first of the Cynics, the dog-like or *kunikos* philosophers. There is a story, sometimes also attributed to Diogenes, that Antisthenes was called a "downright dog" and was so pleased with the epithet that after his death the figure of a dog was carved in stone to mark his final resting place. When he was asked about the height of human bliss, he replied, "to die happy." One day he visited Plato, who was ill and had vomited into a basin. Peering into the vomit, Antisthenes said, "The bile I see, but not the pride."

According to Aristotle in the *Metaphysics*, Antisthenes' philosophical doctrine was that nothing can be described except by its proper name: one name for each thing. In this way, Antisthenes appears to have concluded that contradiction is impossible and falsehood nearly so. To which one is tempted to respond: not true.

When Antisthenes was being initiated into the Orphic mysteries, which were secret rituals connected to the possible passage to the afterlife, the high priest said that those who became initiates would partake of many wonderful things in Hades. To which Antisthenes said to the priest, "Why then don't you die?'

On one occasion, when Antisthenes was old and ill, Diogenes visited him wearing a dagger. When Antisthenes asked what might release him from his pains, Diogenes showed him the dagger, to which the former quipped, "I said from my pains, not from my life." He died of an unspecified disease.

## Diogenes
### (DATE OF BIRTH UNKNOWN, DIED 320 BC)

Contrary to common opinion, cynicism is not cynical in the modern sense of the word. Diogenes the Cynic was once described as "a Socrates gone mad," but this overlooks the sanity of his approach to life and his real affinity with Socrates, the gadfly of the Athenian city state.

When asked what was the most beautiful thing in the world, Diogenes replied, "freedom of speech." His words and actions manifest a single-minded and unending protest against corruption, luxury and hypocrisy. The path to individual freedom requires honesty and a life of complete material austerity. Diogenes credited his teacher Antisthenes with introducing him to a life of poverty and happiness and, like the latter, he willingly accepted the epithet "dog." When Plato called him a dog, he replied, "Quite true, for I come back again and again to those who have sold me."

Diogenes is a source of wonderful stories: he threw away his cup when he saw someone drinking from their hands. He lived in a barrel, rolling in it over hot sand in the summer. He inured himself to cold by embracing statues covered with snow in the winter. He said that one could learn in a brothel that there is no difference between what costs money and what doesn't. He masturbated in the marketplace, saying that he

wished it were as easy to relieve hunger by rubbing his empty stomach. He ate raw squid in order to avoid the trouble of cooking. He mocked the auctioneer while being sold into slavery. When asked by Lysias the pharmacist if he believed in the gods, he replied, "How can I help believing in them when I see a god-forsaken wretch like you." When he was asked what was the right time to marry, he said, "For a young man not yet, for an old man never at all."

Apparently he advocated a community of wives and husbands and thought that children should also be held in common. He also thought there was nothing wrong in stealing from a temple, and eating any flesh whatsoever, including human flesh. When asked where he came from, Diogenes replied that he was a "citizen of the world" or *kosmopolites*. If only more contemporary self-styled cosmopolitans drank water from their hands, ate human flesh, hugged statues and masturbated in public. Indeed, Diogenes' "cosmopolitanism" is much more of an anti-political stance than some sort of banal internationalism.

Diogenes thought Plato's lectures a waste of time. On one occasion, Plato had defined the human being as an animal, a biped and featherless, for which he was warmly applauded. Diogenes plucked a chicken and brought it into the lecture room, declaring, "Here is Plato's man." When Plato was talking in his way about "cupness" and "tableness" in relation to the problem of universals, Diogenes said, "The table and cup I see, but I do not see tableness and cupness."

Diogenes Laertius attributes a number of writings to his illustrious namesake, none of which survive, but listed among them is a treatise on death (as well as something strangely called "Jackdaw").

When Diogenes was asked how he would like to be buried, he said, "Face down." Xeniades inquired after the reason for this, and received the mysterious reply, "Because after a little time down will be converted into up."

Diogenes is said to have been nearly ninety years old when he died. On one account, he died after eating raw octopus and on another he committed suicide by holding his breath.

Lucian depicts Diogenes in Hades ridiculing the once mighty and handsome King Mausolus, who was interred in his vast eponymous Mausoleum after conquering most of Asia Minor. All are equal before death and amount to nothing in Hades. Death makes Cynics of us all.

## Crates of Thebes
### (365–285 BC)

A pupil of Diogenes and another Cynic. Plutarch wrote a *Life of Crates*, which has been lost. Apparently, Crates spent his days in poverty and laughter. Knowing that he was dying, Crates would chant to himself the charm, "You are going, dear hunchback, you are off to the house of Hades, bent crooked by age."

## Hipparchia
### (DATES UNKNOWN, FLOURISHED LATE THIRD CENTURY BC)

Hipparchia is the first female philosopher to be mentioned by Diogenes Laertius. As a young woman Hipparchia became enamoured of the philosophy and person of Crates, who was considerably older than her. Refusing many suitors of high birth and wealth, she demanded to marry Crates. In despair, Hipparchia's parents summoned Crates in order to dissuade her. He failed and, in a last gesture, Crates ripped off all his clothes and said,

This is the bridegroom, here are his possessions; make your choice accordingly; for you will be no helpmeet of mine, unless you share my pursuits.

Hipparchia chose and from that moment she lived with and dressed like Crates and followed the life of the Cynic. According to the testimony of Sextus Empiricus in the second century, Crates and Hipparchia partook of the unusual habit of having sex in public. The manner of her death is unknown.

## Metrocles
### (DATES UNKNOWN, LATE THIRD CENTURY BC)

Metrocles was Hipparchia's brother. He reportedly farted when rehearsing a speech. This drove him into such despair that he tried to starve himself to death. Crates came to visit the distraught Metrocles and made him a meal of lupins. Of course, as lupins are members of the bean family or *fabaceae*, this merely caused him to repeat the indiscretion. For reasons that escape me, lupins were very popular amongst the Cynics and are mentioned by Diogenes in Lucian's *Dialogues*.

Eventually, Crates consoled Metrocles that such gaseous indiscretions were nothing to be ashamed of and Metrocles, formerly a pupil of Theophrastus, became a follower of Crates. Thus, philosophy begins in farting, and some might say that hot air at one end of the body is simply accompanied by hot air at the other end.

Metrocles died in old age, "having choked himself," as Diogenes Laertius curtly notes. One hopes that the cause wasn't lupins.

This puts me in mind of the following passage from Aristophanes' *The Clouds* where Socrates, in the role of the charlatan Sophist, is trying to convince the gullible Strepsiades of the cause of thunder. Socrates says,

First, think of the tiny fart that your intestines make. Then consider the heavens: their infinite farting is thunder. For thunder and farting are, in principle, one and the same.

Which is to say that thunder storms are nature's flatulent way of making a philosophical point.

## Menippus
(FLOURISHED THIRD CENTURY BC)

He was a Phoenician and originally a slave who practised usury, apparently with great success, and became a citizen of Thebes, presumably a rich one. So the story goes, he was robbed of all his money and hanged himself in despair. Menippus was a follower of Diogenes and perhaps the most cynical, in the modern sense, of the Cynics. He was certainly the Cynic most prone to laughter, a delightfully cruel ribaldry. Although none of his writings survives, he is known through a literary genre that he inspired: Menippean satire, whose great exponents are Petronius and Lucian. In the latter's *Dialogues of the Dead*, Menippus is the consummate anti-hero, summoned down to Hades to laugh at the complaints of the formerly rich and powerful, like Midas and Croesus, and the inanities of the philosophers like Socrates, who is depicted chasing boys in Hades (old habits die hard). Menippus refuses to pay Charon, ferryman to the underworld, and acquires the admiration of Cerberus, the three-headed hellhound. It is a case of one dog admiring another. Cerberus concludes their dialogue by saying,

> You alone were a credit to your breed—you and Diogenes before you, because you came in without having to be forced or pushed, but of your own accord, laughing and cursing at everyone.

I would now like to turn to three philosophical schools that exerted a vast influence in later antiquity and beyond: Scepticism, Stoicism and Epicureanism.

# Sceptics, Stoics and Epicureans

## Anaxarchus

(DATES UNKNOWN, FLOURISHED FOURTH CENTURY BC)

He was a follower of Democritus and the teacher of Pyrrho. Anaxarchus claimed that he knew nothing, not even the fact that he knew nothing.

Although he was known as "the happy man," the eudaimonist, he didn't come to a happy end. Like Pyrrho, he travelled with the conquering armies of Alexander the Great. It is said that during a banquet with Alexander he insulted Nicocreon, the tyrant of Cyprus. The tyrant never forgot the insult and when bad weather forced Anaxarchus to land his ship in Cyprus, he was seized. Nicocreon ordered that Anaxarchus be placed in a huge mortar and pounded to death with iron pestles. At which point, Anaxarchus exclaimed, "Pound, pound the pouch containing Anaxarchus, you do not pound Anaxarchus."

When Nicocreon ordered that his tongue be cut out, it is said that, like Timycha, Anaxarchus bit off his own tongue and spat it at the tyrant.

## Pyrrho
(360–262 BC)

Pyrrho was the founder of the hugely important tradition of ancient scepticism. As he left no writings, his ideas come down to us through his pupil Timon, a professional dancer turned philosopher, who called himself "Cyclops" because he only had one eye.

But the clearest and most powerful account of Pyrrhonian scepticism can be found in Sextus Empiricus, a physician from the second century. As with the other sceptics, we know very little about Pyrrho's life. It is said that he lived to be ninety years old. We do know that he travelled with Alexander the Great as a court philosopher to India and allegedly met with the naked ascetics whom the Greeks called "Gymnosophists." As Jonathan Barnes notes, "It is by no means impossible that Pyrrhonism has an Indian godfather."

Timon, the one-eyed ex-dancer, says that "Truly, no other mortal could rival Pyrrho," and he was famous for always maintaining the same tranquil state. Aboard a ship, during a ferocious storm that terrified the other passengers, Pyrrho pointed to a pig that calmly went on eating and said that this is how the wise person should behave. When he was badly bitten by a dog and momentarily frightened, he apologized by saying that "it was difficult to strip oneself of being human." Such tranquillity of mind is the goal of ancient scepticism, for it is here that we find well-being. In this, it differs dramatically from the modern connotations of scepticism. We normally connect it with radical doubt about the existence of the material world, God or the soul. In modern philosophy, in Descartes and Kant for instance, scepticism represents a dangerous and dizzying threat that has to be answered by discovering certainty. By contrast, in antiquity, scepticism *is* the answer and it was not some academic experience of doubt, but the expression of an entire way of life. Scepticism is eminently practical.

In Greek, *skeptikos* means "inquirer" and the sceptic is

someone who does not claim to know, but who persists in their inquiries. There are two sides to every story; that is, we can assemble evidence that would justify belief *x* or its negation *y*. To borrow some of the more colourful ancient examples, the Persians believed that there was nothing unusual about having sex with their daughters, while Chrysippus believed that it was a matter of indifference whether one had sex with one's mother, whereas mainstream ancient Greek opinion and law would have winced at both these beliefs.

By contrast, the sceptic is simply sceptical about the possibility of belief as such. Their counsel is to look at both sides of an issue and practise a suspension of judgement, or what was called an *epoché*, in all matters. In Philo's words, "There is nothing firm we can say about anything." The sceptic neither declines nor chooses, but simply suspends judgement and practises silence or *aphasia*. Thus, the sceptic refuses to either assert or deny that there is life after death, whether the soul is separate from the body or whether there is a heaven or a hell. In neither asserting nor denying anything, one lives in a tranquillity that is open to all forms of inquiry and an utter stranger to any species of dogmatism. Appropriately enough, it is not known how Pyrrho died, although it would be taking his scepticism too far to deny that it occurred.

## Zeno of Citium
(335–263 BC)

The founder of Stoicism, who was fond of eating green figs and basking in the sun. He was swarthy, with a twisted neck and by all accounts rather harsh in manner. Interestingly, Zeno was not a Greek, but a Phoenician who ended up in Athens, poverty-stricken, because of a shipwreck off Piraeus, the port of Athens, with a cargo of purple. Of course, Plato's *Republic* takes place at Piraeus, and it was against Plato that Zeno wrote his own *Republic*, which was extremely radical, greatly admired and established his philosophical reputation. According to Plutarch, Zeno argued that political organization should not be based on cities, each marked out by its own legal system,

but instead all human beings should be regarded as fellow citizens. In a highly un-Greek manner, citizenship was extended
to women and slaves. Zeno also argued against the building of
temples and lawcourts and denounced the use of money. He
was in favour of an open community of wives and husbands
and advocated unisex clothing. It is probable that he also
defended incest and cannibalism. True, Zeno's radicalism was
a source of embarrassment to the later Roman Stoics, like
Seneca and Marcus Aurelius, when Stoicism enjoyed imperial
approval at the very highest echelons of society.

Zeno was famously frugal, eating raw food and wearing a
thin cloak. He was seemingly oblivious to the effects of rain,
heat and painful illness. Returning to our theme of lupins,
there is a story of Zeno getting drunk and nicely happy at a
party. When he was challenged as to how much his usual
unpleasant manner was changed, he replied, "Lupins too
are bitter, but when they are soaked they become wet."

Zeno gave his lectures on the *stoa*, the covered walkways
or porticos that surrounded the Athenian marketplace. His
followers were first called Zenonians and later Stoics. He
presided over his school for fifty-eight years and the manner
of his death at the age of ninety-eight is bizarre. One day, as
he was leaving the school, he tripped and fell, breaking a
toe. Lying there in pain, he struck the ground with his fist
and quoted a line from the *Niobe* of Timotheus, "I come of
my own accord; why then call me?" He died on the spot
through holding his breath.

Interestingly, the manner of his death illustrates well the
Stoic belief that virtue consists in following the law of nature
and that all natural events and entities—lupins included—
are the expression of divine providence.

### Ariston

(FLOURISHED THIRD CENTURY BC)

A pupil of Zeno, known as "The Bald," who proclaimed indifference towards all things. He said that the end of life was the
cultivation of indifference towards vice and virtue where one

could be equally disposed to both and neither. The story goes that, being bald, he died of sunstroke. To which Diogenes Laertius devotes the worst of his terrible verses:

> Wherefore, Ariston, when old and bald did you let the
>     sun roast your forehead?
> Thus seeking warmth more than was reasonable, you
>     lit unwillingly upon the chill reality of death.

## Dionysius
### (FLOURISHED THIRD CENTURY BC)

For some reason, he was known as "The Renegade." He committed suicide by starving himself.

## Cleanthes
### (331–232 BC)

Zeno's successor, second leader of the Stoics and originally a professional boxer.

Cleanthes was a philosopher of great patience and slow wit (it is not known whether pugilism was the cause). As he was something of a plodder, Cleanthes was sometimes known as "The Ass."

Like Zeno, he believed that happiness could be defined as "a good flow of life." For lack of money, he wrote down Zeno's lectures on oyster shells and ox bones. He enjoyed the respect of his faster-thinking pupil, Chrysippus, although they had a curious disagreement about the nature of walking: Cleanthes said that walking was breath extending from what the Stoics called the "commanding faculty" of the soul to the feet. Chrysippus maintained that walking was the commanding faculty itself.

In his old age, Cleanthes suffered from extreme inflammation of the gums and refused all food. After being treated successfully by doctors, he persisted with his fast, arguing that he had already walked too far down the road to death. He starved himself until he expired.

## Chrysippus
(280–207 BC)

The third leader of the Stoics, from 232 until his death, of whom it was said, "If there had been no Chrysippus, there would be no Stoa."

Chrysippus was a philosopher of great brilliance and some arrogance who allegedly wrote 705 books dealing extensively with logic and the nature of propositions. Here are some examples of his deftness in matters logical:

> What is not in the city is not in the house either: now there is no well in the city, ergo there is none in the house either.

And again, even more bewilderingly,

> There is a certain head, and that head you have not. Now this being so, there is a head which you have not, therefore you are without a head.

Wonderful how logic helps one to know oneself!

Diogenes Laertius scandalously reports that Chrysippus permitted marriage with mothers, daughters and sons, and in the third book of his *On Justice*, he allowed eating the corpses of the dead. One dreads to think about the catering at Chrysippus' family funerals.

There are two stories of his death, both involving alcohol. In the first, he took a draught of sweet wine unmixed with water, was seized with dizziness and died five days later. But the second is even better: after an ass (presumably not his old teacher, Cleanthes) had eaten his figs, he cried out to an old woman, "Now give the ass a drink of pure wine to wash down the figs." Thereupon, he laughed so heartily that he died.

But perhaps the last laugh is on us, for if we pick our way through the small thicket of fragments that are all that survive of Chrysippus' writings, he can be seen to advance the following theses. (i) Death is the separation of the soul from the body. (ii) For the Stoics, the individual soul or *microcosmos* is part and parcel of the "world soul" or *macrocosmos*, which is identical with God or the divine principle. (iii) As such, the life of the soul does not end with death, but is part of what the Stoics saw as the eternal and eternally recurring cycle of the world order. (iv) Therefore, in a fragment from Lactantius, Chrysippus concludes, "It is evidently not impossible that we too after our death will return again to the shape we now are, after certain periods of time have elapsed." We can therefore perhaps look forward to seeing more of Chrysippus in the future.

## Epicurus
(341–271 BC)

The Stoics were bitterly opposed to the Epicureans. The latter's founder, Epicurus, was called "the preacher of effeminacy" by Epictetus, and his views on the nature of the gods were derided by Cicero. Clement of Alexandria, the Christian, called Epicurus "The Prince of Atheism." Timocrates claimed in his *Merriment* that Epicurus used to vomit twice a day from overindulgence. In response to the nauseating abuse of one Nausiphanes, Epicurus called the latter "a jelly-fish, an illiterate, a fraud and a trollop"—and he was only warming up.

Other Stoics were more conciliatory and Seneca writes in *On the Happy Life* that Epicurus does not at all deserve his bad reputation. What is most surprising in Diogenes Laertius' ten books of turgid reportage is the strength and length of his defence of Epicurus. "These people are stark mad," Diogenes says to Epicurus' accusers, and he gets the longest and

most detailed treatment of any philosopher in *Lives*, running
to 154 pages.

Epicurus was a prolific author, and his main treatise on
natural philosophy extended to a massive thirty-seven volumes. All that survive are four letters and scattered fragments
and testimonies, preserved largely thanks to Diogenes Laertius, who says of him, "His goodness was proved in all ways."

A large part of the problem with Epicurus is with the
connotations surrounding the word "Epicurean." If, as we
saw above, the Cynics were not cynical, then Epicurus was
far from being an Epicurean. On the contrary, he advocated
abstemiousness in all things. He said that he was prepared to
compete with Zeus in happiness as long as he had a barley
cake and some water. Epicurus adds, "Send me a little pot
of cheese; then, when I like, I may feast sumptuously." Epicureanism is concerned with the cultivation of happiness,
which is understood as the state of bliss that would accompany a life without wants, worries and, most of all, anxiety.
A person will never be happy if they are anxious about what
they do not have. To live without anxiety is to enjoy the bliss
of the gods.

So, Epicureanism is not about drinking, partying, enjoying boys and women, or consuming fish and the other dain-
ties of an extravagant table. It is concerned with *prudence* in
all matters. The wise Epicurean will not marry or rear a family, nor will he "drivel when drunken." As for fornication,
Epicurus says, "No one was ever the better for sexual indul-
gence." Of course, given Epicurus' extremely ascetic understanding of pleasure, it is not at all clear why anyone should
want to become a hedonist.

The Epicureans lived in small communities, modelled on
the one that Epicurus established on the outskirts of Athens,
called "The Garden." We know very little about the life of
these communities, except that they included household servants and women on equal terms and they placed a very high
value on friendship. Epicurus says that the greatest blessedness in human life is the possession of friendship and that
the wise man "will on occasion die for a friend."

The painful truth of Epicurus' purported pleasure-seeking can be seen in the circumstances of his death, some seven years after that of Plato. Epicurus was a notoriously sickly character and there was even a book written by his disciple Metrodorus called *On the Weak Constitution of Epicurus.* He died in excruciating pain from renal failure after two weeks of suffering caused by kidney stones. But he expired cheerfully, surrounded by his friends and disciples. In a final letter to Hermarchus, Epicurus writes,

> On the happiest, and the last, day of my life. I am suffering from diseases of the bladder and intestines, which are of the utmost possible severity.

But he goes on, amazingly,

> Yet all my sufferings are counterbalanced by the contentment of soul which I derive from remembering our reasonings and discoveries.

Two millennia later, in 1649, with the rise of the modern scientific view of the world, it was this contentment of soul that fascinated Pierre Gassendi in his extended defence of the life and opinions of Epicurus that I discussed above (p. xxxv). In my view, there is no more relevant ancient philosopher for our time than Epicurus, for he combines a thoroughly atomistic, scientific view of nature with an ethical stance that aims at prudence, calm and overcoming the terror of annihilation. Epicurus' view of death is plain and powerful and it was touched on in the introduction to this book (pp. xxix–xxx):

> Against other things it is possible to obtain security. But when it comes to death we human beings all live in an unwalled city.

In contrast to the Pythagoreans, Platonists and Stoics, death is understood as complete extinction and the soul is

nothing more than a temporary amalgam of atomic particles.
The vital moral corollary of this view is that it is the fear of
death and the longing for immortality that ruins life. What
must be cultivated is the idea that death is nothing to us, certainly nothing to be feared. As Epicurus puts it, "To practise
living well and to practise dying well are one and the same."
If life can be lived as a practice for death, then Epicurus'
"contentment of soul" might be more than a vain wish.


## Lucretius, Titus Carus
### (FLOURISHED FIRST CENTURY BC)

With Epicurus, we are finished with the long line of ancient
Greeks. We know almost nothing about the author of the
long, didactic Latin epic devoted to the teaching of Epicurus,
*De Rerum Natura* (*On the Nature of the Universe* or *On the Nature of
Things*). But there is the infamous statement of St. Jerome,
who writes four centuries after Lucretius in an entry under the
year 94 BC,

> The poet Titus Lucretius Carus was born. A love potion
> drove him mad, and he composed, in the intervals of his
> insanity, several books which Cicero corrected. He com-
> mitted suicide aged 43.

We have no reason to either believe or disbelieve this story,
although it would obviously suit Jerome's Christian purposes
to denounce the hedonistic excesses of the great pagan poet.
But the story of Lucretius being driven mad by a love potion
passed into legend; Tennyson wrote his "Lucretius" in 1868. In
this poem, he imagines the story from the perspective of
Lucretius' wife, one Lucilla, who "found her master cold."
This was not for want of love on the poet's part, but because he
was "buried in some weightier argument," such as the roll of
the Latin hexameter or the 300 scrolls left behind by his master Epicurus, "whom he held divine." Unwilling to accept
such coldness, Lucilla grew wrathful and petulant, employing
the services of a witch to brew a love philtre. Far from induc-

ing the desired amorous effect, the potion produced in
Lucretius a horrific vision of the Epicurean universe with
atoms colliding randomly in the void. In his raving madness,
Lucretius' passion is directed not at his wife, but to the highest
Epicurean virtue of tranquillity, whom he personifies and
addresses in a pained paean:

> O thou Passionless bride, divine Tranquility
> Yearn'd after by the wisest of the wise
> Who fail to find thee.

After acknowledging his failure to woo divine tranquillity,
he drives a knife into his side and expires. Lucilla must have
remained somewhat sexually frustrated by this outcome.

Whatever the validity of Jerome's story, we find Lucretius'
views on death powerfully expounded at the end of Book 3 of
*De Rerum Natura*. Having argued for the mortality and indeed
materiality of the soul, Lucretius joins his master Epicurus
in claiming that "Death is nothing to us." It is nothing to
fear, because

> One who no longer is cannot suffer, or differ in any way
> from one who has never been born, when once this mortal
> life has been usurped by death the immortal.

So, why weep and wail over death? It is nothing. It is less
than sleep, which is its resemblance. The difference is simply that in death we don't wake and our bodily form disperses
into "the seething mass of matter." An eternity passed before
we were born. Is that a source of anxiety? Of course not.
Then why should the eternity that will pass after our death
be any greater source of anxiety? We should also have no fear
of what will happen to our body after death, and Lucretius
writes, with a rude realism,

> For if it is really a bad thing after death to be mauled and
> crunched by ravening jaws, I cannot see why it should not
> be disagreeable to roast in the scorching flames of a

funeral pyre, or to lie embalmed in honey, stifled and stiff
with cold, on the surface of a chilly slab, or to be squashed
under a crushing weight of earth.

Whether squashed, scorched, stifled or soaked in honey,
the philosopher knows when to die and does not appeal
against his sentence when it has been passed. Epicurus is
mentioned just once in Lucretius' poem in connection with
his preparedness for death. To run away from death is to run
away from oneself, to succumb to the desire for immortality,
against which Lucretius offers a mathematical argument:
the amount of time one is alive is not going to reduce the
eternity of one's death:

> So an unquenchable thirst for life keeps us always on the
> gasp. By prolonging life, we cannot subtract or whittle
> away one jot from the duration of our death. However
> many generations you may add to your store by living,
> there waits for you nonetheless the same eternal death.

What is a year or a decade more or less in comparison to
the length of time spent dead? Viewed from the standpoint
of eternity, what Spinoza calls *sub specie aeternitatis*, life's
brevity or longevity is nothing in comparison to the eternity
of our death. Moreover, this eternity is nothing to fear, but is
the basis for contentment and calm.

# Classical Chinese Philosophers

Classical Chinese philosophy belongs to two rich and complex historical epochs: the later part of the "Spring and Autumn" period (722–481 BC) and the "Warring States" period (403–221 BC), which ended with the unification of China under the Qin Dynasty, the installation of the first emperor, and the completion of the Great Wall. It is also known as the period of the "Hundred Philosophers," the first and most prominent of whom was Master Kong or Kongzi.

## Kongzi or Confucius
### (551–479 BC)

Without doubt, no philosopher has influenced more human beings than Kongzi and he is inseparable from whatever "Chineseness" has meant for the past two and a half millennia. The suffix "Zi" or "Tzu" means teacher or master, and Kongzi's name was Latinized by Jesuit missionaries into Confucius. Apparently his mother used to call him "Qiu," meaning "mound" or "hillock," because of the unusual elevation on the top of his forehead with which he is often depicted.

Like Socrates, Kongzi was not particularly good-looking and he said of himself (and one thinks of the Cynics), "To say that I am like a dog from a bereaved family, that is so indeed, that is so indeed." The great period of classical Chinese philosophy fascinatingly coincides with ancient Greek thought and just as the latter is characterized by intense disagreements between Platonists, Cynics, Stoics and Epicureans, so, too, Chinese thought finds bitter opposition between Confucian, Daoist and Mohist schools.

For Kongzi, birth and death are boundaries and the religious rites for mourning are hugely important occasions for giving proper expression to the value of human life. Kongzi revived the ancient, but in his day forgotten, rituals connected with burial and mourning, some of which still endure in China. When his mother died, she was buried with great splendour and solemnity and Kongzi resigned all his public offices and mourned her in solitude for three years. He also showed extreme grief over the death of his favourite disciple, Yen Yüan, and when his disciples suggested that he was showing undue sorrow, he replied, "Am I? Yet if not for him, for whom should I show undue sorrow?"

Legend has it that Kongzi knew when he was going to die and had the following despairing vision in a dream:

For a long time the world has been unregulated; no one understands how to follow me. Last night I dreamed that I was sitting before the sacrificial offerings between the pillars where the coffin is placed.

Kongzi died at the age of seventy-three surrounded by a large number of faithful disciples, and his coffin was placed between pillars as described in his dream. His disciples mourned him for three years before dispersing to their homes; with the exception of Tze Kung, a very close disciple, who didn't feel that the debt to his master had been paid and mourned for a further three years.

In the *Lun yü* or *Analects*, Kongzi expresses some agnosticism about the possibility of the afterlife. Chi-lu asks Kongzi, "May I ask about death?" to which the latter replies, "You do not understand even life. How can you understand death?"

## Laozi or Lao Tzu
### (FLOURISHED IN THE SIXTH CENTURY BC)

It is altogether unclear whether Laozi really existed, and the connection between such a person and the author of the *Tao Te Ching* is weak and embroiled in legend. According to that legend, as preserved by China's first great historian, Sima Qian, Kongzi went to visit Laozi and they disagreed strongly about the importance of ritual. When the kingdom of Zhou was disintegrating in war, Laozi left his post as imperial librarian and travelled west on a buffalo. When he came to the Han Gu Pass, the border guard understood that Laozi was leaving for ever and asked him to write down some of his wisdom. Laozi immediately complied and thus the *Tao Te Ching* came into being. When he finished, Laozi got back on his buffalo and was never seen again. No one knows where he died.

He wrote,

I suffer great disaster because I have a body. When I have no body, what disaster can there be?

Laozi was turned into a heavenly body when asteroid 7854 was named after him. 7853 is named after Kongzi.

# Mozi

(DATES UNCERTAIN, SOME SOURCES SAY 470–390 BC)

So the story goes, Mozi was the founder of Mohism, a philosophical school devoted to frugality, self-reflection and what would now be called distributive justice. Mozi, the neglected rival of Kongzi, believed the Confucian concern with ritual consumed too much money and impoverished the people.

Zhuangzi makes the following quip at the expense of Mozi:

> He would have men toil through life, with a bare funeral at death. Such teaching is too barren. He considered self-suffering as the ideal.

The Mohists were bitterly opposed to what they saw as the bureaucratic elitism of Confucianism with its contemptuous and patronizing idea of the common people or "Min." The Mohists were the proletarians and democrats in classical Chinese philosophy and their views were progressively marginalized by successive imperial dynasties. As a consequence, we know next to nothing about Mozi's life. It appears that Mozi was a craftsman from the lower classes who ended up holding an official position because of his expertise in fortification. Indeed, there is much debate about the meaning of the name "Mozi." Initially, it was thought that "Mo" was the family or clan name and "Ti" or "Zi" his personal name. But recent scholarship suggests that "Mo" is the generic name for someone who has been branded as a criminal slave. On this interpretation, the disciples of the Way of Mo opposed the power of the ruling class by declaring themselves followers of slaves. He led an itinerant lifestyle. Huai Nantze remarks, "Mozi did not retain a single seat long enough to make it warm."

## Mengzi or Mencius
(372–289 BC)

Mengzi, a defender of an idealized and lofty version of Confucianism against the Mohists, proclaimed the goodness of human nature and sought to cultivate rightness or proper conduct in all things, what he saw as the way of Heaven or "Tian."

On one occasion, Mengzi writes,

> I desire fish and I desire bear's paws. If I cannot have both of them, I will give up fish and take bears' paws.

Mengzi pursues the analogy by claiming that one may desire life and rightness. If one cannot have both of them, then one should give up life and pursue rightness. Therefore, as much as one may detest death, one can detest something more than death, namely not doing the right thing. He concludes, typically,

> Thus, there are things that we desire more than life, and things that we detest more than death. It is not only exemplary persons who have this in mind; all human beings have it. It is only that the exemplary persons are able to avoid losing it, that is all.

As a non-exemplary person, I'll take fish and life and politely pass on rightness and bears' paws.

## Zhuangzi or Chuang Tzu
(369–286 BC)

To my mind, Zhuangzi is by far the most intriguing, deep and witty of the classical Chinese philosophers. Unlike the lofty moralism of Mengzi, the gnomic utterings of Laozi

and the moral propriety of Kongzi, the philosophical universe of Zhuangzi is linguistically dazzling and philosophically unsettling.

The core of Zhuangzi's version of Daoism is the belief that everything should be allowed to behave according to its nature. Right behaviour consists in allowing things to be, without forcing them to be something else through an effort of will or engaging in empty speculation. This is one way of approaching the idea of "non-action" or "*wu wei*," which does not mean doing nothing, but only doing what accords with a thing's nature. Thus, for Zhuangzi,

> The great earth burdens me with a body, forces upon me the toil of life, eases me in old age, and calms me in death. If life is good, death is good also.

When Zhuangzi was about to die, his disciples wanted to prepare a lavish funeral in the Confucian style. But he refused, saying, "The sun and earth will be my coffin." When his disciples objected, saying, "We are worried that your body will be eaten by crows and eagles," Zhuangzi offered the remarkable reply,

> An unburied body will be consumed by crows and eagles, but a buried body will be eaten up by ants. So you're snatching food from the mouths of crows and eagles and feeding it into the mouths of ants. Why are you showing favours to ants?

For Zhuangzi, there is nothing in existence that is not good. Death is nothing more than a change from one form of existence to another. If we can find happiness in this existence, then why can't we also find happiness in a new form of existence as antfood, crowfood or even bearfood? Existence is defined by its transitions from one form to another and all forms have to be accepted for what they are. Thus, Zhuangzi writes,

> Death and life are never-ceasing transformations. They are not the end of a beginning. If we once understand this principle we can equalize life and death.

We have met this idea of the equality of life and death once or twice already in this book, but Zhuangzi is making an even more radical claim: if life and death are equal, then the dead shouldn't be mourned, but their passing should be accepted and even celebrated. This can be illustrated with the following extraordinary anecdote. After Zhuangzi's wife died, Hui Tzu visited him to offer his condolences. He found him sitting with his legs sprawled out, pounding on a tub and singing, "You lived with her, she brought up your children and grew old." When Hui Tzu suggested that this was perhaps a little disrespectful, Zhuangzi protested, saying,

> When she first died, do you think I didn't grieve like anyone else? But I looked back to her beginning and the time before she was born. Not only the time before she was born, but the time before she had a body. Not only the time before she had a body, but the time before she had a spirit. In the midst of the jumble of wonder and mystery a change took place and she had a spirit. Another change and she had a body. Another change and she was born. Now there's been another change and she's dead. It's just like the progression of the four seasons: spring, summer, autumn, winter. Now she's lying peacefully in a vast room. If I were to follow after her bawling and sobbing, it would show that I don't understand anything about fate. So I stopped.

Ashes to ashes, dust to dust, antfood to antfood, one might mutter. Existence is the passage from the formlessness that precedes life to the formlessness that succeeds death. One must ring the changes, pound the tub and sing.

In a debate about death among four masters, Master Lai says, "If I think well of life, for the same reason I must think well of my death." We mustn't disturb the process of change from life to death, but affirm it, for it is a necessary transformation. When Master Yu fell ill, he was not sad, but genuinely curious about what change awaited him: maybe the creator would transform his left arm into a rooster, in which case he would be able to watch all night; or his right arm might become a crossbow pellet, in which case he'd be able to shoot down an owl for roasting; or his buttocks might be turned into cartwheels, in which case he would save a huge amount of money on underwear. Master Lai looked at Master Yu and said,

> How wonderful the creator is! What is he going to make of you next? Where is he going to send you? Will he make you into a rat's liver? Will he make you into a bug's arm?

It is not difficult to imagine how such behaviour infuriated the moral propriety of Kongzi, who allegedly exclaimed,

> What sort of men are they anyway? . . . They look upon life as a swelling tumor, a protruding wen, and upon death as the draining of a sore or the bursting of a boil. To such men as these, how could there be any question of putting life first or death last?

Unlike Kongzi, who ended up a police commissioner, Zhuangzi refused all public office and spent his whole life in destitution and often appeared malnourished. One day, when Zhuangzi was fishing in the Pu River, Lord Wei from the state of Chu sent two ministers to invite him to run the state's affairs. Holding the fishing rod in his hands, Zhuangzi said,

> I've heard that there is a sacred turtle in the state of Chu, which was dead for three thousand years. The lord keeps it

in a bamboo case covered with a kerchief. Would this tur-
tle prefer to be dead and kept in such a grand style or to be
alive and drag its tail through the mud?

The ministers said, "It would prefer to be alive and drag its
tail in the mud." To which Zhuangzi replied, "Please go
away, then. I'd rather drag my tail in the mud." Even if our
buttocks might have been transformed into cartwheels, I suggest that we follow Zhuangzi and drag our tails through the
mud.

## Han Feizi
### (280–233 BC)

Han Feizi was the author of *The Way of the Ruler*. He met an
ugly end at the hands of a wayward ruler. In an age when
eloquence was the most potent political weapon, Han Feizi
stuttered badly. However, he wrote well, but this was the
cause of his undoing. His writings fell into the hands of the
King of Qin, who would eventually ascend the throne as
the first Emperor of China, Qin Shi Huang. The king
expressed his deep admiration for Han Feizi's writings to
his minister, Li Si. Now, Li Si was a former fellow student
of Han Feizi and bitterly jealous of the latter's literary
brilliance. Sometime later, the King of Qin had laid siege to
the ruler of Han, King An, who had always refused to
follow the Way of Han Feizi. In the hope of saving his
state from destruction, King An dispatched Han Feizi to
the King of Qin, who was initially delighted. However,
green-eyed Li Si persuaded the king that Han Feizi would
always have the interest of the enemy Han at heart and never
the king. Han Feizi was imprisoned and before the king
had the chance to regret his decision (which he apparently
did), Li Si sent poison to the prison. Han Feizi drank it and
died. Li Si became prime minister to the first Emperor of
China. This is another reason why philosophers should keep
out of politics.

## Zen and the Art of Dying

I am not an expert in Zen Buddhism and some of its Western variants invite my scepticism. Yet what is fascinating is the tradition of Japanese death poems written by Zen monks on the verge of death. In addition to leaving the usual will, Zen monks would write a farewell to life in the form of a haiku or other short elegiac poem. Ideally, the dying monk would anticipate the moment of his death, write his poem, set aside his ink brush, cross his arms, straighten his back, and die.

An extreme and slightly comical example of this can be found in Eisai (1141–1215), one of the founders of Japanese Zen. He went to Kyoto to show people how to die. To this end, the monk preached to the crowd, sat still in the Zen position and died. But when his followers complained that his death had been too sudden, he revived and died in exactly the same way five days later. These death poems display extreme economy, formal rigour and beauty, such as in the following haiku from Koraku (*d.* 1837).

> *The joy of dewdrops*
> *In the grass as they*
> *Turn back to vapour.*

Or this, from Dokyo Etan (*d.* 1721),

> *Here in the shadow of death it is hard*
> *To utter the final word.*
> *I'll only say, then,*
> *"Without saying."*
> *Nothing more,*
> *Nothing more.*

However, many of these death poems are wonderfully self-deprecating and humorous, as in the following haiku from Mabutsu (*d.* 1874):

*Moon in a barrel:*
*You never know just when*
*The bottom will fall out.*

Or the following excerpt from Kyoriku's *kyoka* death poem which reminds us of Zhuangzi's idea of the corpse as antfood:

*Till now I thought*
*That death befell*
*The untalented alone.*
*If those with talent, too,*
*Must die*
*Surely they make*
*Better manure.*

# Romans (Serious and Ridiculous)
## and Neoplatonists

### Cicero, Marcus Tullius
(106–43 BC)

Moving back from east to west, it is time to turn to Rome and consider what it might mean to die like a Roman. As we shall see, it is a fairly bloody business. In *De Finibus Bonorum et Malorum* (*About the Ends of Goods and Evils*), Cicero writes,

> A great commander's death is famous; but philosophers mostly die in their beds. Still it makes a difference how they die.

Cicero is thinking of the death of Epicurus, whose intellectual pleasure mastered his extreme physical pain. However, far from his bed, the violent death of Cicero more resembles the demise of a commander than a philosopher. He died nobly among the disintegration of the Roman Republic that he had always sought to defend against its slide into despotism. Although Cicero had no prior knowledge of the plot to murder Caesar on the Ides of March, Brutus was an intimate friend and indeed shouted Cicero's name as he waved the blood-stained dagger (hardly politically discreet behaviour). In his final philosophical work, *De Officiis* (*On*

*Duties*), Cicero tirelessly justifies Caesar's murder as a legitimate act of tyrannicide. But any idea of a restoration of the Roman Republic was short-lived. Brutus and the other "liberators" were chased out of Rome, and the consul, Mark Antony, clearly intended to take Caesar's place.

Knowing he was in danger, Cicero planned to escape Rome for Greece in July 44 BC. Yet—inexplicably—Cicero returned, initially in triumph. He denounced Antony in a series of four orations, called the Philippics in memory of Demosthenes' denunciations of Philip of Macedon. After a new Roman triumvirate had been formed, composed of Octavian, Antony and Lepidus, proscriptions were issued for Cicero's execution. His brother and nephew met the same fate. A band of soldiers, led by the centurion Herennius, battered down the door to Cicero's house, but he was not at home. A freed slave, Philologus, who had been educated by Cicero, informed the soldiers that his master had just escaped and was heading towards the sea.

Perceiving that Herennius and his men were pursuing him, Cicero confronted his assailants. Herennius then killed him, first cutting off Cicero's head and then, by the order of Antony, his hands, the very hands that had written the Philippics against Antony. Cicero's head and hands were sent to Antony in Rome who ordered that they be fastened above the rostra where the Roman orators spoke. As one might imagine, this was something of a disincentive to free speech.

For his betrayal, Philologus was ordered by Cicero's sister-in-law to cut off his own flesh piece by piece, and then roast and eat it—the world's first self-service barbecue.

## Seneca, Lucius Annaeus
### (4 BC–AD 65)

Seneca writes, "It is not that we have a short time to live, but that we waste a lot of it." The problem with life is not its brevity, but the fact that we squander it as though it was never going to end, as though life were in infinite supply. We live in a counterfeit immortality, believing our desire to be immortal and concealing the fear of death that underpins it. Seneca writes, "You act like mortals in all that you fear, and like immortals in all that you desire." The correct philosophical attitude is exactly the other way around.

For Seneca, the philosopher is the person who is at home to all human beings and who will always make time. As Wittgenstein remarks in *Culture and Value*, "This is how philosophers should greet each other: "Take your time!" The philosopher will show you how to take time and will teach you how to die. For Seneca, anxiety is caused by fear for the future, and this fear is the cause of the weeping over the shortness of life. He gives the example of the Persian emperor Xerxes, deploying his huge army over the vast plains, who wept because in a hundred years not a soul in that body of men would still be alive. Most of us have imagined the world without us or those we love in it. Yet, such anxiety over the future is paralysing and the cause of the feeling of life's brevity.

The philosopher, for Seneca, enjoys a long life because he does not worry over its shortness. He lives in the present and, in my view, the only immortality that philosophy can promise is to permit us to inhabit the present without concern for the future. All honours and offices of state are soon forgotten, monuments and public buildings fall into ruin. But not so the philosopher, Seneca says,

> So the life of the philosopher extends widely: he is not confined by the same boundary as others. He alone is free from the laws that limit the human race, and all ages serve him as though he were a god. Some time has passed: he grasps it in recollection. Time is present: he uses it. Time is to come: he anticipates it. This combination of all times into one gives him a long life.

What the philosopher seeks and tries to teach is something "great and supreme and nearly divine." It is a steady firmness of mind, a tranquillity, in which the mind seeks to

follow a steady course, remaining in a state of equilibrium. But this is not the tranquillity of Lucretius and Epicurus, with their materialist belief in the mortality of the soul. For Stoics, like Seneca, Epictetus and Marcus Aurelius, the human being is a compound of soul and body where death is the separation of one from the other. But although Stoicism influences Christianity, this notion of the soul is not Christian. The soul for the Stoics is "divine breath" that is evidenced in our rationality, what is also called "the commanding faculty." This rational soul is part of the world soul, which is divine. Thus, in an image much used by the Stoics and that we saw above in Chrysippus, the individual soul is the microcosm of the divine animating macrocosm. At the point of death, it is into this macrocosm that we return, this universal and ultimately divine substance.

Seneca wrote: "He will live badly who does not know how to die well." The important thing is to be prepared for death, to be courageous. Death might come at any moment. Seneca concludes his essay "On Tranquility of Mind" with stories of philosophers who remained calm in the face of fortune. When Zeno of Citium lost all his possessions in a shipwreck, he said, "Fortune bids me a less encumbered philosopher," a remark later echoed by Spinoza. When philosophers are threatened by emperors or would-be emperors, what must be maintained at all times is tranquillity.

When Julius Caesar condemned Julius Canus to death, what was most remarkable was how calm he remained while awaiting his execution. Canus was playing a game of draughts when the call came for him to be killed. He counted the pieces and said to his companion, "See that you don't falsely claim after my death that you won." Upon seeing the sorrow of his friends, he said to them, "Why are you sad? You are wondering whether souls are immortal: I shall soon find out." Seneca concludes, "No one ever pursued philosophy longer."

Sadly, Seneca's own death is more tragicomic than heroic. Having received the order from Nero that he should take his life, Seneca spoke calmly to his friends and embraced his wife, Paulina, urging her to endure a husband's loss with honourable consolations. She refused all consolation and decided to take her own life along with her husband. At one and the same moment, they slit the arteries of their arms with daggers and began a peculiarly tedious process of dying. Tormented by his wife's suffering, Seneca asked for her to be removed into another chamber. Then came word from Nero forbidding Paulina's death. Soldiers bound up her arms and staunched the bleeding. Apparently, she lived on for several years.

Seneca seems to have had considerable difficulty dying. Tacitus reports that, unable to die by bleeding to death, because of an aged frame attenuated by a frugal diet, he asked for poison, of the same kind administered to Socrates. He drank it in vain, however, and death stubbornly refused to come. Eventually, he was placed into a bath of hot water and suffocated with steam by his servants. As he had requested in his will, his body was burnt without any of the usual funeral rites.

## Petronius, Titus Niger
### (DIED 66)

Petronius was Nero's *arbiter elegantiae*, his adviser in matters of luxury and extravagance. He was a notoriously debauched man, who passed his days in sleep and his nights in excessive pleasure. Like Seneca, and on suspicion of treason, Petronius was obliged to commit suicide. However, unlike Seneca, his death was elaborately staged as a kind of anti-Socrates, making fun of the ideal of the philosophical death. Tacitus writes that, having made an incision into his veins, Petronius bound them up, only to reopen them and bind them again, according to his humour. Petronius did not expound on the immortality of the soul or the theories of philosophers, but chatted with friends, told jokes and sang light and playful songs. To some of his servants he gave generous presents, to others he gave a flogging. He dined, drank, indulged in sleep and eventually passed from this life in much the same manner as he had lived it.

Petronius was also the author of *The Satyricon*, a biting satire that was intended not so much to produce mirth as a comic disgust with humanity. The anti-hero of *The Satyricon* is Trimalchio, the base and vulgar slave who crawls to the top of the social hierarchy and who is intended to be a caricature of Emperor Nero. Compared to a "great shining pig," Trimalchio writes his own epitaph, composed in what Beckett would call "pigsty Latin." It reads,

> Here Lies C. Pompeius Trimalchio
> He could have had any job in Rome
> But didn't.
> Loyal, brave and true,
> He started with a nickel in his pocket,
> And left his heirs thirty million;
> AND HE NEVER ONCE LISTENED TO A PHILOSOPHER.

## Epictetus
### (55–135)

Originally a Roman slave, Epictetus' extremely popular lectures were posthumously published as *The Discourses* and the short didactic moral manual *The Enchiridion*, by his student Arrian (himself the author of the most important extant account of the campaigns of Alexander the Great). Epictetus was lame, possibly because of maltreatment when he was a slave. He lived a life of great simplicity in a hut with a simple rush mat and earthenware lamp (apparently his iron lamp had been stolen).

The Emperor Domitian, a horrid thug and a cruel tyrant, was deeply suspicious of philosophers and he exiled them all from Rome in 95, Epictetus included. He founded a highly successful philosophical school in Nicopolis, Greece, which was eventually visited by the Emperor Hadrian.

Although a hugely influential figure in subsequent centuries, Epictetus is something of a master of Stoic moral truism, delivered in a mild-mannered yet assured and highly accessible way. He encouraged self-reliance, acceptance of providence and forbearance in all things.

The manner of his death is unrecorded, but there are some pithy remarks on mortality, one of which interestingly ends up as the epigraph to Laurence Sterne's monumental literary oddity, *The Life and Opinions of Tristram Shandy, Gentleman* (1759–67):

> Men are disturbed not by things [ *pragmata* ], but by the opinions [*dogmata*] which they have of things. Thus death is nothing terrible, else it would have appeared so to Socrates. But the terror consists in our opinion of death, that it is terrible.

Terror of death, then, lies in the opinion we have of death, the dogmas that we take to be true. If we look hard at the things themselves, the *pragmata*, then the terror falls away. If we keep death constantly before our eyes and in our mouths, then our terror of it and our attachment to worldly things will fall away. The thought is completed in a later remark from *The Enchiridion*:

> Let death and exile, and all other things which appear terrible, be daily before your eyes, but death chiefly; and you will never entertain any abject thought, nor too eagerly covet anything.

Of course, it is no small irony that this thought should end up as the epigraph to *Tristram Shandy*. For what is that novel but an extraordinary and exhausting exploration of the fact that human beings are more troubled with opinions, with what Sterne calls their "hobby horses," than with the things themselves? The universe of Tristram's loquacious father, Walter Shandy, is entirely made up of bizarre opinions: on names, on noses, on the best technique for birth in order to protect the delicate web of the cerebellum, and so on, and on, and on for hundreds of pages.

Sterne's riposte to Epictetus would seem to be that human beings simply cannot *help* but submerge themselves in opinions and that's the reason why we remain terrified of death.

## Polemo of Laodicea
### (BORN 85)

An obscure, talkative Sophist whose extraordinary death is recorded in Philostratus' *Lives of the Sophists*.

Polemo loved to declaim and vowed, "Never shall the sun behold me reduced to silence!" To make his point, he ordered his family to bury him alive. As he was being walled into the sepulchre, he cried, "Make haste, make haste!" When the job was done, his voice could be heard from inside the tomb: "Give me a body and I will declaim."

This story rather confirms Clement of Alexandria's jibe at the Sophists that they are like old shoes: "The rest of them has weakened or admits water; only the tongue is left."

## Peregrinus Proteus
### (100–65)

Peregrinus was a Cynic who started out as a Christian and styled himself "Proteus," after the Homeric character capable of many sudden transformations. His final, fatal and most famous transformation was to cremate himself in the manner of Empedocles by jumping into the Olympic flame in 165. However, unlike Empedocles, Peregrinus did not immolate himself far from the madding crowd, but in full public view. Even worse, Peregrinus had already declared that he was going to turn himself into a human Olympic torch in a number of pathetic public speeches. The satirist Lucian actually witnessed this event and in *The Passing of Peregrinus* he declares, "Oh, the stupidity! Oh, the vainglory!" Lucian explains Peregrinus' suicide by a love of fame and a sheer desire for attention. After having witnessed the auto-cremation, Lucian addresses a number of Cynics standing around the pyre:

> Let us go away, you simpletons. It is not an agreeable spectacle to look at an old man who had been roasted, getting our nostrils filled with a villainous reek.

## Marcus Aurelius
### (121–80)

"The greatest of men" according to Voltaire, "the perfect man" according to Oscar Wilde. From the opposite end of the social scale to the slave Epictetus, Marcus Aurelius was Roman Emperor from 161 until his death in Vindobona (modern Vienna) in 180. His *Meditations* were written during military campaigns in the last ten years of his life. Indeed, Marcus Aurelius sees life as warfare, "a brief sojourning in an alien land; and after repute, oblivion." In such a world, where can one find something solid to guide and guard one's path? The answer is clear, and clearly Stoical:

> In one thing and one alone: Philosophy. To be a philosopher is to keep unsullied and unscathed the divine spirit within him, so that it may transcend all pleasure and all pain.

Such a view of philosophy culminates in having the right attitude towards mortality. Marcus Aurelius says that the philosopher must "wait with good grace for death." This means cultivating the sentiment of tranquillity that we have already seen in Seneca:

> To live each day as though one's last, never flustered, never apathetic, never attitudinizing—here is perfection of character.

Naturally enough, the *Meditations* ends with a meditation on death. Marcus Aurelius asks, "Why do you hunger for length of days?" The point of life is to follow reason and the divine spirit and to accept whatever nature sends you. To live in this way is not to fear death, but to hold it in contempt. Death is only a thing of terror for those unable to live in the present. Marcus Aurelius concludes, "Pass on your way, then, with a smiling face, under the smile of him who bids you go."

## Plotinus
### (205–70)

With the last great (some would say greatest) pagan philosopher, we can detect a decided shift in the philosopher's relation to death, a shift that both anticipates and influences Christianity. This is partly because of the nature of Plotinus' philosophy, with its strongly Platonic emphasis on the separation of the immortal soul from the mortal body, but more so because of the way in which his life was commemorated.

An important biography of Plotinus was written by his pupil Porphyry (232/3–305), who was also the editor of his writings, collected as *The Enneads*. Porphyry's text is very much akin to a gospel and Plotinus is described as a "godlike man," endowed with supernatural powers. Porphyry even claims to have experienced a mystical communion with Plotinus after his death. Many of these traits are taken up into the lives of the saints and the tradition of hagiography which I will turn to in the next chapter.

An adulatory mysticism infuses both Porphyry's biography and the organization of his master's writings. *The Enneads* were quite artificially divided into fifty-four treatises, made up of six sets of nine. The reason for this is numerological; as Porphyry explains, "It gave me pleasure to find the perfection of the number six along with the nines." (Porphyry is himself a fascinating figure and author of a monumental fifteen-volume work with the rather direct title *Against the Christians*. Unsurprisingly, the Christians ordered it to be burnt in 448.)

Porphyry begins his biography with the words "Plotinus, the philosopher of our times, seemed ashamed of being in the body." The primary goal of Plotinus' philosophy is to overcome individuality by using the intellect to achieve union with what he called the "One." It is this "One" or divine universal intellect in which the individual participates and that can be rejoined after death. In this regard, Plotinus' death scene is rather revealing. As he was at the point of expiring, Plotinus made the gnomic pronouncement, "Try to bring back the god in us to the divine in the Whole." With these words, a snake crept under the bed on which Plotinus was lying and disappeared into a hole in the wall and he breathed his last.

What might this mean? Perhaps this: the intellect is the god within us that can rejoin the divinity of the Whole, just as a snake can shed its skin and slip back into its hole—but then again, perhaps not.

Interestingly, Plotinus also anticipates Christianity in his prohibition of suicide. As we have seen in numerous examples, most recently in the odd couple of Seneca and Petronius, there was absolutely no shame in suicide in the ancient world. At the end of the first *Ennead*, Plotinus asks, "How does the body depart?" That is, how does the immortal soul separate from the mortal body? Plotinus answers that this separation takes place when "the body is unable to bind" the soul.

But suppose that someone contrives to destroy his body through a suicidal act? Plotinus insists that we must on no account force the body to leave the soul, citing as authority the Chaldean oracle "You shall not take out your soul."

Turning from our souls to arseholes, Porphyry notes that his master often suffered from a disease of the bowels. But on no condition would Plotinus submit to an enema, saying that it was unsuitable for an elderly man to undergo this sort of treatment. For the good of our souls, then, the care of our arseholes should not be permitted to block our passage to the Whole.

## Hypatia
(370–415)

According to the evidence assembled by Gilles Ménage in *The History of Women Philosophers*, Hypatia succeeded Plotinus to the chair of the Platonic school and philosophers flocked from everywhere to hear her. Although little is known of her work, it would appear that she was a Platonist and a devoted and brilliant exponent of the views of Plotinus. Apparently, she lectured and published extensively on mathematics and astronomy.

There is a possibly apocryphal story in the Suda *Lexicon* that when one of her students fell in love with her, Hypatia showed him some cloths covered with menstrual blood and said, "This is what you love, young man, but you do not love beauty for its own sake."

This remark both cured the young devotee of his passion and reinforced the Plotinian distinction between the mere appearance of beauty and its true form. According to one source, Hypatia had lovers, while another says that she remained a virgin. Either way she seems to have inspired jealousy and this led to her violent death.

Hypatia was a close friend of Orestes, the pagan prefect of Alexandria, and there was gossip that she was the reason for Orestes' opposition to Cyril, who was elected to the patriarchate of Alexandria in 412. After Christian mobs had burnt the famous Library of Alexandria and destroyed Jewish synagogues, which led to the forced expulsion of the Alexandrian

Jews in 414, they turned their attention to the city's most famous philosopher. On her way to the lecture theatre, Hypatia was pulled from her carriage by a gang of Christians and dragged to the Church of Caesareum. After being stripped naked, Hypatia was killed with pieces of broken pots. After her skin was stripped with oyster shells, her body was cut into several pieces and burnt at a place called Cinaron. She was forty-five years old. A statement attributed to Hypatia reads, "To teach superstitions as truth is a most terrible thing."

With the oddly reversed martyrdom of Hypatia at the hands of Christians, we pass from paganism to Christianity. What is the relation between the classical philosophy of antiquity and Christianity? This is a vast question, but in the *Stromateis* (*Miscellanies*) from the very early third century, Clement of Alexandria claims that philosophy was to the Greek world what the law of Moses was to the Jews, "a tutor escorting them to Christ." On this view, philosophy is not wrong as such, it is simply a preparation for the *true* philosophy, namely Christianity. As we shall see, this is a view with some fatal consequences.

# The Deaths of Christian Saints

## St. Paul
(10?–67?)

St. Paul was the second and arguably most important founder of Christianity. In a characteristic turn of phrase, he called himself "a Hebrew of Hebrews" and was trained in the tradition of Pharisaic oral law. Yet Paul quotes the Hebrew scriptures in Greek translation and he was even a Roman citizen, which was remarkable for a Jew at that time. Furthermore, it is through Paul's extraordinarily itinerant activism that Christianity developed from a local cult that originated in the villages of Palestine to a religion that became established in the most important cities of the ancient world.

Some, perhaps many, professional philosophers might dispute the claim to understand Paul as a philosopher. True, Paul was no lover of philosophy and he thought (like many present-day evangelical Christians) that he was living in the last days of the end of history. Happily for us, he was mistaken. However that may be, it is difficult to think of a Western thinker whose concepts have had a greater influence, an influence that is still felt in modern philosophy as either repulsion (Nietzsche) or attraction (Kierkegaard).

The logic of Paul's language is deeply antithetical, what Luther calls "a delicious language . . . an unheard-of speech which human reason simply cannot understand." Nowhere is this truer than when Paul writes about death. Sin came into the world through the action of one man, Adam, and with sin comes death. For Paul, sin and death go out of the world through the action of another man, Christ, the second Adam, who dies for our sins. As Paul puts it in *Romans*:

> Then as one man's trespass led to condemnation for all men, so one man's act of righteousness leads to acquittal and life for all men.

It is Christ's death in the crucifixion that puts an end to sin and death in order that we may live, that we may be born again. Paul says of Christ:

> For if we have been united with him in a death like his, we shall certainly be united with him in a resurrection like his.

Therefore, what dies on the cross is not just Christ the God-man, but our former sinful, death-bound existence. Through the identification with the passion of the Christ, Christians die to their selves in order to be born into eternal life. Thus, to put the central paradox of Christianity at its most stark, Christ puts death to death and in dying for our sins we are reborn into life. To be a Christian, then, is to think of nothing else but death, for it is only through a meditation on mortality that the path to salvation might be sought. In which case, and this is the question that Kierkegaard will ask eighteen centuries later: how many so-called Christians are really Christian?

The "actual" life of Paul is recorded in Acts of the Apostles, traditionally thought to have been written by the same author as Luke's Gospel. However, Acts does not give an account of Paul's death, but instead ends with him languishing for two years in Rome, under house arrest. However, Paul was still apparently free to write and preach the Gospel, and Acts ends with the words "boldly and without hindrance he preached the kingdom of God and taught about the Lord Jesus Christ."

Paul had wound up in Rome after having been imprisoned for two years in Casaerea in Palestine for giving an unsuccessful speech in Aramaic where a mob tried to kill him. Because he was a Roman citizen, he had the right to trial in Rome, which accounts for his final journey in which he takes the Gospel to the very heart of the Empire.

According to Eusebius in *The History of the Church*, Paul met a grisly death under the orders of Nero (who is now responsible for three deaths in this book): "It is recorded that in his reign Paul was beheaded in Rome itself." The traditional tale is that Paul was interred in the catacombs and that some centuries later the Basilica of St. Paul Outside the Walls was built over the site of his sarcophagus. Are we to believe such tales of martyrdom? According to Voltaire, "We can only guffaw at all the humbug we are told about martyrs." However, one should never underestimate the power of humbuggery.

## Origen
### (185–254)

In *Against the Christians*, the pagan Porphyry expresses his exasperated admiration for the Christian Origen as "the most distinguished philosopher of our time." St. Gregory of Nyssa calls him "The Prince of Philosophers," and for St. Jerome he was the greatest teacher in the early Christian church. Like Plotinus, Origen was a pupil of the philosopher Ammonius, but unlike Plotinus, he was led to clarify Christian doctrine and provide the most detailed textual criticism of the Old and New Testaments.

Many stories are told about Origen's extraordinary chastity. In the Gospel according to St. Matthew, Christ says,

> For there are some eunuchs, which were so born from their mother's womb: and there are some eunuchs, which were made eunuchs of men: and there be eunuchs, which have made themselves eunuchs for the kingdom of heaven's sake. He that is able to receive it, let him receive it.

Unfortunately, Origen seems to have interpreted these words literally, and when he was teaching in Alexandria he castrated himself in order to work freely with female students of Christian doctrine. Although the courage required to perform this act makes cowards of us all, Origen's faith was so strong that he was certainly able to "receive it." Eusebius euphemistically describes Origen's self-castration as "a headstrong act." It prevented him from being ordained and he was never canonized. In Deuteronomy it is written,

> No man whose testicles have been crushed or whose organ has been removed shall become a member of the assembly of the Lord.

Origen met his death in a particularly gruesome manner. After Decius became emperor in 249, he began his brief reign with widespread persecution of Christians. As Eusebius relates in his extended biographical account, terrible sufferings befell Origen:

> Chains and bodily torments, agony in iron and the darkness of his prison; how for days on end his legs were pulled four paces apart in the torturer's stocks.

Origen apparently faced these horrors with courage before he eventually expired.

# St. Antony
## (251–356)

Bishop Athanasius' elegantly recounted *Life of Antony* is the founding text of Christian monasticism. "Monachos" in Greek means "living alone" and the monastic life meant withdrawal from the world, chastity, constant prayer and manual labour. For Antony, this withdrawal meant long years spent deep in the arid mountains of the Egyptian desert.

The *Life of Antony* became an immediate best-seller and exerted enormous influence from Augustine to Luther and beyond. It became the model for hagiography. My reason for including Antony is to show the self-conscious connection between the death of the Christian saint and that of the philosopher, exemplified by Socrates. What Antony represents, in my view, is the Christianization of the philosophical death through which "the lives of the philosophers" become "the lives of the saints."

There are many striking parallels between Antony and Socrates: rejecting normal values, both of them live a life of personal austerity and intellectual humility. But this humility is combined with devastating perceptiveness. On one occasion, two pagan philosophers came to visit Antony out of curiosity. Antony asked them why these wise men wanted to speak to someone as stupid as himself. To which the philosophers courteously replied that Antony was not stupid but exceedingly wise. Antony then immediately made the following inference:

> If you have come to see a stupid man, your effort is wasted; but if you think that I am wise and possess wisdom, it would be a good idea to imitate what you approve of, for it is right to imitate good things. If I had come to you, I would imitate you, but since you have come to me in the belief that I am wise, you should be Christians like me.

The pagan philosophers departed, amazed at Antony's mental agility. On another occasion, a group of old men came to visit Antony for counsel and he decided to test them by asking about the meaning of a passage of Scripture. Each man gave his opinion until the last was asked and he said simply, "I do not know." Like Socrates, Antony said this was the only true answer.

With Antony, the death of the Christian saint takes over and transforms the "art of dying" or *ars moriendi* of the pagan philosopher. Antony knew when he was going to die and insisted to his followers that he did not want his body embalmed and mummified in the Egyptian fashion. He asked for a simple earth burial and bequeathed his worn tunic and old sheepskin rug to Athanasius, his biographer. When he had finished speaking, "he stretched his feet out a little and looked upon death with joy."

The sublime simplicity of Antony's death can be compared with the death of St. Benedict in Gregory the Great's hagiography from the late sixth century. Benedict predicts the day of his death, surrounds himself with his disciples, his body too weak to stand without support. In Gregory's words, he "arms himself" for death by "partaking of the Lord's body and blood." Spiritually nourished, his hands raised up to heaven, he breathes his last in the middle of a prayer.

It is important, I think, in cultures like our own where Christianity has become so trivialized, to remind oneself of this considerably more rigorous and demanding Christian attitude towards death. In this regard, the sayings of the Desert Fathers from the fourth and fifth centuries are absolutely fascinating. Evagrius, a follower of Origen, says,

> Always keep your death in mind and do not forget the eternal judgment, then there will be no fault in your soul.

John the Dwarf says,

> Renounce everything material and that which is of the flesh. Do your work in peace. Persevere in keeping vigil, in hunger and thirst, in cold and nakedness, and in suffer-

ings. Shut yourself in a tomb as though you were already dead, so that at all times you will think death is near.

The Christian attitude to death can also lead to what sounds like cold callousness to modern ears. There is a story told of Cassian from the early fifth century, where he is reported as saying:

> There was a monk living in a cave in the desert. His relations according to the flesh let him know, "Your father is very ill, at the point of death: come and receive his inheritance." He replied to them, "I died to the world before he did and the dead do not inherit from the living."

As we saw with St. Paul, to be Christian is to die to the self and the world in order to be born again. From the worldly, fleshly point of view, the true Christian is already dead and therefore relations with one's family members have no importance. But we are going to see such Christian austerity interestingly compromised in the next two entries.

## St. Gregory of Nyssa
### (335–94)

One the most brilliant and influential of the Church Fathers, Gregory left an extraordinarily tender piece of writing on the life and death of St. Macrina, his sister. He visits her convent, where she is already terribly afflicted. In plain and subtle detail, Gregory recounts her last days and hours. Her final prayer displays the severity of the Christian attitude to death:

> Thou, O Lord, hast freed us from the fear of death. Thou hast made the end of life the beginning to us of true life. Thou for a season restest our bodies in sleep and awakest them again at the last trump.

Therefore, one should not fear death, as it is not the end but the beginning of the true life that will reach fruition with the

Second Coming of Christ and the resurrection of the dead. Gregory witnessed Macrina's death and described it in a language at once hagiographic and personal:

> Meanwhile evening had come and a lamp was brought in. All at once she opened the orb of her eyes and looked towards the light, clearly wanting to repeat the thanksgiving sung at the Lighting of the Lamps. But her voice failed and she fulfilled her intention in the heart and by moving her hands, while her lips stirred in sympathy with her inward desire. But when she had finished the thanksgiving, and her hand brought to her face to make the Sign had signified the end of the prayer, she drew a deep breath and closed her life and her prayer together.

## St. Augustine
### (354–430)

Gregory's account of the death of his sister finds an even more powerful echo in Augustine's famous description of the death of his mother, Santa Monica, at the end of Book 9 of the *Confessions*.

Monica's final wish was to see her son converted to Christianity, and when this had taken place in the manner that Augustine dramatically describes in Book 8 of the *Confessions*, she asks, "What am I doing here?" Monica falls into a fever and when it is clear that she is dying, Augustine's brother asks her—in a vain offer of comfort—if she minds being so far from home, in Ostia near Rome rather than back in Thagaste, in modern Algeria. She replies,

> Nothing is far from God. I need not fear that he will not know where to raise me up at the end of the world.

Like others we have seen in this book, Monica expresses no concern for the care of her corpse—"put this body anywhere"—and only asks to be "remembered at the altar of the Lord."

Yet, Augustine is not assuaged by his mother's final words and falls into deep grief. He asks himself, in a characteristically self-lacerating question, revealing a subjective depth arguably never seen prior to Augustine and only rarely equalled since, for example in Rousseau,

> What was it, therefore, that grieved me so heavily, if not the fresh wound wrought by the sudden rupture of our most sweet and dear way of life together?

He goes on to say that his heart was "ripped asunder" by his mother's death, "for out of her life and mine one life had been made." Augustine feels as if his individuality has been divided by his mother's death. He feels as if part of his self is missing or, indeed, already dead, and this pains him immeasurably. Augustine has already grieved for the death of his dear, but unnamed, friend in Book 4 of the *Confessions*. He writes that his heart was "made  dark by sorrow, and whatever I looked upon was death." In his wretchedness, Augustine makes the following astonishing remark,

> Well has someone said of his friend that he is half of his soul. For I thought that my soul and his soul were but one soul in two bodies.

Augustine sees his soul as sundered and his life as a half-life. Interestingly, this is also the reason why Augustine fears death: if he dies then the friend whom he loved so much would also wholly die. Love half-alive is still better than love fully dead.

Yet, the profound grief in Book 4 of the *Confessions* is that of a pagan. The issue becomes radically different after his conversion to Christianity. The pain that Augustine feels over his mother's death is a double pain, for he also feels *guilt* for the depth of his grief. Why? Because it shows how far he is still in the grip of human feelings and not sufficiently attached to God. He writes, in an extraordinary sentence:

> I sorrowed under my sorrow with an added sorrow, and I was torn by a twofold sadness.

His sorrow for his mother becomes twofold at the sorrow he feels for not dying to his self and living in Christ. This is a fascinating moment, for although Augustine knows that his mother will live eternally through Christ, he cannot assuage his grief. This is why he feels guilt and an existential need to open himself up further in an act of confession to God:

> Now, Lord, I confess to you in writing. Let him read it who wants to, let him interpret it as he wants. If he finds sin in it, that I wept for my mother for a small part of an hour, for that mother now dead to my eyes who for so many years had wept for me so that I might live in your eyes, let him not laugh me to scorn. But rather, if he is a man of large charity, let him weep over my sins before you, the Father of all brothers of your Christ.

It must sound mystifying to the eggshell egos and their easy tears that populate so much contemporary popular culture that Augustine should feel shame for weeping "a small part of an hour" over his mother's death. But this has to be explained in Christian terms: he feels grief because of the fact of sin that still corrodes Augustine's nature and makes him imperfect.

To say it once again, it is not easy being Christian. The properly Christian attitude to death is revealed in Augustine's reaction to the seemingly tragic death of his son, Adeodatus, at the age of seventeen. Augustine confesses that his son was "born of me in the flesh out of my sin" through his first wife. But Augustine is able to look on his death with peace of mind because he and his son had been baptized together a couple of years earlier: "Anxiety over our past life fled away from us."

The *Life of St. Augustine* was written by Bishop Possidius thirty years after his death. Augustine fell ill with a terrible fever during the fourteen-month siege and blockade of Hippo by "a mixed group of savage Vandals and Alans, together with a Gothic tribe and people of different races." When asked by Honoratus whether or not bishops and clergy should withdraw from the Church in the face of an enemy, Augustine wrote a long and withering rebuke, arguing that it was the obligation of the clergy to stay with their flock and not hand them over to the pagan "wolf."

Augustine died at the age of seventy-six, having served as bishop or priest in Hippo, in modern Algeria, for forty years. As he was dying, he requested solitude and seclusion. Augustine had the psalms of David copied and he read them "with copious and continual weeping." He left no will, because as a poor man he had nothing to leave.

## Boethius, Ancius Manlius Severinus
### (DATE OF BIRTH UNKNOWN, POSSIBLY AROUND 475, DIED 524)

Boethius, traditionally known as the last of the Romans and the first of the Medieval Scholastics, was a hugely important philosopher, as it was through his translations that Aristotle's logical works survived in the West. Boethius planned to translate all of Plato's and Aristotle's work into Latin, a project brought to an end by his violent death while he was still in his forties. *The Consolation of Philosophy* was one of the most important books in the Middle Ages and beyond, existing in hundreds of manuscript copies. Sometime later, in

1593, an elderly Elizabeth I translated the *Consolation*, allegedly in twenty-four (some say twenty-seven) hours.

Like Cicero and Seneca before him, Boethius was a very important political figure. He gained the confidence of the Ostrogothic king Theodoric, who governed Italy and much of the Western Roman Empire after the capital had been moved to Constantinople. By the age of thirty, Boethius became *magister officiorum*, head of civil and military affairs, who controlled access to the king. The details of his rapid fall from power are not clear, but it seems that he was implicated in a plot to undermine Theodoric. The senate at the time was little more than the plaything of the king, and Boethius was arrested, condemned to death and sent into exile to await execution. It was in this period of anxious waiting that Boethius wrote *The Consolation of Philosophy*.

When reading *Consolation*, it should not be forgotten that this is a book written by a man who believes himself unjustly condemned to death. It is in a prison cell, then, that Philosophia appears, personified as a woman and offering consolation. And what a woman she is: "Sometimes," Boethius writes,

> she was of average human size, while at other times she seemed to touch the very sky with the top of her head.

Boethius is full of righteous indignation and he says to Philosophia,

> And now you see the outcome of my innocence—instead of reward to true goodness, punishment for a crime I did not commit.

The form of the book is a dialogue between Boethius and Philosophia about the nature of happiness. And herein lies the main riddle of the text: Boethius is ostensibly a Christian in an empire that was by that time fully Christianized, yet Christ is never so much as mentioned. Indeed, the conception of philosophy offered by the fifty-foot woman is highly

Platonic. This is most obviously the case with the endorse-
ment of Plato's conception of creation where eternal matter
is formed by the hands of the demiurge or craftsman of the
world, as opposed to the Judaeo-Christian God who creates
the universe out of nothing. Philosophia also claims that
happiness, goodness and God are identical and that we can
participate in them not through the mediation of Christ, but
much more Platonically by turning our intellect towards the
emanations from their substance.

What consolation does philosophy offer to the man condemned to death? The book finishes with a distinction
between human and divine judgement. Although human
judgement, in the case of Theodoric, can often be unjust,
Philosophia insists that this is ultimately overridden by "the
sight of a judge who sees all things." Philosophy's consolation is the knowledge that God rewards the good and pun-
ishes the wicked—if not in this world, then in the next.

The extent of Boethius' consolation by philosophy is not
known. He was cruelly tortured before being bludgeoned to
death.

With Boethius' bludgeoning and the collapse of learning in
what remained of the classical world, I'd like to begin a journey through medieval philosophy. This will take us first to the
barbaric north of England and Ireland, the Islamic and
Judaic south of Córdoba, Baghdad and Persia, and then to the
great medieval universities of Paris and Oxford. It's quite a
journey.

# Medieval Philosophers: Christian, Islamic and Judaic

## The Venerable Bede
### (672/3–725)

Bede is the only Englishman who made it into Dante's *Paradiso*. Some might consider this a little too generous. However, the news that Bede made it to paradise is particularly welcome as he seems to have expressed some anxiety about death during his demise. In St. Cuthbert's hagiographical letter on Bede's death, we find a tone that is strikingly different from what we saw in Antony and Augustine. As he was dying, Bede liked to quote Paul's words, "It is a fearful thing to fall into the hands of the living God." In an unusually and powerfully human moment in the death of the saint, Bede is shown breaking down and weeping over the dread departure of the soul from the body and the prospect of God's judgement. Cuthbert records a beautifully economical and unsentimental death song that Bede spoke in his native Northumbrian dialect:

*Before the unavoidable journey there,*
*No one becomes wiser in thought*
*Than him who, by need, ponders,*
*Before his going hence,*
*What good and evil within his soul,*
*After his day of death will be judged.*

## John Scottus Eriugena
### (810–77)

His name is a pleonasm, meaning "John the Irishman, native of Ireland (Erin)." In the ninth century, Ireland was called "Scotia Maior" and "*scottus*" meant an Irishman (some centuries later it came to refer to someone from Scotland, as we see with John Duns Scotus or John the Scot).

Eriugena is the greatest and most original European philosopher in the long, dark centuries that separate Augustine and Anselm. For some, he only has his equal in Aquinas. His writing dazzles with dialectical brilliance and deep learning, with a perfect knowledge of Ancient Greek, a language which had more or less died out in the West apart from among Irish monks. The reasons for Eriugena's neglect are manifold. Matters were not helped by the fact that his major philosophical work, *Periphyseon: On the Division of Nature*, was placed on the Index of Forbidden Books by the Catholic Church. In the thirteenth century, Pope Honorius III described Eriugena's writing as "swarming with worms of heretical perversity"—praise indeed!

The Church's problem with Eriugena lay in his deeply Neoplatonic conception of nature, which included both God and creation. Nature is the whole and is understood as a dynamic process of emanation from the divine One. This position brings Eriugena dangerously close to the accusation of pantheism, or the identity of God with nature. As such, Eriugena can be seen as a precursor of "heretics" like Giordano Bruno, "atheists" like Spinoza and "godless dialecticians" like Hegel. As Feuerbach would write a thousand years later, "Atheism is reversed Pantheism."

Eriugena enjoyed the munificent patronage of King Charles the Bald and spent his entire adult life in France. There is a story relating to an incident when the bald monarch and the Irish philosopher were seated at a table across from each other. The king said, "*Quid distat inter sottum et Scottum?*" ("What separates a fool from an Irishman?") To which Eriugena quipped, "Only a table." The contemporary Irish poet Paul Muldoon gives an updated version of this joke in his audacious *Madoc* (an alternative history of philosophy from the Greeks onwards):

"What is the difference between an Irishman and a puddle?" And a voice pipes up, "The bottle."

William of Malmesbury tells the doubtless apocryphal tale that Eriugena was summoned to England by Alfred the Great and subsequently stabbed to death by his pupils, presumably some unsatisfied English monks. Apparently, the murder weapons were not knives but writing *styli*. Further proof, if proof were needed, that the pen is mightier than the sword.

## Al-Farabi
### (870–950)

The complex and hugely important story of the place of philosophy or what Muslims call "*falsafa*" in the Islamic world cannot be told here. Although many readers know nothing of this period in the history of philosophy, it is only through the monumental labour of the great medieval Islamic philosophers that knowledge of Greek philosophy, particularly Aristotle, was transmitted to the Christian West. This tradition is usually considered to begin with Al-Farabi, known as the "Second Master" (second, that is, only to Aristotle). Avicenna, Averroës and Moses Maimonides all acknowledge their debt to the Second Master, and many of his writings were translated into Latin.

Al-Farabi's fame rests largely on his commentaries on Aristotle, particularly his logical works, but also the *Rhetoric* and *Poetics*. But the word "commentary" has unfortunate connotations and understates the originality of Al-Farabi's philosophy. His work is an extraordinarily ambitious attempt to combine the logical rigour and empiricism of Aristotle with the more mystical intuition of the One in Plotinus and Neoplatonic thought.

The title of one of Al-Farabi's works from 900 makes this ambition plain: *The Harmonization of the Opinions of the Two Sages, the Divine Plato and Aristotle*. The goal of such a philosophical harmony cannot be separated from the more religious ambition of the salvation of the soul in the next life.

We do not know if Al-Farabi made it to the next life and we know very little about his life on earth. He was born in Turkestan, educated in Damascus and Baghdad and worked in Aleppo in northern Syria. According to one source, he died in Aleppo after a long trip to Egypt, but according to some medieval biographers he was violently murdered by highwaymen on the road from Damascus to Ashkelon.

## Avicenna or Ibn Sina
### (980–1037)

If we don't know enough about the life of Al-Farabi, then perhaps we know a little too much about Avicenna. He began to write an autobiography, which was completed by his disciple Al-Juzajani. He was born in Bukhara in modern Uzbekistan and worked at various courts in Persia before enjoying the patronage of Abu Ya'far, the Prince of Isfahan. Avicenna wrote some 450 books, ranging widely from metaphysics to medicine, including *The Canon of Medicine*, the standard medical textbook in Europe for seven centuries. Sadly, however, the physician doesn't seem to have been able to heal himself. Towards the end of *The Life of Ibn Sina*, his disciple writes:

> The Master was vigorous in all his faculties, the sexual faculty being the most vigorous and dominant of his concupiscible faculties, and he exercised it often.

However, such was Avicenna's sexual appetite that his priapic performances made him ill and he was grievously afflicted by what his disciple vaguely calls "colic." "Therefore," Al-Juzajani continues,

> he administered an enema to himself eight times in one day, to the point that some of his intestines ulcerated and an abrasion broke out on him.

The story continues,

> One day, wishing to break the wind of the colic, he ordered that two *danaqs* [a measure in Arabic] of celery be included in the enema.

However, Avicenna's instructions were not followed and the doctor threw in "five *dirhams*" (another Arabic measure, from which we get the word "dram") of celery seed, which aggravated the abrasions. In addition, one of his servants, who had stolen a large sum of money from Avicenna, gave him a huge quantity of opium in order to try to kill him.

In this perilous state, Avicenna journeyed to Isfahan, but he was so weak that he was unable to stand. However, he continued to treat himself until he could walk. Yet, Al-Juzajani continues, "He did not take care and frequently had sexual intercourse." Eventually, Avicenna gave in to his illness saying, "The governor who used to govern my body is incapable of governing." He died a few days later at the age of fifty-eight and is reported to have said, "I prefer a short life with width to a narrow one with length." When Avicenna was asked about his excesses, he said,

> God, Who is exalted, has been generous concerning my external and internal faculties, so I use every faculty as it should be used.

His disciple concludes his biography with the words "May God find his deeds worthy."

## St. Anselm
### (1033/4–1109)

 Justly or unjustly, Anselm is famous for one argument, what a later philosophical tradition called the ontological argument for the existence of God. It is an argument of singular elegance designed to persuade the fool whom the psalmist quotes as saying, "There is no God."

For Anselm, one can conceive of that than which nothing greater can be thought. If that is true, then one is obliged to accept that such a conception exists in the understanding. Even the fool would agree. But if one can conceive of that than which nothing greater can be thought, then does this conception only exist in the understanding? Must it not also exist in reality, which is greater? If it did not exist in reality, then it would not be that than which nothing greater can be thought. Why? For the simple reason that there would be something greater than that which only exists in the understanding. Therefore, if one can conceive of that than which nothing greater can be thought, then assuredly it must exist in reality as well as the understanding. Now, God is that than which nothing greater can be thought. Therefore, God exists in both conception and reality. No one who is able to form the conception of God can deny that such a being exists, not even a fool.

To which I am tempted to reply: I am not even a fool. For what is it to *conceive* of God? What does it mean for the conception of God to somehow *exist* in the understanding, wherever the latter might be located? Whether God exists or not, I would simply deny that we can conceive of such a being in much the same way as I do not think we can conceive of death, that death cannot be located in the understanding. In a deep sense, I can conceive of neither death nor God. They both passeth understanding.

Although born in Piedmont, northern Italy, in 1033 or 34, Anselm was chosen to succeed Lafranc as Archbishop of Canterbury in 1093. Sadly, his time as Archbishop was marked by serious political conflicts with two English monarchs: William Rufus and Henry I. As a consequence, Anselm spent many years in exile and died in Rome shortly before Easter, 1109. A few days before Anselm's death, with his bed surrounded by fellow monks, one of them remarked that he would probably die by Easter. Apparently, Anselm replied,

> If it is His will I shall gladly obey, but if He should prefer me to stay with you just long enough to solve the question of the origin of the soul which I have kept turning over in my mind, I would gratefully accept the chance, for I doubt whether anybody else will solve it when I am gone.

Sadly, God didn't allow Anselm the extra days and, as he predicted, no one has subsequently been able to solve the problem.

## Solomon Ibn Gabirol or Avicebron
### (1021–58)

Born in Málaga in Muslim Spain, the great Jewish Neoplatonist and poet was, according to legend, murdered by an envious Muslim poet who buried him beneath a fig tree.

Oddly, the tree bore fruit of such sweetness that suspicion was aroused, the corpse of Ibn Gabirol unearthed, and the perpetrator apprehended and hanged (although not from the tree, it would appear).

## Peter Abelard
### (1079–1142)

Abelard was described by Peter the Venerable as "The Socrates of the Gauls, Plato of the West, our Aristotle, prince of scholars." In his *Historia calamitatum* or *Story of His Misfortunes*,

Peter Abelard describes Origen as "The greatest of Christian philosophers." The cutting irony here is that Abelard met a similar fate to Origen, the difference being that whereas Origen castrated himself in order to devote himself to teaching female students, Abelard was castrated because of an inability to restrain his desire for one of his.

After defeating William of Champeaux in public disputations, Abelard was seen as the leading philosopher in Paris, without a rival. He relates that "I began to think of myself as the only philosopher in the world." At the peak of his fame, when he was in his mid-thirties, he began a passionate sexual affair with a young student, Héloïse, who was seventeen years old at the time. Peter writes that "Our desires left no stage of love-making untried, and if love could devise something new, we welcomed it." Héloïse was the niece of one of the canons at Notre-Dame, Fulbert, who some suspect was really her father, such was his possessiveness and rage against Abelard.

Héloïse became pregnant and Abelard removed her to his home country in Brittany, where she gave birth to a son, inexplicably called Astralabe, presumably in honour of that ancient astronomical computer for determining the position of the stars.

Fulbert was furious and Abelard offered to marry Héloïse, provided it was kept secret in order to protect his reputation. Fulbert initially agreed. In one of her letters, Héloïse writes that she would rather be Abelard's whore than his secret bride. Incidentally, what strikes the reader in their famous correspondence is the direct warmth and intelligent power of Héloïse's language as opposed to the impersonal, self-protective and rather priggish arrogance of Abelard.

Some time later, Fulbert broke his agreement with

Abelard and began to spread the news of their marriage. Abelard responded by removing Héloïse to a convent, where they continued to meet and are reported making passionate love in the convent refectory.

Fulbert suspected, not without reason, that Abelard was trying to get rid of Héloïse and save himself by making her a nun. Enraged, Fulbert sent some of his servants and friends to break into Abelard's lodgings. In Abelard's words, "They cut off the parts of my body whereby I had committed the wrong of which they complained." As with Origen, this act prevented Abelard from being ordained.

Although Abelard returned to teaching and writing, his fate was sealed. He entered into a famous debate with Bernard of Clairveaux, powerful leader of the Cistercians, which effectively ended up as Abelard's trial. At Bernard's bidding, Abelard's theological views were condemned as heretical by the pope in 1140. His books were burnt, his followers were excommunicated and he was confined to a monastery in perpetual silence.

Abelard died eighteen months later at the monastery in Chalon-sur-Saône, where he had been sent by his friend and protector, Peter the Venerable. Peter's final letter to Héloïse describes a peaceful death, surrounded by his books. Héloïse died twenty-one years later on 16 May 1163 or 64. Some say she died, like Abelard, at the age of sixty-three.

## Averroës or Ibn Rushd
(1126–98)

Averroës and Avicenna both made it into Dante's *Limbo*, along with the pagan philosophers, although Avicenna, as we have seen, possibly deserved something worse.

Born in Córdoba in Muslim Spain, Averroës became known in the Christian West as "The Commentator" for his extensive explanations of Aristotle. Averroës' influence on the development of Medieval Christian philosophy, first on Albert the Great and later on Aquinas and others, cannot be overstated. This influence was also hugely controversial and led to the development of "Averroism" among Christian philosophers.

Roughly and readily, Averroists defended the autonomy of philosophy and its separation from questions of theology and religious faith. The most extreme of the Averroists was Siger of Brabant, who met a sticky end, as we will see below. In 1277, Pope John XXI asked the Bishop of Paris to look into the possible heresies that were being propagated at the University of Paris. The worry was that philosophers like Averroës were being employed to produce purely philosophical and hence untheological interpretations of Aristotle and much more besides. After a significant investigation, a commission of sixteen theologians issued a highly influential condemnation against any concept of philosophy that claimed to be independent of Christian theology.

These events echo a debate that Averroës had with Al-Ghazzali (1058–1111), who was known as "The Proof of Islam." The latter had written a powerful attack on philosophy in *The Incoherence of Philosophers* (*Tahafut al-Falasifah*), where he had accused the philosophers of infidelity (*al-kufr*) and teachings inimical to Islam. Although the main target of Al-Ghazzali's attack was Avicenna, Averroës wrote a detailed reply wonderfully entitled *The Incoherence of the Incoherence* (*Tahafut al-Tahafut*). He argued that philosophy is not forbidden by the Koran, but on the contrary is to be encouraged by those with adequate intellectual ability.

Be that as it may, around 1195 Averroës seems to have become the victim of political harassment and was exiled from the court of the sultan in Marrakech in modern Morocco to a small town near to Córdoba. Happily, his disgrace was short-lived and he returned to the sultan's court, where he ended his days.

Although he was initially buried in Marrakech, his remains were later taken to Córdoba on a mule. The story goes that the weight of his bones was balanced on the back of the mule by his works of philosophy. It is unclear whether this means that he wrote too much or weighed too little.

# Moses Maimonides,
# Rabbi Moshe ben Maimon
(1135–1204)

It is an irony from which the contemporary world might learn that the person whom many regard as the greatest Jewish philosopher of all time should have emerged from the Islamic world. In addition to his extensive work on Jewish law and the Torah, his major philosophical work, *The Guide for the Perplexed*, written in Arabic, shows the influence of Aristotle in arguing for a rational philosophy of Judaism. Maimonides was referred to as "Rabbi Moyses" with great respect by Albert the Great and Aquinas.

Like Averroës, Maimonides was born in Córdoba, then a flourishing centre of Jewish culture and learning under the Almoravid caliphate, which granted citizens complete religious freedom. Matters changed dramatically with the conquest of Spain by the intolerant and fanatical Almohads in 1148, who required either the forced conversion of all non-Muslims or expulsion.

Faced with this choice, Maimonides' family was offered refuge by Averroës. The family decided to disguise themselves as Muslims when in public, while continuing to practise and study Judaism privately. They remained in Córdoba in this manner for another eleven years before fleeing to Fez, which was also under Almohad rule, but where, being strangers, they might go unrecognized. When a rabbi with whom Maimonides had studied was arrested and executed in 1165, the family fled first by boat to Palestine and then to Egypt where they settled in Al-Fustat, now part of modern Cairo.

Some years later, Maimonides was chosen to be head of the Jewish community in Al-Fustat. In straitened financial circumstances, he made a living as a physician, eventually ending up as court doctor to the Sultan Saladin. Maimonides was buried in Tiberias in modern Israel, where his tomb is still visited as a shrine. In his commentary on the

Mishna, he famously formulated thirteen principles of faith that all Jews should follow. The thirteenth concerns belief in the resurrection of the dead—lucky for some.

## Shahab al-din Suhrawardi
### (1155–91)

An Iranian Sufi who developed an influential mystical philosophy and was founder of what became known as the School of Illumination. He was executed in Aleppo, in modern Syria, on the order of the son of Saladin for cultivating heretical mystical beliefs. He is sometimes simply called Maqtul, "The Slain."

# Philosophy in the
# Latin Middle Ages

## Albert the Great or Albertus Magnus
### (1200–80)

Albert received the title of *Magnus* from his contemporaries before his death. He was also known as *Doctor Universalis* (Universal Doctor). Although his philosophical influence has been felt mainly through the writing of his long-time student Thomas Aquinas, he was a powerful philosopher in his own right. At the request of his Dominican brethren, he was asked to provide an explanation of the new interpretation of Aristotle that had emerged from Jewish and Arabic sources in Spain. His explanation ran to some thirty-nine volumes.

During a lecture in 1278, Albert's memory suddenly failed and the strength of his mind rapidly deteriorated. According to Butler's *Lives of the Saints*, he died peacefully and without illness, sitting in his chair, surrounded by his brethren in his home town of Cologne.

## St. Thomas Aquinas
### (1224/5–74)

St. Thomas Aquinas, the most influential philosopher and theologian of the Christian West, was known as *Doctor Angelicus*

(Angelic Doctor). There is a doubtless apocryphal story that when he was at the Sorbonne in Paris, Thomas was asked for his views on the nature of the Sacrament in the Christian Mass. Apparently, Thomas was sunk in prayer and contemplation for an unusually long time before writing down his opinion on the matter. When he had finished, he reportedly threw down his thesis at the foot of a crucifix and buried himself once more in prayer. The other Dominican friars reported that Christ descended from the cross, picked up the scroll, read it, and said, "Thomas, thou hast written well concerning the Sacrament of My Body." At which point, Thomas was miraculously borne up into mid-air.

Now, this was no mean miracle, as Thomas was not a small man. He was, in G. K. Chesterton's words, "a huge bull of a man, fat and slow and quiet." Large chunks had to be sawn out of dining tables so that Thomas could sit and eat with his brethren. Because he was so big and quiet, Thomas was called "the dumb ox" by his fellow students in Paris. Albert the Great retorted, "You call him a dumb ox; I tell you that the dumb ox will bellow so loud that his bellowing will fill the world." And Thomas certainly bellowed. He wrote over eight million words, two million on the Bible, one million on Aristotle and the rest devoted to university teaching and compendia for use by students of theology. As Timothy McDermott points out, "The largest of these works read like an internet encyclopaedia," with articles like Web pages with links to other topics and articles to be read in parallel.

Given the volume of Thomas's writing, it is pointless trying to offer a summary. It is often said that Thomas's achievement is a synthesis of Aristotle and Christianity. But what does this mean? Let's go back to Averroës and his separation of philosophy and theology or the realms of reason and faith. Thomas rejects this separation, arguing that although theology begins from the revealed truths of faith, it proceeds to its conclusions using reason. If reason without faith is empty, then faith without reason is blind.

Thomas always argues against the separation of the natural and the spiritual and in favour of their continuity. In this way, the empirical Aristotle-influenced activity of philosophy and natural science need not be seen as heretical or atheistic, but as a path to God.

This continuity of the natural and the spiritual can be seen in Thomas's conception of the human being situated amphibiously at the juncture of these two realms. We are a composite of soul and body, but the soul is not some immaterial substance located in our brain or beneath our left nipple. On the contrary, and here Thomas follows Aristotle, the soul is the form of the body. The soul is that which individuates each of us and animates this indistinct lump of matter that I am (and as we have already said, Thomas was quite a large lump of matter). Wittgenstein unwittingly adopts this position when he writes that "the human body is the best picture of the human soul."

On 6 December 1273 during Mass in Naples, something devastating happened to Thomas that some commentators see as a mystical experience and others see as a cerebral stroke. Either way, Thomas was afterwards unwilling or unable to write and the massive labour of the *Summa Theologiae* was suspended at Part 3, Question 90, Article 4.

In response to the protestations of his secretary, Reginald of Piperno, that he should complete the work, Thomas answered,

> Reginald, I cannot . . . in comparison with what I have seen in prayer all that I have written seems to me as if it were straw.

Admittedly, it is an awful lot of straw. Despite his transformation, he was summoned by the pope to attend the Council of Lyons. On the way, it seems that he was injured by the bough of a tree and died at the age of forty-nine, twenty-five miles from his birthplace in Roccasecca, halfway between Rome and Naples. On his deathbed, Thomas dictated a brief commentary on Solomon's Song of Songs, which sadly has not survived.

## St. Bonaventure or Giovanni de Fidanza
### (1217–74)

*Doctor Seraphicus* (Seraphic Doctor) was to the Franciscans what Aquinas was to the Dominicans. Bonaventure and Aquinas were both recognized as Regent Masters of the University of Paris on the same day in 1257. (Incidentally, the present pope, Benedict XVI, wrote his "Habilitation," or second doctoral thesis, on Bonaventure.) Like Thomas, Bonaventure was highly critical of Averroism, a tendency which he thought would lead to the separation of the worlds of faith and reason and would ultimately culminate in atheism. But unlike Thomas, Bonaventure was much more suspicious of the rationalism of Aristotle and much closer to Augustine and Neoplatonism in arguing that the emanations of the divine had to be experienced at all levels of reality. In 1273, Pope Gregory X made Bonaventure into a cardinal and soon afterwards they travelled to the Second Council of Lyons. In the midst of Council activities, Bonaventure died suddenly at the age of fifty-seven. Some say that he was poisoned.

## Ramon Llull or Raymond Lully
### (1232/3–1315/16)

Llull was a great Majorcan polymath and author of 290 works, written in Catalan, Latin and Arabic. He is famous for his *ars magna* or great art, what Leibniz later baptized an *ars combinatoria* or combinatory art. The purpose of this art was to show that the entirety of human knowledge was derivable from the logical combination of several basic concepts. He also invented machines for this purpose, which some have seen as the first computers, making Llull the father of computer science. However, the purpose of these logic machines was highly specific: the conversion of infidel Muslims to the truth of Christianity by the use of logic and reason. Llull's entire life was spent in a battle with Islam. He went on numerous missions to North Africa to convert Muslims and fought the Islamic-influenced Averroism at the University of Paris when he taught there.

There is a widely told, but probably fallacious, story that he was stoned to death during one of his missions to Tunis. Brucker recounts that Llull was captured, tortured and expelled from Tunis and escaped with his life only through the intercession of Genoese traders.

Although he was never canonized, he received the title of a Blessed and is known as *Doctor Illuminatus* (the Most Enlightened Doctor). However, Schopenhauer tells the characteristically misogynistic story that Llull was converted to Christianity in the following terms: Llull was from a wealthy, aristocratic family and as a young man he led a life of hedonism and dissipation. However, one day Llull was finally admitted to the bedroom of a woman he had long been wooing. When she opened her dress, she showed him her breast eaten away with cancer. "From that moment," Schopenhauer continues, "as if he had looked into hell, he was converted; leaving the court of the King of Majorca, he went into the wilderness to do penance."

## Siger of Brabant
### (1240–84)

As we have seen, Aquinas, Bonaventure and Ramon Llull were united in their hostility to Averroism and its separation of philosophy and theology or reason and faith. Siger was the most radical, charismatic and influential of the Paris Averroists. His main philosophical concern was establishing the truth of what the ancient philosophers wrote, especially Aristotle. If the latter was at odds with the teaching of the Church, as he often was, then so much the worse for the

Church. In this view, Aquinas's proposed marriage between Aristotle and Christianity was doomed to end in divorce. Needless to say, the Church was not too pleased and Siger was forced to flee Paris for the safety of Orvieto in Italy, where the pontifical curia generously allowed him to stay and even provided him with a secretary. Sadly, his secretary went mad and stabbed Siger to death.

## St. John Duns Scotus
(1266–1308)

Very little can be said with certainty about the life and death of John the Scot. The name "Duns" might refer to the present village of Duns in Berwickshire in southern Scotland, but even that is not certain. He was known as *Doctor Subtilis* (Subtle Doctor) and the undoubted difficulty of his work has led to widely differing evaluations of its importance. Some see nothing but hair-splitting in his voluminous arguments pro and con with objections, replies and endless debates with unnamed contemporaries. Indeed, followers of John the Scot were known as "Duns men," from where we get the notion of the "dunce" or stupid fellow who believes himself subtle.

However, other philosophers see John the Scot in very different terms. The great American philosopher Charles Sanders Peirce called him "the profoundest metaphysician that ever lived" and Heidegger wrote his doctoral thesis on John the

Scot's theory of meaning, which was important for the development of Heidegger's early views on the question of being.

John the Scot famously developed the notion of "haecceity" as a way of giving expression to the uniqueness or the indivisible "thisness" of a person.

His own uniqueness was cut short prematurely at a Franciscan study house in Cologne. There is a horrifying story that John the Scot was buried alive. Apparently, he had fallen into a coma, was believed dead, and was buried. However, when his tomb was reopened, his body was found outside its coffin and his hands were bloody from his unsuccessful attempts to escape.

## William of Ockham
(1285–1347/9)

The most influential philosopher of the fourteenth century was a native of Ockham, a small village in Surrey. Disputative, abrasive and polemical, with a predilection for empirical evidence and logical analysis as a way of cutting through nonsense, William of Ockham is often seen as a precursor to modern philosophers such as the logical positivists.

Although Ockham never uses the term, his name is associated with "Ockham's razor." This is best understood as a principle of parsimony, where nothing should be assumed as necessary unless it is given in experience, established by reasoning or required by faith. Ockham famously writes, "It is useless to do with more what can be done with fewer."

His polemics against what he saw as the errors of previous philosophers like Aquinas and Duns Scotus got him into trouble and he was charged with heresy by John Lutterell, former Chancellor of Oxford. Ockham travelled to Avignon in 1324, at that time the seat of the papacy, where he was detained for four years although no agreement could be reached as to whether or not he was a heretic.

Fearing the worst, Ockham fled Avignon with some fellow Franciscans and eventually found sanctuary in Munich thanks to the holy Roman emperor, Ludwig of Bavaria. Charged with apostasy and excommunicated, Ockham spent the remainder of his life in Munich writing polemical tracts against the papal pretensions to political power. Ockham argued that the pope should limit himself to theological issues, "lest he should turn the law of the Gospels into a law of slavery."

Ockham was a victim of the Black Death that ravaged the fourteenth century and brought about an intellectual and cultural decline that lasted for a century.

# Renaissance, Reformation and Scientific Revolution

## Marsilio Ficino
### (1433–99)

Let's pick up the thread of our story in the warm glow of the Italian Renaissance in Florence. Thanks to the patronage of Cosimo de' Medici, ruler of Florence, Ficino founded the Platonic Academy of Florence in 1462. He completed the first complete translation of Plato's dialogues in Latin before moving on to Plotinus. Ficino's commentaries on Plato were hugely influential and, in his celebrated interpretation of Plato's *Symposium*, he coined the concept of "Platonic love." The latter does not simply mean friendship or non-physical love, but divine love, and this idea was at the centre of Ficino's understanding of Platonism (he even wrote an astrological chart determining the position of the stars at the time of Plato's birth).

Ficino writes in a letter on the Platonic function of the philosopher,

> Since philosophy is defined by all men as love of wisdom and wisdom is the contemplation of the divine, then certainly the purpose of philosophy is knowledge of the divine.

For Ficino this is also the reason why the philosopher should
meditate upon death, for it is through such a meditation
that "we are restored to the likeness of God." Philosophy,
then, is nothing less than an imitation of God and the
philosopher is a "demi-god" or intermediary between the
human and the divine. It is hardly surprising, on this strato-
spherically metaphysical interpretation of Plato, that the
core of Ficino's Platonism is the doctrine of the immortality of the soul.

As for Ficino himself, he was slightly less than divine in
physical appearance. According to Giovanni Corsi's *Life of
Marsilio Ficino* from 1506, he was very short, slender, slightly
hunched and stuttered. He had persistent stomach problems, was cheerful in company and liked to drink, but was
given to solitude and melancholy. As to the cause of his
death, Corsi claims that it was possibly his lifelong stomach
complaint, or possibly just old age.

## Count Giovanni Pico della Mirandola
### (1463–94)

This brilliant philosophical meteor of the Italian Renaissance
led a short, extraordinary life. Pico was the most famous student of Ficino, one in whom could be seen "powers which were
almost divine," according to Corsi. His approach to philosophy
was as metaphysical as Ficino's, but much more syncretic, since
he read Hebrew, Arabic and Aramaic as well as Latin and Greek.
In addition to Plato, Aristotle and the medieval Islamic and
Scholastic philosophers, Pico drew on the most diverse sources:
Hermetic, Zoroastrian, Orphic, Pythagorean and Cabbalistic.
He believed that each of these positions possessed a grain of
truth and assembled some 900 theses that, with a delightfully
naive arrogance, he decided to debate in Rome against all
comers. Unsurprisingly Pope Innocent VIII decided that Pico
was guilty of heresy. He fled to France, was arrested and only survived because of the protection of Lorenzo de' Medici. He died
in suspicious circumstances at the age of thirty-one and it was

rumoured that, like Siger of Brabant, he had been poisoned by his secretary. On the day of his death, Charles VIII of France entered Florence after the sorry capitulation of the Florentine Republic.

## Niccolò Machiavelli
(1469–1527)

Looked at disinterestedly, and from a certain Martian distance, what generalizations might one make about human beings? As one might expect, in giving advice to his imagined prince, Machiavelli doesn't exactly mince his words:

> They are ungrateful, fickle, liars and deceivers, they shun danger and are greedy for profit.

If a prince treats people well, then the people are his and they will proclaim that they will risk their lives for him. But this only lasts for as long as danger is remote. When the prince himself is in danger, the people will turn against him. This is why the prince has to use fear of death as a means of political control. If the prince expects to govern by being loved, then he will be greatly disappointed. Human beings— wretched creatures that they are—will always break the bond of love when it is to their advantage to do so. What is required, then, is a fear of death, "strengthened by a dread of punishment which is always effective."

If political control requires the fear of death, then the problem that this raises—as is evidenced in contemporary suicide bombers—is that such control cannot be exercised over someone who lacks a fear of death. Thus,

Princes cannot escape death if the attempt is made by a
fanatic, because anyone who has no fear of death himself
can succeed in inflicting it.

This question of punishment was not simply a theoretical
issue for Machiavelli. In 1513, he was imprisoned on charges
of conspiracy and tortured. There are reports that he was subjected to the delights of "strappado," where the prisoner's
hands are tied behind his back and attached to a rope and
then the prisoner's body is hoisted off the ground.

There is a doubtless fallacious story that Machiavelli
thought that one should fake one's death in order to fool one's
enemies. The truth in his case is a little less dramatic. Machiavelli died a disappointed man, leaving his family in utter
poverty. In his last years, he was denied the governmental post
he desired because of his past connections with the Medici
dynasty, who had finally been ousted from power in Florence.

Machiavelli has enjoyed a uniquely evil reputation since
the time of his death, and Shakespeare speaks in *Henry VI* of
the "murtherous Machevil." I am more inclined to Rousseau's
assessment of Machiavelli as "an honest man and a good citizen." In a letter written a couple of months before his death,
Machiavelli wrote about Florence, "I love my native city more
than my own soul." Sadly, this doesn't prevent the citizens of
one's city from being ungrateful, fickle, liars and deceivers.

## Desiderius Erasmus
### (1469–1536)

Unlike his close friend Thomas More, Erasmus seems to have
met an uneventful end in the turbulent times of the early
Reformation. The *Moriae Encomium* or *Praise of Folly*, a delightfully stinging satire, is dedicated to More and its title is a pun
upon his name.

Personified as a woman, Folly speaks and defends madness
against the purported wisdom of philosophers and theologians. This got Erasmus into enormous trouble, and in a letter
to Martin Dorp he says that "I almost regret that I published

*Folly*." But the emphasis here should be placed on the word "almost," for in praising folly Erasmus defends the only possibility of salvation that, for him, was available, what Paul calls in *Corinthians* the "folly of the cross." Lest it be forgotten, the central paradox of Christianity is that God becomes a fool in the person of Christ and is crucified in order to redeem the folly of humanity and free us from sin and death. As Folly says, "What else can that be but madness?"

## St. Thomas More
(1477–1535)

In John Aubrey's (1626–97) wonderful *Brief Lives*, he tells the following story of how More nearly became no more. When he was elderly and serving as Lord Chancellor of England, a "Tom of Bedlam," or lunatic, burst into More's house, threatening to throw him out of the window. Although physically much weaker than the madman, the author of *Utopia* thought quickly on his feet and pointed towards a little dog that he owned. More suggested that they first throw down the dog, as "This is very fine sport." After defenestrating the poor creature, More told the madman to run downstairs and repeat the jest. While the madman was descending, More followed, fastened the door shut, and called for help. Aubrey concludes that "my Lord ever after kept the door shut."

The full story of how More ended up behind shut doors in the Tower of London cannot be told here. After refusing to bless Henry VIII's marriage to his second wife, Anne Boleyn, because it would entail a repudiation of papal authority, More was sentenced to a traitor's death. This meant being gruesomely hanged, drawn and quartered, although Henry VIII in his infinite mercy commuted the sentence to beheading. More wrote a beautiful dialogue in the Tower called "A Dialogue of Cumfort [*sic*] against Tribulation." The dialogue ends with an extended meditation on the prospect of a painful death. More heroically argued in his conclusion that a consideration of the painful death of Christ is sufficient to make us content to suffer a painful death for his sake. He writes,

Remembre that yf yt were possible for me and you alone,
to suffre as mych trowble as the whole world doth together / all that were not worthy of yt selfe, to bryng vs to
the ioy which we hope to haue euerlastyngly / And therfor
I pray you let the consideracion of that Ioy, put all worldly
trowble out of your hart . . .

When on the scaffold, More said to the lieutenant, "See
me safe up and for my coming down let me shift for myself."
In a dramatic alteration to the usual execution ritual, More
blindfolded himself and calmly awaited his deathblow. After
beheading, More's body was interred in a church in Chelsea,
while his head was stuck on a pike on London Bridge.
Aubrey tells the chilling story of More's daughter who, while
crossing the bridge and seeing her father's head, said,
"Would to God it would fall in my lap as I pass under." Her
wish came true and her dead dad's head fell into her lap—
thud! She preserved the head in spices before it was interred
at St. Dunstan's Church in Canterbury.

## Martin Luther
(1483–1546)

In sharp opposition to the rationalism of many of the medieval Christian philosophers we
have encountered, for Luther
the truth of the Gospel is justified by faith and by faith alone.
That said, Luther's interpretation of the New Testament, for
example Paul's Letter to the
Galatians—to which Luther
confessed himself "betrothed"—
is full of audacious reasoning.
For Luther, as for Paul, the death of Christ was the death of
death itself and the advent of eternal life. Delighting in paradox,
Luther writes,

Thus death killed death, but this death which kills death is life itself. But it is called the death of death, by an exuberant indignation of the spirit against death.

Luther's later years were played out in a minor key. The firebrand monk denounced as a heretic for his implacable opposition to the Catholic Church showed himself an irascible, unpleasant and reactionary figure in his final years. His views on the Jews as "poisonous envenomed worms" whose synagogues and schools should be burnt are clearly incendiary. The same Luther who made the Bible accessible to the common people through his German translation called for the nobility to crush the Peasants War in 1524–5, an uprising which was to some extent inspired by his teaching. His wife, Katy, once said to him, "Dear husband, you are too rude."

Although there was a rumour, circulated by Catholics, that he had committed suicide, Luther died of a heart condition, complicated by kidney stones. In a letter from his last years, he movingly wrote,

I desire that there be given to me a good little hour when I can move onward to God. I have had enough. I am tired. I have become nothing. Do pray earnestly for me so that the Lord may take my soul in peace.

## Nicolaus Copernicus
### (1473–1543)

With Copernicus, we begin to enter the modern world and the effect is not reassuring, it is bewildering. The Copernican revolution changed thinking in two distinct but related ways:

(i) In physics, the hitherto immovable and central earth is shown to be in movement around the sun. With Copernicus, but more radically with Bruno and Galileo, the closed meaningfulness of the medieval worldview begins to open up to an infinite and potentially meaningless universe. As Pascal will write in the following century, "The eternal silence of infinite spaces fills me with dread."

(ii) In metaphysics, the Copernican revolution is a turn away from God as the still point in a turning world and towards the self. Yet, this self is not some triumphal and self-assured individual, it is rather something that is revealed through Pascal's feeling of dread. The self only becomes itself by throwing everything into doubt and embarking on a quest for certainty. The self is not given, then, but is rather a question mark among other question marks.

There is a story that after Copernicus lost consciousness from a stroke, a newly published copy of his decisive astronomical work *On the Revolutions of the Celestial Spheres* was placed in his hands. So the legend goes, he regained consciousness just long enough to realize that he was holding his magnum opus and immediately expired. He perished as he published and published as he perished.

## Tycho Brahe
### (1546–1601)

Apparently, the great Danish astronomer lost his nose in a drunken duel and wore a false one for the rest of his life. Initially, it was believed that Tycho's nose was made of gold and silver, but apparently when his coffin was opened in 1901, the nasal opening in his skull was tinted green, providing evidence of exposure to copper.

Tycho died in strange circumstances some years after he left Denmark for Prague in 1599. Apparently, his bladder burst during a banquet because he thought it would be the height of bad manners to relieve himself during the festivities. Another story says that he died from internal bleeding because he overate and his digestive tract ruptured. Either way, our copper-nosed friend died in agony some days later.

## Petrus Ramus or Pierre de la Ramée
### (1515–72)

Although largely forgotten, Ramus was a hugely influential philosopher during the sixteenth and seventeenth centuries. Most famous for his work on logic, which was a defence and updating of Aristotle, Ramus published over fifty books, many of which ran into several editions. He had an impressively bushy black beard which he washed daily in water and white wine. Nancelius reports that he only took a bath once a year.

Ramus was murdered during the St. Bartholomew's Day massacre that began at dawn on 24 August 1572. With the connivance of Catherine de' Medici and the French Catholic nobility, some 70,000 Huguenot Protestants were slaughtered in Paris and throughout France in a frenzy of killing that lasted several months. Ramus was mutilated and his fine beard and the head to which it was attached were cut off and thrown into the Seine. News of the massacre was welcomed by many Catholics and Pope Gregory XIII had a medal struck to commemorate the event.

## Michel Eyquem de Montaigne
### (1533–92)

We have already met Montaigne in this book (p. xvi). His meditation on death is marked by a hunger for life. He writes in an intimate tone with which we have long become familiar but of which Montaigne was the inventor:

> I was born between eleven o'clock and noon on the last day of February, 1533. It was only just two weeks ago that I passed the age of thirty-nine years and I need at least as many more.

Sadly, Montaigne's wish was not granted and he died six months short of his sixtieth birthday. Echoing the wisdom of Sophocles, he writes a short essay entitled "That Our Happiness Must Not Be Judged Until after Our Death." Now, if this is right, then the manner in which one ends one's life is absolutely crucial to that judgement. Montaigne says he has known good people who have died badly and bad people who have died well. He speaks of the tragi-comic death of his valorous brother at the age of twenty-three, fatally struck by a tennis ball just above his right ear. In stark contrast:

> In my time three of the most execrable and most infamous persons I have known in every abomination of life have had deaths that were ordered and in every circumstance composed to perfection.

He concludes by thinking of his own demise:

> In judging the life of another, I always observe how it ended; and one of my principal concerns about my own end is that it shall go well, that is to say quietly and insensibly.

It seems that Montaigne's wish to die quietly was granted, although not at all in the manner he had hoped. He suffered from many different illnesses in his last years, and like Epicurus was plagued by kidney stones. He died after an attack of quinsy (peritonsillar abscesses) that completely deprived

him of speech. Elsewhere in his *Essais*, he writes that the most horrible death would be to have one's tongue cut out, to die without the power of speech. Montaigne seems to have died in dumb silence, which is an awful end for such a creature of words. However, he seems to have shown no dread of death at the end, as if responding to a line from his essay on fear, "The thing I fear most is fear."

True enough, Montaigne's reflections on death, written in the prime of life, can seem like a piece of "stoic bravura," as Terence Cave notes. However, Montaigne had a near-death experience a few years prior to the writing of "To Philosophize Is to Learn How to Die." While out riding just a league from his home, one of Montaigne's servants, riding at full gallop, and bearing down like a colossus, collided head-on with Montaigne, leaving both horse and rider unconscious. In his essay "On Practising," he writes, with great impersonality, as if it had happened to someone else,

> So there was the horse lying stretched out unconscious and me ten or a dozen paces further on, dead, lying on my back, my face all bruised and lacerated . . . showing no more signs of movement or feeling than a log of wood.

Montaigne suffered severe amnesia and the memory of the accident only gradually returned over time. When he eventually did recall the memory of "the horse bearing down on me," Montaigne "took himself for a dead man." He then adds the extraordinary thought,

> It felt as if a lightning flash was striking my soul with a shuddering blow and that I returned at that moment from the other world.

What is fascinating about this incident is that Montaigne insists that he felt no fear throughout. The imminence of death was faced with equanimity.

The genius of Montaigne consists in the way in which his highly personal style does not at all appear self-indulgent, but rather speaks to something shared in our experience. Pascal is right when he says, "It is not in Montaigne, but in myself, that I find all that I see in him." For Montaigne, the manner of writing is as important as the matter. What he develops is an experimental style that is able to map the movement of the mind, "to penetrate into the opaque depths of its recesses; to tease out and pin down so many of its subtle shades and stirrings." What we see in Montaigne is something utterly modern: an attempt to write in such a way that captures and evokes the wanderings of the mind, its digressions, its assertions and its hesitations.

Although Montaigne was an admirer of Seneca and the Stoics, towards the end of his life he decided that Sceptics like Pyrrho "were the wisest party of philosophy." The ancient sceptics declared that certainty with regard to knowledge was unattainable and they gave to Montaigne the question with which he is most identified and which marks out a true philosophical attitude, "*Que sais-je?*" (What do I know?) Montaigne's approach to death also shows the strong influence of Epicureanism, and he adopts Lucretius' argument against immortality: "Imagine honestly how much less bearable and more painful to man would be an everlasting life."

Philosophy is the way in which a human being can prepare him- or herself for death. For Montaigne, the study necessary for philosophy is both an apprenticeship for death and its semblance. To study is "to draw our soul out of us" and "to keep it busy outside the body." From Aristotle onwards, the most sublime happiness that philosophy promises is the life of contemplation, the *bios theoretikos*, the stillness of the soul's dialogue with itself. More closely considered, the contemplative life is the very image of death. It is the achievement of a calm that accompanies existing in the present without forethought or regret. I know of no other immortality.

## Giordano Bruno
### (1548–1600)

If Copernicus ignited a revolution in astronomy and our entire thinking about the universe, then it was Bruno who spread that fire all across Europe and who was finally engulfed by the conflagration. His theories of an infinite universe and a multiplicity of worlds, combined with his fascination with the hermetic tradition of magic and the arts of memory, led to multiple charges of heresy.

Following his excommunication in Italy and an accusation of murder, Bruno settled for a time in Paris, London, Oxford and various university towns in Germany. During an extended and highly influential stay in England, where he befriended Sir Philip Sidney and might even have met Shakespeare, he famously quarrelled with the Oxonian doctors.

In 1591, he made the fatal move of returning to Italy, where he was tried for heresy briefly in Venice and for seven long years in Rome. After being condemned to death for refusing to retract his views, he famously said to his judges, "Perhaps your fear in passing judgement on me is greater than mine in receiving it." He was gagged and burnt alive on the Campo de' Fiori.

Bruno was the magus of a hermetic tradition of the arts of memory. In Frances Yates's words, its central doctrine is:

> All is in all in nature. So in the intellect all is in all. And memory can memorize all in all.

The human being is the microcosm of the divine macrocosm of nature and through the techniques of memory can achieve absolute knowledge and become divine. Bruno has also always been viewed as the dissenting hero of political radicalism and an enemy of the Catholic Church. In many small Italian towns the Piazza Giordano Bruno, often at the initiative of the local communist party, stands directly opposite the main Catholic church.

## Galileo Galilei
### (1564–1642)

He was threatened with the same fate as Bruno, but, as is powerfully dramatized in Brecht's *Life of Galileo*, he recanted his Copernicanism under threat of torture by the Inquisition. There is a legend that, after his retraction, he muttered, *"Pero si muove"* ("Still it moves"): still the earth moves and is not a fixed point at the centre of the universe.

Although Galileo is largely responsible for the rise of empirical observation and the separation of physics from philosophy, in his 1623 text *The Assayer* he writes, "Philosophy is written in this grand book, the universe, which stands continually open to our gaze." He spent the last eight years of his life under house arrest until his blindness put an end to his experiments with telescopes and he died of something described as a "slow fever."

## Francis Bacon
### (1561–1626)

In Bacon's view, the field of "natural philosophy" had made no progress since the ancient Greeks. Not one for understatement, Bacon proposed a *Novum Organum* (1620) or new instrument or tool that would supersede the *organon* of Aristotle and allow human beings to regain their mastery over the natural world. It has become a banality to say that "knowledge is power," but we owe this idea to Bacon.

In his view, the traditional speculative philosophers were like spiders spinning webs of fine and marvellous complexity from out of their own bodies. The problem is that these cobwebs fail to touch reality and are easily blown away. By contrast, the true philosopher should be like a bee, working together with others, conducting experiments and amassing data that can guarantee knowledge and power over nature.

True to his word, it was as a consequence of conducting such an experiment that Bacon met his end. We owe the story to John Aubrey, who insists that he heard it from no less an authority than Thomas Hobbes. Apparently, during a particularly cold winter in London with snow on the ground, Bacon was travelling with a Scottish physician and fell upon the idea that flesh might as well be preserved in snow as in salt. They both got out of the carriage at the foot of Highgate Hill and bought a hen from a poor woman who lived there. Bacon then stuffed the hen with snow and was immediately taken ill with a chill. Unable to return home, Bacon was put to bed at the Earl of Arundel's house in Highgate. Sadly, the bed was so damp that his condition worsened and, according to Hobbes, "in 2 or 3 days, he dyed of Suffocation." This is what we might call "death by empiricism."

Aubrey also claims that Bacon "was a *paiderastos*. His Ganimeds and Favourites took bribes." Although the truth of Bacon's sexual predilections cannot be established, he was found guilty of accepting bribes in 1621. He was dismissed from his lofty post of solicitor general, disgraced, and given a huge fine.

There is a less colourful story that Bacon had depended on opiates during his entire adult life and died from an overdose of nitre or opium.

## Tommaso Campanella
### (1568–1639)

After being denounced to the Inquisition for his heterodox views and confined to a convent, Campanella spent twenty-seven years in prison for fomenting rebellion in Calabria in southern Italy against Spanish rule. It was in captivity that he wrote his most famous work, *The City of the Sun*, a communistic utopia in the form of dialogue, strongly influenced by Plato's *Republic*.

After five years of freedom, Campanella was once more threatened with imprisonment and fled to France, where he lived and died under the protection of Cardinal Richelieu.

# Rationalists (Material and Immaterial), Empiricists and Religious Dissenters

## Hugo Grotius or Huig de Groot
### (1583–1645)

The great Dutch theorist of just war, whose views on international law had a profound influence on subsequent jurisprudence and politics, met a suitably international end. Although not a native of Sweden, he had been appointed Swedish ambassador to France in 1634. After some political intrigue and backstabbing, Grotius was recalled to Stockholm by Queen Christina and released from his post. On his return sea voyage to Lübeck in Germany, he was shipwrecked and washed up on the shore. He was taken by open cart to Rostock where he died of his injuries. His final words were "By understanding many things, I have accomplished nothing."

## Thomas Hobbes
### (1588–1679)

In *Leviathan*, Hobbes famously describes life in the state of nature as "solitary, poor, nasty, brutish, and short." Although Hobbes's life was not without drama—his mother went into labour with him because of fright about the Spanish Armada, and his relations with both king and parliament had their dif-

ficulties, to say the least—none of these epithets seems justified. He lived to be past ninety, still writing and publishing extensively. This was nothing short of miraculous in the turbulence of England in the seventeenth century.

The reasons for Hobbes's longevity are described with great wit and tenderness by his younger friend John Aubrey. Even in his youth, Hobbes avoided excesses "as to wine and women" and stopped drinking at the age of sixty. He carefully monitored his diet, eating lots of fish, "especially whitings." Hobbes walked vigorously every day in order to work up a sweat, for he believed that in this way he would acquire heat—for old men are cold—and expel any excessive moisture. When he had got himself into a great sweat, Hobbes would return to his house, "and then give the servant some money to rub him." Until at least seventy-five, Hobbes even played tennis several times a year. Finally, late at night when he was in bed and sure that nobody could hear him, he would sing from books of "prick-song." These were collections of popular, sentimental songs, such as "Phyllis, why should we delay?" and "Gather ye rosebuds while ye may." It was not that Hobbes had a good voice, but he believed that "it did his lungs good, and conduced much to prolong his life."

Of death, he wrote that "we should not mourn too long over one death; otherwise we should have too little time to mourn for others." Hobbes fell ill with "the strangury," or acute pain in urinating, which was probably caused by an ulcerated bladder. He is reported to have said to one of his doctors "that then he should be glad to find a hole to creep out of the world at." He died after suffering a stroke that paralysed the right side of his body.

Hobbes was buried at the local parish church of Ault

Hucknall, Derbyshire, sometimes described as the smallest village in England. According to Aubrey, the company of family and neighbours at his funeral were very handsomely entertained with "wine, burned and raw, cake, biscuit, etc."

If Hobbes's life was not nasty, brutish and short, then neither was it solitary. It appears that he had an unnamed younger female companion when he was in his nineties with whom he was very much in love. Not long before his death, Hobbes composed the following self-deprecating and touching verses:

> Though I am now past ninety and too old
> To expect preferment in the court of Cupid,
> And many winters made me even so cold
> I am become almost all over stupid.
>
> Yet I can love and have a mistress too,
> As fair as can be and as wise as fair;
> And yet not proud, nor anything will do
> To make me of her favour to despair.
>
> To tell you who she is were very bold;
> But if I the character yourself you find
> Think not the man a fool though he be old
> Who loves in body fair, a fairer mind.

In his will, Hobbes leaves 10 pounds to an otherwise unmentioned Mary Dell. Was this his love? We shall never know.

Before his final illness, Hobbes invited his friends to write possible epitaphs to be engraved on his tombstone. His favourite was the following: "This is the true philosopher's stone."

## René Descartes
### (1596–1650)

In stark contrast to Hobbes, Descartes died relatively young, shortly before his fifty-fourth birthday, while in exile in

Stockholm in the coldest winter for sixty years. Descartes
wrote to a friend, "Men's thoughts freeze here during the
winter months in addition to the water." Descartes had just
one friend in Stockholm, the French ambassador, Chanut.
Sadly, it was from Chanut that Descartes caught the viral
infection that brought about his demise. Whereas Chanut
recovered after some blood-letting, Descartes thought such
remedies were nonsensical and hoped to recover naturally.
His fever continued and worsened over a period of ten days.
Before Descartes lost consciousness, he is reported to have
said, in the manner of a Socrates or a Plotinus,

> My soul, you have been held captive a long time. This is
> the time for you to leave the prison and to relinquish the
> burden of this body. You must suffer this rupture with joy
> and courage.

It was Chanut who had encouraged Descartes to accept the
invitation of Queen Christina of Sweden to come and teach
the monarch philosophy. Sadly, this seems to have been a total
failure, for after a couple of sessions Descartes confessed, "I do
not know if she [Christina] has ever learnt anything about philosophy." The pedagogical situation was certainly not helped
by the fact that Christina arranged for her philosophy tutorials
to take place at five o'clock in the morning in the Stockholm

winter. Descartes was apparently not an early riser.

It is unclear why Descartes
accepted Christina's invitation. It is true that she was
insistent, first sending an
admiral to invite him to Sweden and subsequently sending a warship to fetch the
philosopher. Was it the flattery
of being recognized by a
monarch when he felt totally

unrecognized in his native France or his adopted Holland? It is true that the desire for recognition can do terrible things to the soul. But it might also have been some sort of death wish on Descartes's part. According to Desmond Clarke, before he left for Stockholm Descartes had a premonition of death by shipwreck. Of course, this was hardly an unreasonable fear in the seventeenth century, particularly as Grotius had died in that manner just five years earlier after a meeting with the same monarch. Descartes seems to have been entirely unstimulated by Stockholm; he read very little and wrote almost nothing.

Descartes was notoriously itinerant, living at no fewer than thirty-eight addresses during his lifetime. Oddly enough, this pattern seems to have continued after his death and the story of the wanderings of Descartes's corpse borders on the tragi-comic. As Descartes was a Catholic and Sweden was Protestant, he was buried in a cemetery for unbaptized orphans and victims of the plague. According to the Christian theology of the time, this meant that the soul of which Descartes spoke so fulsomely above would not be allowed to enter heaven and would be doomed instead to wander in limbo. In 1666 Descartes's body was exhumed and a long return journey to Paris began. Because of lengthy delays in Copenhagen and numerous interruptions elsewhere, it took fully eleven months for it to arrive in Paris.

But that was not an end to the matter. After initially being placed in the church of Sainte-Geneviève in Paris, it was decided to move his remains to the Panthéon, the great cathedral of the French Revolution. Sadly, this decision was never carried out and after two more temporary residences in Parisian cemeteries, Descartes's remains were finally interred at the former monastery of St.-Germain-des-Prés in 1819.

Intriguingly, the initial inscription on Descartes's grave, which no longer exists, was *Bene qui latuit, bene visit* ("He who hid well, lived well").

# Elizabeth of Bohemia, Princess Palatine
### (1618–80)

In what is possibly the most stupid entry in his *Brief Lives*, Aubrey writes that Descartes was "too wise a man to encumber himself with a wife." Be that as it may, he enjoyed relationships with many women, none more brilliant than the exiled Princess Elizabeth, whose uncle was Charles I of England, rudely but rightly beheaded in 1649. Indeed, in a letter of consolation to Elizabeth after the regicide, Descartes writes that a fast and glorious beheading was preferable to "the death one awaits in bed"—a remark of peculiar irony considering the facts of Descartes's own demise.

Because of the restrictions placed on women's education and role in public and intellectual life until more recently than we might care to imagine, their presence in the history of philosophy tends to find expression not so much in treatises as in other literary forms, such as correspondence. In 1643, when she was twenty-four, Elizabeth began a long and detailed philosophical correspondence with Descartes that lasted until his death. With a rigorous education in science and mathematics, as well as classics and theology, she was Descartes's intellectual equal and he treated her as such. In addition, her letters are marked by a refreshing candour,

warmth and directness that was sorely absent from the courtly language of the seventeenth century.

The question she raises is central to Descartes's dualism of thought and extension—that of the separation of the mind and body. If the thinking mind is separate from the extended body, as Descartes claims, then how do mind and body interact?

Descartes's full response

can be found in his final book, *The Passions of the Soul*, published shortly before his death. He argues that the pineal
gland, a greenish-grey lump of matter about the size of a pea
and located at the centre of the brain, is the locus of the
mind's interaction with the body.

Elizabeth was clearly underwhelmed by René's pineal
gland and her letters show her continually criticizing
Descartes's rationalism and his mechanistic view of the body
in a manner that prefigures much subsequent criticism. At
one point in her disagreement with Descartes about the passions, she writes with irony about the weakness of her sex and
concludes, "I appear to have the wrong body."

Some have claimed that Descartes and Elizabeth were in
love. Whatever the truth may be, it was clearly a very strong
and deep friendship. Elizabeth never married and some
years after Descartes's death she removed herself to a convent and became canoness and abbess at Herford in West-
phalia, where she died.

## Pierre Gassendi
### (1592–1655)

We briefly met Gassendi above (*see* Epicurus). Apparently,
Molière was a student of Gassendi and was inspired by his
teacher to translate Lucretius' *On the Nature of the Universe* into
French. "Gassendism" was very influential and the main rival
to Cartesianism in the seventeenth century as an alternative to
Scholasticism. Indeed, Gassendi raises what Descartes called
"the objection of objections" against his philosophy: namely
that all knowledge, even if clear and distinct, as Descartes
always emphasized, might be about nothing outside our own
minds and have no contact with reality. Descartes replies with
characteristic irritation by refusing to take the objection seriously, saying, if true, "then we have to shut the door
completely on reason, and be content to be monkeys, or parrots, and no longer men." (This is a terrible slur on both
monkeys and parrots.)

The core of Gassendi's philosophy is what he calls "mitigated scepticism." This consists in the rather improbable attempt to reconcile the atomism and materialism of Epicurus with the revealed truths of Christianity. This is an audacious task, particularly when Gassendi argues like a libertine that the highest good is "voluptuousness."

Although he died of a long illness from lung disease, it is perhaps an appropriate immortality for an atomist like Gassendi that his name was given to a large crater on the moon.

## Duke François de La Rochefoucauld
### (1613–80)

A brave, heroic, but unlucky soldier, La Rochefoucauld was shot through the head at the battle of Faubourg St.-Antoine in 1652 and nearly lost his sight, not to mention his life. He was also noted for gallantry in a number of notorious romantic liaisons for which, on one occasion, La Rochefoucauld was imprisoned at the Bastille by Cardinal Richelieu.

In his literary self-portrait, he confesses to his past peccadilloes and, very unusually for the time, describes himself in careful physical detail. He writes, "I am of a medium height, elegant and well-proportioned," with curly black hair and white teeth, "tolerably well-set." He goes on to confess that he is witty, but "of a wit spoiled by melancholy." He was a leading light in the Paris salons of the mid-seventeenth century and his cynical *Maxims* contain some splendidly barbed remarks on death, where his target is the ideal of the philosophical death.

La Rochefoucauld is resolutely against the idea that we have seen in so many ancient philosophers that one can or should have contempt for death. On the contrary, for him, death "is a dreadful thing." Nothing proves more how dreadful death is than the trouble that philosophers take trying to persuade us that it is nothing to fear. Death can only be tolerated by either cultivating one's immortality and posthumous fame or being stupid, which, for the aristocratic La Rochefoucauld, is the great virtue of common people. He writes,

Nothing proves as well that philosophers are not as convinced as they claim that death is not an evil, as the torment they go through in order to establish the immortality of their names by the loss of their lives.

For La Rochefoucauld the philosophers' contempt for death is but a barely concealed desire for glory and posthumous fame. He writes, "We fear all things as mortals, and we desire all things as if we were immortal." By contrast, La Rochefoucauld counsels, we should abandon the hypocrisy of philosophers and "content ourselves in order to bear death well." La Rochefoucauld famously writes that "Neither the sun nor death can be looked at steadily." He died after many years of crippling pain from gout.

## Blaise Pascal
### (1623–62)

In his posthumously published *Pensées*, Pascal writes,

Let us imagine a number of men in chains and all condemned to death, where some are killed each day in the sight of others, and those who remain see their own fate in that of their fellows and wait their turn, looking at each other sorrowfully and without hope. It is an image of the human condition.

There is no more divided genius in modern thought than Pascal and none, in my view, who speaks so powerfully to the condition of his time and ours, torn apart by the rival claims of science and religion.

Pascal wrote his first, groundbreaking mathematical treatise at the age of sixteen; he invented the first calculating machine a couple of years later to help his father with his tax-collecting job; he was at the forefront of experimental and theoretical work on the nature of the vacuum which was a topic that preoccupied the great minds of the day; shortly before his death he invented a large carriage with many seats which would prove to be the world's first bus line, carrying passengers across Paris; and his posthumous glory is evinced by the computer programming language that bears his name.

Although Pascal was a prodigious exponent of the new science, he saw at the same time the deep spiritual crisis it opens up. He writes of Descartes,

> I cannot forgive Descartes: in his whole philosophy he would like to do without God; but he could not help allowing him a flick of the fingers to set the world in motion; after that he had no more use for God.

The problem with Cartesian rationalism is its hubris, namely that it admits of no other limit to explanation than those given by reason. By contrast, for Pascal, reason is limited and cannot establish its own first principles. Therefore, as Pascal writes, "Nothing is so consistent with reason as this denial of reason." But, to be clear, Pascal is not an irrationalist. On the contrary, there are two excesses, "to exclude reason, to admit nothing but reason." If reason is left to itself, then Pascal thinks it leads to endless and unanswerable scepticism. Therefore, he says, "Humble yourself, weak reason." Reason must open its ears to the true master of the human condition: "Hear God."

And Pascal did hear God on the night of 23 November 1654, the famous "night of fire." After his death, a text was found sewn into his jacket which he carried with him at all times. It is the memorial of his conversion and it begins, "Fire. God of Abraham, God of Isaac, God of Jacob, not of philosophers and scholars." Importantly, in a manner that anticipates philosophers such as Kierkegaard, Wittgenstein and Simone Weil, the experience of faith cannot be expressed philosophically. The God of the philosophers is an intellectual misunderstanding of the experience of faith. Inspired by Paul and Augustine, Pascal seeks to defend a Christian understanding of death against the rationalism of Descartes, on the one hand, and the scepticism of Montaigne, on the other.

Interestingly, Pascal writes that Montaigne professes "a cowardly and effeminate" conception of death based in pagan sources and with no concern for our personal salvation. It is an open question posed in this book as to whether Montaigne's vice is not in truth a virtue.

After a lifetime of ill health, Pascal died at the young age of thirty-nine after suffering from intestinal gangrene and a blood clot in the brain.

## Arnold Geulincx
### (1624–69)

The Flemish metaphysician, who incidentally exerted some influence over the young Samuel Beckett, had quite possibly the strangest theory of causation in the history of philosophy. For Geulincx, an action cannot be done unless one has knowledge of how it is done. In his view, human beings, lacking adequate self-awareness, are not in possession of such knowledge. Therefore, we cannot truly be said to act.

Now—and this is the strange move in the argument—the only being that can be said to act is that being who possesses knowledge of how the action is done. That being is God. Therefore, we do not act, God acts through us. God is the cause of the actions whose effects we see in the world.

Geulincx writes, in the guise of a syllogism,

1. I am nothing more than a spectator of the world.
2. Nevertheless, the world itself cannot produce this spectacle.
3. God alone can produce this spectacle.

Of course, this raises a delicate issue in the case of murder. For example, if I kill a grizzly bear with an AK-47 gas-operated assault rifle (not that I possess such a weapon or often frequent the company of bears), then is it truly I that kills the bear?

Geulincx writes, "Men do not, then, properly speaking, kill; they merely *want* to kill." The successful completion of the act of killing depends on the will of God.

Therefore, it is God that kills the bear and not I (it is probably a good thing that most defence lawyers in homicide cases are ignorant of Geulincx).

Geulincx's view of causation also has a strange consequence for how we conceive of death. He writes,

> If death should befall me, what is that to me, since I owe my human condition not to my nature, but to the will of another?

God has a "secret government" over me and death is not in my power, but in the power of God's will. He may decide to join me to another body, transform me into a bear, or—and this would be the ideal for Geulincx—release me from bodily existence altogether. What is certain for Geulincx is that one's own existence does not end in death. By turning itself towards God, the mind turns itself towards that which grants it eternal life.

## Anne Conway, Viscountess Conway
### (1631–79)

Until recently, Anne Conway was a completely neglected figure in the history of philosophy. She was deeply involved in one of the major preoccupations of philosophers in the later seventeenth century: what are the religious consequences of the entirely mechanistic theory of nature advanced by Descartes and Hobbes?

In her posthumously published *The Principles of the Most Ancient and Modern Philosophy*, she argues against materialism and indeed against any distinction between mind and matter. For Conway, the universe consists of one substance: spiritualized matter whose source is divine. Her views exerted a direct influence on Leibniz, and his use of the term "monad," as the simple, perceiving entity out of which he believed the cosmos to be composed, was very probably taken from his reading of Conway.

Excluded from the universities because of her sex, she made her home at Ragley Hall, Warwickshire, into a centre for intellectual discussion and developed a close friendship with the foremost of the Cambridge Platonists, Henry More. After converting to Quakerism, Conway died relatively young, suffering from unbearable headaches. Her epitaph consists of two words: "Quaker Lady."

## John Locke
### (1632–1704)

For many, John Locke is the greatest English philosopher and without doubt the most influential. Although Locke always credited his mature interest in philosophy to his reading of Descartes, his ideas are largely developed in opposition to the Frenchman's. Nowhere is this clearer than in Locke's conception of philosophy itself. Whereas, for Descartes, philosophy is the queen of the sciences that can give us the key to indubitable knowledge in physics and metaphysics, Locke is much more modest and circumspect about the scope of philosophy. At the beginning of his major philosophical work, *An Essay Concerning Human Understanding* (1690), he writes that in the wake of "the incomparable Mr. Newton," the ambition of the philosopher should be that of

an under-labourer in clearing the ground a little, and removing some of the rubbish that lies in the way of knowledge.

For Locke and the empiricist tradition that he inspires, the
philosopher is no longer a Platonic king or a Cartesian master
of nature, but is more of a janitor in the palace of the sciences,
clearing away rubbish and tidying up.

My favourite description of Locke's *Essay* is given by Laurence Sterne. In *Tristram Shandy*, Sterne asks, "Did you ever
read such a book as Locke's *Essay upon the Human Understanding?*" He goes on, "I will tell you in three words what the book
is." Of course, Sterne being Sterne gives the answer in four
words:

> It is a history.—A history! of who? what? where? when?
> Don't hurry yourself—It is a history book, Sir of what
> passes in a man's own mind; and if you will say so much of
> the book, and no more, believe me, you will cut no con-
> temptible figure in a metaphysick circle.

This is a peculiarly apt description of Locke's *Essay*, for his
claim is that human knowledge consists in nothing but what
passes in a man's mind, what he calls "ideas." These ideas are
not, as Descartes thought, innate, but have their source in
either sensation or reflection, that is, in each individual's idiosyncratic history, like young Tristram.

Unlike Sterne, Locke was not much animated by the
philosophical question of death. There is a revealing passage on the question of the immortality of the soul in the
*Essay* where he claims that the idea that the dead will rise is
not a matter of knowledge but a question of faith. His argument is that knowledge only extends as far as one's ideas and
no further. "The modesty of philosophy" requires us to
accept that questions like God and the soul are not capable
of philosophical proof and furthermore belief in such entities does not require proof.

Locke lived amidst the political turbulence of late seven-
teenth-century England and although his *Two Treatises of*

*Government* was only published anonymously in 1690, two years after the Glorious Revolution of 1688, recent scholarship has shown that it was written much earlier. Therefore, Locke did not write in order to justify a revolution that had taken place, but to bring about an insurrection against the Catholic James II, who finally succeeded to the throne in 1685. Indeed, because of his close friendship with Anthony Ashley Cooper, the Earl of Shaftesbury, who was arrested and tried for treason for his opposition to James II, Locke fled to Holland in 1683 and lived for six years under the pseudonym of "Dr. van der Linder."

Locke's fortunes were restored after the Glorious Revolution and he was appointed commissioner for trade in 1696. Exhausted by this work and suffering from asthma, Locke retired to the Essex countryside to live at Oates, the residence of Sir Francis Masham. Locke's letters express evident joy about his freedom from work and being able to ride his horse every day. It was during one of these rides that he discovered a lump on his back, which he thought was responsible for the acute pain he felt in his legs, which eventually prevented him from riding.

He died in the presence of Lady Masham, Damaris Cudworth. She sat in vigil with Locke throughout his last days and nights and gave him whatever food and liquid he could tolerate. After reminding Damaris Cudworth about his instructions for the disposal of his body, he said to her,

I have lived long enough and I thank God I have enjoyed a happy life; but after all this life is nothing but vanity.

At three o'clock the following afternoon, while Damaris was reading from the Psalms, he lifted his hands to his face, closed his eyes and died. He is buried in a very simple but dignified grave in the churchyard of High Laver in Essex. He wrote his own epitaph, which declares,

Near this place lies John Locke . . . contented with his modest lot [. . .]. His virtues, if he had any, were too slight

to serve either to his own credit or as an example to you.
Let his vices be interred with him.

## Damaris Cudworth, Lady Masham
(1659–1708)

She was the daughter of the leading Cambridge Platonist
Ralph Cudworth, and although women were denied access to
university education, she grew up in the Master's Lodge of
Christ's College, Cambridge, and was educated by her father.

When Damaris Cudworth was twenty-two, she began an
intense and revealing philosophical correspondence with
Locke, whom on one occasion she describes as "*un second
père*" ("a second father"). Later, they became lovers, although
he was twenty-six years her senior. Locke admired Damaris
Cudworth enormously and he writes enthusiastically to others of her intellectual brilliance. She went on to publish two
books in later life.

Her philosophical position is the first articulation of a
feminist standpoint. For example, in *Occasional Thoughts in
Reference to a Virtuous or Christian Life* (1705), she argues against
any form of patriarchy and in favour of a vision of Christianity based on complete equality of the sexes.

Given the intensity of the affection between them, it is
unclear why Locke and Damaris Cudworth did not marry.
From some of the letters, it seems that she doubted Locke's
capacity for love and deep feeling. It also appears that Locke
had a change of heart and wanted to wed Damaris, but it
came too late and she married Francis Masham, an older
widower with eight children from his first marriage. Be that
as it may, after 1690, Locke took up permanent residence at
Masham's home.

After his death, Locke left half of his estate to the only son
of Sir Francis and Lady Masham, Francis Cudworth
Masham. He was greatly preoccupied with the boy's education. In 1693, Locke published *Some Thoughts Concerning Education*, where he argues that children's feet should be washed in

cold water daily and they should wear thin shoes that leak and let in water. He also thought that children should be obliged to eat at irregular intervals and on no condition to eat fruit as "a thing totally unwholesome for children." Perhaps it is a good thing that Locke did not have any progeny himself.

The younger Francis Masham died at the age of forty-five and is buried in Matching, Essex. Damaris died in 1708 and was buried in Bath Abbey.

## Benedictus (Baruch) de Spinoza
### (1632–77)

In Book IV of the posthumously published *Ethics*, one of the greatest books of philosophy ever written, Spinoza proposes the following:

> A free man thinks of nothing less than death, and his wisdom is a meditation on life, not on death.

In the demonstration of this proposition, Spinoza argues that a free human being is one who lives according to reason alone and is not governed by fear. To be free is to desire the good directly and to act and live in such a way as to persist in this desire without flinching or failing. This is why the free human being thinks of nothing less than death.

If we employ what Spinoza sees as the native wisdom of the mind, namely reason, then we will be able to overcome the fear of death and achieve what is described in the final pages of the *Ethics* as "joy," a word too little used so far in this book. This joy is the intellectual love of God, and Spinoza writes, "Death is less harmful to us the greater the mind loves God."

Now, this conclusion sounds like a traditional religious sentiment, but appearances can be deceptive. Everything turns on what Spinoza means by God and herein lies the rub. He famously writes, "*Deus sive natura*," that is, either God or nature. What this means is that there cannot be two substances in the universe as Descartes proposed with his distinction of thinking things like us and extended things like trees, rocks and stars. There is only one substance in the universe and all versions of dualistic thinking are rejected by Spinoza's monism.

Now, does this mean that Spinoza is a theist or an atheist? It is a moot point, to say the least. But it is not difficult to see how Spinoza's thought opened the door to an atheistic scientific naturalism. The only things that exist for Spinoza are natural things and the causes of these things can be known through the activity of the mind. The latter is the exercise of reason that, as we have seen, is the ethical activity of a free human being. On this reading, it is knowledge of nature produced by the rational, free mind that allows for what Spinoza calls at the end of the *Ethics* "blessedness."

Whether or not Spinoza was an atheist, the historical record clearly shows that from very shortly after the time of his death, he was viewed as such and a huge conflict erupted in European thought around his name, a conflict that rumbled on into the following centuries. Spinoza is the key figure in what Jonathan Israel has called "the radical enlightenment," the strand of anti-Christian, materialist freethinking that runs like a subterranean stream through the philosophical conflicts of the eighteenth and nineteenth centuries. According to Voltaire, "Spinoza was not only an atheist, but he taught atheism."

Be that as it may, what is most striking about the *Ethics* is its wholesale rejection of Christian virtues like humility, pity and repentance and its argument for a conception of virtue rooted in power and desire, ultimately the desire to persist in one's being, the famous *conatus essendi*. Indeed, this is one way to think about the argument for the eternity of the mind at the end of the *Ethics*. Once again this looks like a theistic argument, where blessedness consists in intellectual love of

God. But once again, if we go back to the proposition *Deus sive natura*, we can claim that the eternity of the mind consists in its being part of nature and nature is eternal. Death, therefore, is not to be feared, but is the transformation of one natural being (a living human being) into another natural being (the corpse as natural being), somewhat in the way we saw in Lucretius and Zhuangzi.

Those wanting to claim Spinoza as a Jewish philosopher would do well to read the text of his excommunication from the Synagogue in 1656:

> Cursed be he [i.e., Spinoza] by day and cursed be he by night; cursed be he when he lies down, and cursed be he when he rises up; cursed be he when he goes out, and cursed be he when he comes in.

That's quite a lot of cursing. Pierre Bayle, in the article on Spinoza in the monumentally important *Dictionnaire historique et critique* (1697), tells the story that Spinoza was initially reluctant to leave the Synagogue and only did so after he was "treacherously attacked, on leaving the theatre, by a Jew who stabbed him with a knife." Although Spinoza was luckily only left with a light flesh wound, he believed that the intent was to kill him and after that he severed all connection with the Synagogue.

The actual facts of Spinoza's death are simple, but their interpretation has been a matter of constant disagreement. After suffering from a lung disease (phthisis) for many years, Spinoza died peacefully enough in his rented rooms at The Hague in Holland while most of the other residents were at church. He was only forty-four years old.

There is a strong tradition that Spinoza died in the company of his physician and friend, Lodewijk Meyer. The source for this story is Spinoza's most famous—and famously inaccurate—early biographer, Johannes Colerus, a Lutheran pastor who ended up living in the same rooms as Spinoza and sleeping in the bed in which the philosopher died. According to Colerus, Meyer fled back to Amsterdam immediately after

Spinoza had died, having stolen a silver-bladed knife and any loose money he could lay his hands on.

What is peculiar about Spinoza is that, having lived a life of carefully guarded seclusion, he immediately became a cult figure, what Jonathan Israel calls a "secular saint and object of hagiography in the eyes of his disciples." Nowhere is this truer than in the case of Jean Maximilien Lucas, who wrote the first biography of Spinoza in French in 1678. Lucas's tone tends towards the hagiographic as he describes the saintly poverty and frugality of Spinoza. For example, when Spinoza found out that someone who owed him 200 francs had gone bankrupt, he said laughingly, somewhat like Diogenes, "I must reduce my daily fare in order to make up for this small loss."

However, Spinoza's secular sanctity should be qualified by the story—reported in some of the biographies, and which seems simply too weird to have been made up—that he would collect and train spiders to fight with one another and watch them doing so with gusto.

The issue that the conflict over Spinoza's death raises is simple and we will see it recur in the following pages: can an atheist die peacefully? That is, without recanting and making his or her peace with God? Stories abound after the time of Spinoza of atheists recanting on their deathbeds, pleading forgiveness from God or converting to Christianity. But how does one die without any faith in God or the afterlife? How can one live knowing that life is snuffed out and thrown away like a piece of rubbish? Can we truly live as mortals, or must we always live in the bad faith of what Sartre calls "counterfeit immortality"? It is in response to such paralysing questions that the lives and deaths of atheist saints like Spinoza assume such importance.

## Nicolas Malebranche
### (1638–1715)

Echoing the somewhat peculiar views of Geulincx, and directly influencing those of Berkeley, Malebranche's principal thesis is that we see all things in God. That is, God is the cause of our perception of the world around us. Now, if we only see the world through God, then it is only through him that we act in it. Thus, truly speaking, it is not we who act, but God who acts through us. Given that God is eternal and we only see things through him, the life and death of the body is of little importance. Crippled with a deformed spine and often ill, Malebranche had little fear of death. One of his Parisian critics, Fontenelle, writes movingly of his death:

> The body, which he so much despised, was reduced to nothing; but like the mind, accustomed to supremacy, continued sane and sound. He remained throughout a calm spectator of his own long death, the last moment of which was such that it was believed he was merely resting.

## Gottfried Wilhelm Leibniz
### (1646–1716)

Lawyer, diplomat, theologian, poet, logician, physicist, historian, theorist of universal language, amateur chemist, probable inventor of the infinitesimal calculus, librarian and court adviser to the Hanoverian dukes, confidant of the Queen of Prussia, founder of the Berlin Academy of Science, and engineer (he was actively involved for years in silver mining projects in the Harz Mountains), it is difficult to know where to begin with Leibniz.

Perhaps we should begin by breaking Leibniz into two pieces, like a biscuit. On the one hand, there is the public Leibniz, who Bertrand Russell declares is "optimistic, orthodox, fantastic and shallow." This is the Leibniz whom Voltaire ridiculed as Doctor Pangloss in *Candide*, declaring to one and all that this the best of all possible worlds as the worst was happening all around. This is the Leibniz who writes the *Theodicy* in order to flatter the ears of his protectress, Queen Sophie Charlotte.

The other, private Leibniz is the one whose innovations in logic are, according to Husserl, the greatest since Aristotle, and to whom Russell devotes an entire (albeit highly critical) book. The problem is that "the private Leibniz" was not considered terribly important by Leibniz himself. From early on—whether from necessity or ambition—Leibniz had devoted himself to a political career. He left important philosophical work unpublished in his desk or indeed buried in secret archives. It was this political career that was Leibniz's undoing.

In 1711, the Royal Society in London decided that it was Newton and not Leibniz who had invented the infinitesimal calculus and more or less accused Leibniz of plagiarism. Whatever the truth of the matter, there is no question that the accusation severely damaged Leibniz's reputation. When his employer, Duke George Ludwig, was invited to become King of England in 1714, Leibniz was left behind in Hanover and forgotten. Despite his bewildering assertions of divine providence in the *Theodicy*, he became known as an atheist. The name "Leibniz" was popularly derided as *"glaubt nichts,"* or unbeliever. He died alone and was buried at night with only one friend in attendance. No pastor was present at the funeral.

In a cruel twist of fate that really does take the biscuit, his immortality lives in the name of a German butter biscuit, *Leibniz-Butterkeks*, produced by the Bahlsen Company since 1891.

### Giambattista Vico
#### (1668–1744)

In the first sentence of *Finnegans Wake*, James Joyce speaks of "a commodious vicus of recirculation." This is an allusion to

Vico's cyclical theory of history, which provided a template for Joyce's wonderfully wayward masterpiece.

Vico believed that history passed through four stages: beasts, gods, heroes and men, which is presumably where we currently find ourselves. Unless the cycle of history is broken by the action of divine providence, there is a constant danger of a cataclysmic return to a new age of the beasts. The first real philosopher of history and what we would now call cultural anthropology, Vico exerted considerable influence after his death on Herder, Hegel, Comte and Marx, which far outweighs the obscurity of his life.

Vico was born into a life of grinding poverty in Naples; he was largely self-taught, and saw his philosophical career defined by disappointment. He held a minor position in rhetoric at the University of Naples. Passed over for the prestigious chair of law, predeceased by most of his children, and forced to sell the little he owned in order to publish his major work, the *New Science*, he spent his last days in melancholy, stupefaction and silence.

After his death, the university refused to accept the costs of his burial, as was the custom of the time, and his body was left in the house until his son Gennaro obtained burial for his father in the Church of the Oratorians. Since the stairway to his house was too narrow, his coffin had to be ignominiously lowered to the street through a window before his remains could be interred.

## Anthony Ashley Cooper, Third Earl of Shaftesbury
### (1671–1713)

A pupil and close confidant of Locke, he was a philosopher of great refinement, to whom we owe, among many other things, the first philosophical theory of humour. In a way that would influence Hume, Shaftesbury saw humour as the expression of what he called *sensus communis*: a shared, public sensibility or moral feeling, rather than mere "common sense."

He thought that humour was an essential ingredient in

the life of a free society. In Shaftesbury's view, humour should be permitted in the discussion of religion, because there can be no better test of a belief than to see if it can withstand mockery. With Shaftesbury, we begin to see the first glimpse of a separation between a liberal public morality and private religious belief that many of us take for granted and which recent political events have seriously thrown into doubt.

Sadly, Shaftesbury's end was not very humorous. After lengthy illness and lung problems, he retired from public life and settled, like Vico, in Naples in 1711. He died two years later. It is unclear whether Shaftesbury was the originator of the phrase "*Vedi Napoli e poi muori*" ("See Naples and die").

## John Toland
### 1670–1722)

Political life in England in the decades and indeed centuries after the Glorious Revolution of 1688 was defined by the conflict between Whigs and Tories, or liberals and conservatives. This very English problem finds philosophical expression in the writings of two brilliant and opposed Irishmen, John Toland and George Berkeley, Bishop of Cloyne. Indeed, Berkeley invented the term "freethinker" to describe radicals and infidels like Toland until he thought it too complimentary, replacing it with the epithet "minute philosopher."

However, there was nothing minute about Toland. The bastard son of an Irish cleric and a prostitute in Derry, and christened "Janus Junius," he converted to Protestantism and studied in Scotland before travelling to Holland and immersing himself in the radical ideas emanating from the writings of Spinoza and Pierre Bayle.

His most famous work, *Christianity Not Mysterious*, was published when he was just twenty-five years old. Toland was charismatic, handsome and a lover of wild conversation. He invented the term "pantheism" to describe his idea that there is no God but only the vital and dynamic matter of the universe. This led to the familiar accusations of atheism, but Toland's was a rather spiritual materialism.

Although widely seen as a Spinozist, Toland owed a great deal to the writings of Giordano Bruno and was fascinated by the beliefs of the ancient Irish and even wrote a history of the Druids. Politically, he became a prominent Whig writer and enjoyed the patronage of Shaftesbury.

Although Toland had won the affection of Sophie Charlotte, the Queen of Prussia, on visits to Hanover and Berlin, he came to a very sad end. He died in London in such dire poverty that no grave marker was placed at his burial spot. Immediately before expiring, Toland was asked whether he wanted anything. He replied that he only wanted to die. Toland's self-written epitaph concluded with the words "If you would know more of him, search his writings."

## George Berkeley
### (1685–1763)

The conflict between a radical like Toland and an archconservative like Berkeley turns on the question of matter. Berkeley was against what he saw as the rising tide of materialism in early eighteenth-century Britain. This meant both the philosophical materialism of someone like Toland and other "atheists," but equally the socioeconomic materialism that he witnessed firsthand in London in 1720 with the South Sea Bubble, the first stock market crash in history. It was in response to the unchristian greed of such materialism that Berkeley conceived the most dramatic philosophical move imaginable: he simply denied the existence of matter.

For Berkeley, *esse est percipi*, to be is to be perceived. The only access that human beings have to reality is through perception. This theory of perception, combined with its critique of abstract ideas, was very influential on Hume and thereby on Kant. But Berkeley adds the crucial caveat that we saw anticipated by Malebranche, that all perceptual impressions have their source in God. Nature, for Berkeley, is God's *sensorium*, the divine environment that gives rise to everything that we experience. On this view, there is no reason at all to presuppose any material reality outside of God. Furthermore, Berkeley insists, the independent reality of the material world is nowhere affirmed in the Bible.

What, then, of death? It is true to say that Berkeley was of a sunny disposition and not much concerned with the philosophical question of death. It is not difficult to see why: if matter does not exist and the body is only sustained by the perception of God, then death is of little consequence — provided, of course, that one is a Christian.

In a letter to Samuel Johnson, Berkeley writes, "I see no difficulty in conceiving a change of state as well without as with material substance." Johnson famously responded to Berkeley's immaterialism by kicking a stone and exclaiming, "I refute it *thus*." Berkeley kicked the bucket in a characteristically immaterial style one Sunday evening on a visit to Oxford while his wife read him a sermon.

# Philosophes, Materialists and Sentimentalists

### Charles-Louis de Secondat,
### baron de La Brède et de Montesquieu
(1689–1755)

Montesquieu's literary fame was established in 1721, when he published *Persian Letters* at the age of thirty-two. The decadent world of eighteenth-century Paris, particularly the court of Louis XIV, is seen through the eyes of two Persian visitors, Rica and Usbek, and subjected to the most delightful satirical inversions. Accustomed to the world of eunuchs and the seraglio, the visitors remark on the strange reversal of the Persian custom by giving trousers to men and skirts to women. The pope is described as a great conjuror,

who makes people believe that three are only one, and that the bread that one eats is not bread and the wine one drinks is not wine, and a thousand other things of the same sort.

European customs concerning death are mocked, too. Usbek attacks the prohibition against suicide:

> Life was given to me as a blessing; when it ceases to be so I can give it up: the cause ceasing, the effect ought also to cease.

Usbek also insists that all funeral pomp should be abolished: "Men should be bewailed at their birth and not their death."

The uncomfortable truth of Montesquieu's satire is to show that so-called "oriental despotism" is not some exotic other to occidental reason, but is at its heart. The seraglio is precisely the Paris of Louis XIV. Montesquieu sought to address this despotism in *The Spirit of Laws* (1748), with its highly influential doctrine of the separation of powers into legislative, judiciary and executive authority. The only way of checking power is by turning another power against it.

Montesquieu died tastefully enough in the arms of his lover, Madame Dupré de Saint Maur, leaving unfinished an essay on taste for the *Encyclopédie* of Diderot and d'Alembert.

## François-Marie Arouet de Voltaire
### (1694–1778)

Stories abound around the death of Voltaire in Paris at the ripe old age of eighty-four. According to Condorcet in his *Life of Voltaire*, a certain Abbé Gaulthier received a confession and profession of faith from Voltaire on his deathbed, where he declared that he wanted "to die in the Catholic religion in which he was born." On hearing this news, the parish priest of Saint-Sulpice was so enraged that he demanded a more detailed theological discussion with the sceptical *philosophe*. Knowing that Voltaire had denied the divinity of Christ in his tireless tirades against the Catholic Church, apparently the parish priest kept shouting in Voltaire's ear, "Do you believe in the divinity of Christ?," to which Voltaire replied,

In the name of God, Monsieur, don't speak to me any more of that man and let me die in peace.

In another account, as Voltaire lay dying, the bedside lamp suddenly flared up and he declared, "What? The flames already?" As he makes clear in his *Philosophical Dictionary*, Voltaire thought that hell was a pretty silly idea designed to dupe the poor and uneducated.

But Voltaire was no atheist. Earlier in the *Dictionary*, he expressed doubts as to whether a society of atheists could exist and added, doubtless thinking of the fate of Boethius,

I should want no dealings with an atheist prince who thought it useful to have me pounded in a mortar: I am quite sure that I would be pounded.

Voltaire was a deist with a belief in natural religion. He had strong sympathies with the Quakers, whose beliefs and practices he thought accorded with the Christianity of the Gospels and, interestingly, he also thought Confucius the wisest of mortals.

According to his secretary, Wagnière, Voltaire expired in perfect tranquillity after having suffered great pain. Ten minutes before he died, Voltaire took the hand of Morand, his valet-de-chambre, pressed it, and said, *"Adieu, mon cher Morand, je me meurs"* ("Adieu, my dear Morand, I am dying").

After a lifetime of exile, imprisonment and harassment by the Church and state in France, Voltaire was not allowed to be buried in Paris. His corpse was secretly removed by friends and interred at the Abbey of Scellières, a hundred miles from the capital. His remains were returned to Paris with great ceremony in 1791 and placed in the Panthéon, shrine to the Revolution. The funeral procession was led by an entire cavalry troop, four men in theatre costumes carried a golden statue of Voltaire followed by members of the Académie Française and a golden casket containing the recently published collected works in ninety-two volumes.

Sadly, some members of a royalist religious group, the "Ultras," stole Voltaire's remains in 1841 and dumped them in a garbage heap. Happily, the heart had already been removed from Voltaire's corpse and can be found today at the Bibliothèque Nationale in Paris.

## Count Alberto Radicati di Passerano
### (1698–1737)

Including this rather obscure Italian philosopher enables me to raise a question about death that is still very much alive: the right to suicide. This is a theme that we saw prefigured by Montesquieu, where it is indirectly put into the mouth of a Persian visitor to Paris, and which will be taken up directly by Hume. Why should suicide be seen as illegal, immoral or irreligious? As we have already seen, it was rather popular among the ancients, particularly the Romans. So, what's the problem with suicide?

Radicati was born into an aristocratic family in Piedmont. He converted to Protestantism and took up voluntary exile in London. In his ninety-four-page pamphlet, *A Philosophical Dissertation upon Death* (1732), Radicati seeks to defend and legitimize suicide against Christianity and the state. The pamphlet caused a huge stir in London and was declared by the attorney general, at the repeated prompting of the Bishop of London, "the most impious and immoral book." Radicati was taken into custody, given a substantial fine and then made his escape to the Netherlands sometime in 1734. He died in complete destitution in Rotterdam, attended by a Huguenot preacher. The latter declared that, shortly before his death, Radicati was filled with dread, renounced all he had written, and was reconfirmed in the Protestant faith.

Radicati's simple thesis is that individuals are free to choose their own death. This right to death is based on a radically materialist conception of nature and inspired by Epicurean and Stoical arguments that suicide is an honourable gesture: the legitimate withdrawal from a state of unbearable pain. Such views were rejected as paganism by the Christian tradition, notably in Augustine and Aquinas, although, as we have already seen, one already finds arguments against suicide in Plotinus. For the Christian, life is something given, it is a *datum*, over which we have the right of use (*usus*), but not governance (*dominion*), which is the prerogative of God. A true Christian must battle with suffering like a Christian soldier. This attitude began to be challenged in the seventeenth century with the rise of science and a materialist conception of nature, broadly Hobbes's idea of reality as matter and motion and the atheistic interpretation of Spinoza's identification of God with nature. On this view, death is nothing but the dissolution of atom clusters. It is the transformation of one lump of matter into another, from a living human being to antfood. Radicati rewrites the wisdom of Epicurus in the following way: "We cease to exist in one sort, in order to begin to exist in another."

But if this is the case, then why do people fear death? This is also where things start to get rather interesting. By definition, the fear of death cannot be based in experience as no one experiences death twice, as it were. Nor can the fear of death be ascribed to our natural constitution. Therefore, the fear of death has been imposed on humankind by

Ambitious Men, who, not contenting themselves with the State of Equality which Nature had given them, took it into their heads to thirst for Dominion over others.

Radicati is alluding to the *Traité des trois imposteurs* (*Treatise of the Three Impostors*), also known as *L'Esprit de Spinosa* (*The Spirit of Spinoza*). Written in French and published anonymously in the Netherlands probably in the 1690s, the *Traité* is possibly the most dangerous, heretical text of the eighteenth century. It embodies the radical tradition of Enlightenment thought that we have already seen with Spinoza and Toland. The *Traité* argues that Moses, Jesus and Muhammad are three impostors who have deceived humankind by imposing their "silly ideas of God" and teaching "the people to receive them without examination." Central to this imposition is the cultivation of the fear of death, a belief that the three impostors propagate through the offices of their priestly castes.

What is fascinating in Radicati's text and the radical context that surrounds it is the connection between materialism, Spinozism, freethinking and the right to suicide.

But this was (and remains, moreover) no mere theoretical debate. In April 1732, shortly after the publication of Radicati's pamphlet, the shocking suicide of the Smith family was widely reported in England. Richard Smith and his wife, living in dreadful poverty in London, had shot their daughter before hanging themselves. In his extended and carefully reasoned farewell letter, Smith, a bookbinder by trade, makes allusion to Radicati's pamphlet. He writes that he and his family had decided to take leave of this friendless world rather than live in misery. They made this decision in complete cognizance of the laws prohibiting suicide, adding that it was "indifferent to us where our bodies are laid." The Smiths' only wish was for an epitaph, which reads,

> Without a name, for ever silent, dumb;
> Dust, Ashes, Nought else is within this Tomb;
> Where we were born or bred it matters not,
> Who were our parents, or hath us begot;
> We were, but now are not; think no more of us,
> For as we are, so you be turned to Dust.

## Madame du Châtelet, Gabrielle-Émilie Le Tonnelier de Breteuil
### (1706–49)

Madame du Châtelet was an extraordinarily gifted woman who wrote influential works on the philosophy of physics and mathematics and translated Newton's *Principia Mathematica* with a commentary. Her work did a great deal to promote the new physics in France. When she was twenty-seven years old, the mother of three children and a wife in the usual loveless marriage of the time, Madame du Châtelet began an affair with Voltaire. This turned into an abiding intellectual relationship that lasted sixteen years, during which time they lived together with the full knowledge of her husband. Voltaire wryly said of her that she was "a great man whose only fault was being a woman." She had other lovers aside from Voltaire and her last affair was with the Marquis de Saint-Lambert. She became pregnant, bore the child and died six days after the birth from an embolism.

But the importance of Madame du Châtelet should not be judged in terms of her relationships with men. In a letter to Frederick the Great of Prussia, she writes with great audacity,

> Judge me for my merits, or lack of them, but do not look upon me as a mere appendage to this great general or that great scholar, this star that shines at the court of France or that famed author. I am in my own right a whole person, responsible to myself alone for all that I am, all that I say, all that I do. It may be that there are metaphysicians and philosophers whose learning is greater than mine, although I have not met them. Yet, they are but frail humans, too, and have their faults; so, when I add the sum total of my graces, I confess I am inferior to no one.

## Julien Offray de La Mettrie
### (1709–51)

Physician, philosopher, polemicist and gourmet, La Mettrie is a novel figure in the history of philosophy. He was the first philosopher to draw the full moral consequences of the scientific rejection of metaphysics and theology. He argued unapologetically for an atheistic and hedonistic materialism. La Mettrie was considered immoral by Diderot, frenetic by Baron d'Holbach, and Voltaire called him "the maddest, but the most ingenious of men." The furore caused by his 1745 book, the *Natural History of the Soul*, led to a warrant being issued for his arrest.

In this book, he argued—in what is today the most widely accepted banality of medical science—that psychic phenomena are directly related to brain states and the nervous system. La Mettrie escaped France for the more tolerant climes of Leiden in the Netherlands, where he wrote his most famous work, the materialist manifesto *The Man-Machine* (1748—followed by *The Man-Plant* in the same year). After receiving a hateful reaction and several death threats, La Mettrie escaped under cover of darkness for Germany, where Frederick the Great, Voltaire's patron, had offered him protection.

La Mettrie led a free, wild and Bohemian existence in Berlin, where he turned his attention to matters moral. He argued for an Epicurean position on the relation between matter and morality. But where Epicurus was content with a barley cake, La Mettrie had rather more elaborate tastes. He died after eating a huge dinner at the house of the French ambassador to Berlin, Monsieur Tirconnel. Strangely enough, the ambassador had arranged a feast in order to thank La Mettrie for curing him from an illness. Apparently, La Mettrie expired from the effects of indigestion caused by eating a substantial amount of slightly dodgy truffle pâté.

The Catholic Church claimed it was the hand of God, or at least the pâté of God. Voltaire reports that although Frederick the Great was greatly concerned with the manner of the philosopher's death, he said,

> He was merry, a good devil, a good doctor, and a very bad
> author. By not reading his books, one can be very content.

And yet, the enlightened German despot added, "This gourmet died as a philosopher." In his *System of Epicurus*, La Mettrie writes,

To tremble at the approach of death is to behave like a child who is scared of ghosts and spirits. The pale phantom can knock at my door whenever he wishes and I will not be afraid. The philosopher alone is brave where most brave people become cowards.

## David Hume
### (1711–76)

Whether judged as "the Great Infidel" or "*le bon David*," the question that Hume's death raises is simple: can an atheist die happy? That is, can an atheist embrace the prospect of annihilation without recanting his heresies and embracing God in a last-minute confession?

For Hume, the great advantage that arises from the study of philosophy is that it frees the mind from superstition and the claims of false religion. Although only published posthumously by his literary executor, Adam Smith, Hume's essays, "Of the Immortality of the Soul" and "Of Suicide," show him cutting through cant at his philosophical best. Examining the arguments in favour of the soul's immortality, Hume remains sceptical:

> By what arguments or analogies can we prove any state of existence, which no one ever saw, and which no wise resembles any that was ever seen?

One is thus obliged to conclude that the soul is mortal and dissolves with the body at the moment of death.

If there is no immortal soul and no God to punish us, then what possible prohibition can there be against suicide? None. For Hume, like Radicati, suicide is an act that should not be punished, for it is an entirely reasonable response to intolerable suffering. Hume adds, "I believe that no man ever threw away life, while it was worth keeping." Our horror of death is such that people will not kill themselves willy-nilly. But if life has become a burden that we cannot bear, then Hume thinks we are justified in taking it.

James Boswell was famously perturbed by Hume's atheism and requested, and was granted, an audience with the philosopher on two occasions, the second being shortly before Hume died. Boswell asked Hume whether the thought of annihilation terrified him, to which Hume replied, "Not the least; no more than the thought that I had not been, as Lucretius observes."

Boswell then asked whether it might be possible that there is an afterlife, to which Hume answered that "It was possible that a piece of coal on the fire would not burn." Hume went on to say that he had never entertained any religious belief since reading Locke and added, in words that would still get him into trouble in many parts of the contemporary world:

> The morality of every religion was bad, and that when he heard that a man was religious, he concluded that he was a rascal, though he had known instances of some very good men being religious.

Boswell was deeply shocked by Hume's persistence in his unbelief. He asked his mentor Samuel Johnson for counsel and the latter said, "Why should it shock you, Sir? Hume never owned that he had read the New Testament with attention." In other words, you can't believe what an atheist says because he *is* an atheist.

In his brief autobiographical remarks, Hume notes that he was "struck with a disorder in my bowels" in 1775 and goes on to add that it has "become mortal and incurable. I now reckon upon a speedy dissolution."

What is astonishing is Hume's calm in the face of his demise, his contentment in accepting his fate. In Adam Smith's exchange of letters with Hume's physician, the word that recurs is "cheerfulness" and Smith depicts Hume happily reading Lucian's *Dialogues of the Dead* a few days before his own journey to Hades. Thus, Hume the atheist dies cheerfully, in good humour and without anxiety. Smith concludes,

I have always considered him, both in his lifetime and since his death, as approaching as nearly to the idea of a perfectly wise and virtuous man, as perhaps the nature of human frailty will permit.

Adam Smith died with the same calm as his mentor on 17 July 1790, in the company of a few close friends.

## Jean-Jacques Rousseau
### (1712–78)

It is quite possibly the greatest understatement of the last few hundred years of philosophy to suggest that Rousseau was a difficult man. In 1765, Hume bravely helped Rousseau escape from Switzerland and France, where he had been persecuted for sedition and impiety. In his infinitely resourceful paranoia, Rousseau turned on Hume, accusing him of conspiring with his enemies. As rumours of Hume's supposed treachery spread across the Channel, he calmly penned a refutation of Rousseau's accusations, calling the whole thing "a miserable affair." As Samuel Johnson remarked to Boswell about Rousseau during his stay in England,

I think him one of the worst of men. Three or four nations have expelled him; and it is a shame that he is protected in this country.

Hume's autobiographical essay, "My Own Life," covers a bare ten pages and begins,

It is difficult for a man to speak long of himself without vanity; therefore, I shall be short.

Such was Rousseau's vanity that he spoke very long of himself and wrote three substantial autobiographies. This is not the place to ruminate on the details of Rousseau's sexual masochism in *The Confessions* and his submissive desire to be spanked. Nor shall I consider Rousseau's bizarre dialogue with himself in *Rousseau, Critic of Jean-Jacques* that he deposited on the altar in Notre-Dame in Paris. Instead, I'd like to turn to the last in his trio of self-portraits, *Reveries of the Solitary Walker*. After the storm of his earlier revelations, a mood of calm pervades the *Reveries*. He writes, "If an old man has something to learn, it is the art of dying; we think of anything rather than that."

Of course, Rousseau being Rousseau, matters are not straightforward. On Thursday 24 October 1776, Rousseau set out on a long walk into the hills and countryside that still surrounded Paris at that time. He indulged the great passion of his later life, botany, stopping now and again to pick plants and flowers.

At about six in the evening, Rousseau was walking back into Paris and was descending the hill on Rue Ménilmontant. Suddenly, a Great Dane came hurtling towards him at such a pace that neither creature could avoid the other. Rousseau felt neither the impact of the mastiff nor the fall and it was nearly midnight before he regained consciousness. His jaw, bearing the full weight of his body, had hit the cobblestones. He later discovered that his upper lip was split up to the nose and four teeth had been knocked in on his top jaw. His face and head was swollen, his left thumb badly damaged and his left arm and knee severely sprained. One might imagine that Rousseau was greatly traumatized or at least somewhat upset by the canine collision. Not at all. As he regains consciousness on the cold cobblestones, he writes, in one of the most extraordinary prose passages I know,

> This first sensation was a moment of delight. I was conscious of nothing else. In this instant I was being born again, and it seemed as if all I perceived was filled with my frail existence. Entirely taken up by the present, I could remember nothing; I had no distinct notion of myself as a person, nor had I the least idea of what had just happened

to me. I did not know who I was, nor where I was. I felt neither pain, fear, nor anxiety. I watched my blood flowing as I might have watched a stream, without even thinking that the blood had anything to do with me. I felt throughout my whole being such a wonderful calm, that whenever I recall this feeling I can find nothing to compare with it in all the pleasures that stir our lives.

Rousseau experiences the eternity of the present without past and future unencumbered by any sense of self. The feeling it produces in him is a beatific calm. The most intense pain produces the greatest imaginable pleasure. Perhaps readers would like to test the truth of Rousseau's experiment with a large compliant dog.

As he was such a famous — indeed infamous — public figure, rumours began to circulate around Paris that Rousseau had died or even killed himself. Apparently even the King and Queen of France were certain of Rousseau's death and obituaries began to appear in the press, most of them extremely unfavourable and insulting. Rousseau even learnt that a subscription had been established for the sale of his posthumous, unpublished manuscripts; texts, moreover, that he had not written. Thus, Rousseau is the only example I know of a philosopher who lived his own posterity. He knew that he was damned to an awful fame and that the immortality of his bad name would engulf him. Rousseau writes, in typical self-pitying hubris, "God is just; his will is that I should suffer, and he knows my innocence." Rousseau died of a massive cerebral bleeding two years later, which was possibly a consequence of his encounter with the Great Dane.

## Denis Diderot
### (1713–84)

Diderot's last words, spoken to his daughter, Mme. Angélique de Vandeul, were "The first step towards philosophy is incredulity." Although there is a little incredulity concerning the facts of Diderot's death — its precise date, location and

whether or not he was visited by a priest—the testimony of his daughter is extremely moving. Diderot famously said, "The object of my desires is not to live better, but not to die." Denis expressed some anxiety about ageing and his future demise in a letter to his sister, Denise:

I am beginning to feel that I am growing old: soon I will have to eat mush like children. I shall no longer be able to speak, which will be a rather great advantage for others and but a small inconvenience for myself.

However, he met his end with great dignity. After an exhausting return trip from St. Petersburg, at the invitation of his patron, Catherine the Great of Russia, Diderot became ill, took to his bed, and decided to stop speaking. He enjoyed a brief respite from his illness and was able to sit at table with his wife. He ate soup, boiled mutton and chicory and then took an apricot (some sources claim it was a strawberry). Angélique takes up the story:

My mother wanted to stop him from eating that fruit. "But what the devil kind of harm do you expect it to do to me?" He ate it, leaned his elbow on the table to eat a compote of cherries, coughed gently. My mother asked him a question; since he remained silent, she raised her head, looked at him, he was no more.

As Diderot was the great *encyclopédiste* and advocate of science, he had insisted his body be dissected after his demise. It was discovered that his head was as well preserved as a man of twenty's, that his gall bladder was dry, there being no more bile, and that his heart was two-thirds bigger than normal size.

# Many Germans and
# Some Non-Germans

## Johann Joachim Winckelmann
(1717–68)

Winckelmann was the originator of the classical Greek ideal in Western art and aesthetics, the arguable founder of modern art history whose *History of the Art of Antiquity* (1764) was published to wide acclaim and established him as one of the most celebrated intellectuals of his time. He was stabbed to death by a piece of rough trade in a hotel room in Trieste.

Although he left Germany to pursue a long and highly successful career in Rome as librarian and president of antiquities at the Vatican, he decided to return home for the first time in 1768. However, having reached Munich, he suddenly broke off his journey and seems to have experienced a mental breakdown. Leaving the company of his travelling party, Winckelmann returned incognito to Italy, arriving at Trieste in July. He lodged at the city's largest inn and began an affair with a certain Francesco Arcangeli. After several nights of passion, Arcangeli was desirous not of Winckelmann's person but his medals and finery. He strangled Winckelmann and stabbed him repeatedly in the genitals. Arcangeli was later apprehended and executed by being broken on the wheel.

## Immanuel Kant
(1724–1804)

The life of the philosopher is often that of the neurotically obsessive. This is particularly true of Kant. At 4:55 a.m. Kant's footman, Lampe, would march into his master's room and cry, "Herr Professor, the time is come." Kant would be seated at his breakfast table by the time the clock struck five. He drank several cups of tea, smoked his only pipe of the day, and began to prepare his morning lecture.

Kant would go downstairs to his lecture room and teach from seven until nine and then return upstairs in order to write. At precisely 12:45, Kant would call to his cook, "It has struck three-quarters," which meant that lunch was to be served. After taking what he referred to as a "dram," he would begin lunch at precisely one o'clock. Kant eagerly anticipated lunch, both because it was his only real meal of the day and, his being gregarious, it was an occasion for conversation. Indeed, Kant believed—and I think he is right—that conversation aided digestion. He followed Lord Chesterfield's rule, which meant that the number of guests should never be fewer than the graces or more than the muses and was usually between four and eight. Kant never talked philosophy and women were never invited.

After the meal was over, Kant would take his famous walk, by which the good wives of Königsberg would be able to tell the time (the one time he missed his walk was when he was too absorbed in the reading of Rousseau's *Émile*). Kant walked alone so that he could breathe through the mouth, which he thought healthier. He was disgusted by perspiration, and during summer walks would stand perfectly still in the shade until he dried off. He also never wore garters, for fear of blocking the circulation of the blood.

After an evening of reading, writing and reverie, he would go to bed at exactly ten o'clock. Kant would then proceed to enswathe himself in the bedclothes in a very

exact manner, like a silkworm
in its cocoon, and repeat the
name "Cicero" several times.
He slept extremely well.

Kant's decline was slow and
harrowing and is described in
powerful, poignant if slightly
plodding detail by his former
student and servant Wasianski.
The latter's memoir was translated with interpolations by
Thomas de Quincey as *The Last
Days of Immanuel Kant.*

Kant had suffered from a
stomach affliction for many
years, which eventually robbed
him of all appetite except for
bread and butter with English
cheese. He suffered from frequent and dreadful nightmares
with the constant apparition of murderers at his bedside.
What was worse, Kant was fully cognizant of his decline and
had little desire to see friends and enjoy the pleasures of
company.

On his last day, Kant was speechless and Wasianski gave
him a tiny quantity of water mixed with sweet wine in a
spoon until he whispered his last word, *"Sufficit"* ("It is
enough"). Against his wishes for a simple funeral, Kant lay in
state for sixteen days and the lavish funeral procession was
attended by thousands. Kant fever continued to spread across
the German-speaking world and the rest of Europe.

Although at times a great stylist, the body of Kant's philosophy is too often clothed in the rather elaborate formal academic dress of its time. Kant was the first major modern
philosopher to make his living as a professional teacher of
the subject in a way that would be followed by Fichte, Hegel
and others (although Kant also taught a dazzling range of
other subjects: geography, physics, astronomy, geology and

natural history). Sadly, this professional deformation makes much of what Kant says appear unduly abstruse.

If one were forced to try to summarize Kant's mature philosophy in a sentence, one could do worse than follow the great Kant scholar W. H. Walsh in saying, "He wished to insist on the authority of science and yet preserve the autonomy of morals." This is the gigantic task that still faces us: how are we to reconcile the disenchantment of the universe brought about by the Copernican and Newtonian revolution in natural science with the human experience of a world infused with moral, aesthetic, cultural and religious value? Is such reconciliation possible or are science and morals doomed to drift apart into a general nihilism? Such is still, I believe, our question. Hölderlin, the great German poet, called Kant the "Moses of our nation." One wonders which of his many successors fancy themselves as Christ.

### Edmund Burke
(1729–97)

The artist Joseph Farington writes rather flatly of the death of Burke,

> He died of an atrophy and suffered little pain. He had spit blood and wasted away.

The probable cause was tuberculosis of the stomach and reports suggest that Burke was lucid until the end, being read to in his final hours. By contrast, in his *Reflections on the Revolution in France*, Burke's description of the death of Marie Antoinette positively oozes sentimentality and a florid nostalgia. Burke describes her as the most "delightful vision" who ever "lighted on this orb," which "she hardly seemed to touch." Burke goes on, melodramatically, in classical Tory fashion,

> The age of chivalry is gone; that of sophisters, economists and calculators has succeeded, and the glory of Europe is extinguished forever.

# Mary Wollstonecraft
### (1759–97)

It is precisely such sentimentality and veneration of tradition and the status quo against which Mary Wollstonecraft would rail in *A Vindication of the Rights of Men* (1790). She wrote the latter as a direct reply to what she saw as Burke's shallow emotionalism and support for social inequality. Wollstonecraft followed it up with *A Vindication of the Rights of Women* (1792), arguably the most important work in feminist moral and political philosophy.

Wollstonecraft's overriding concern was to show that women are self-governing, autonomous moral beings who can attain political equality through the use of reason and the availability of education. Burke's Tory sentimentality simply reinforces women's submissive position in society and justifies what Wollstonecraft saw as the legal prostitution of conventional marriage, where the wife was effectively the husband's chattel. The root of women's oppression lies in the belief that they are morally inferior to men. Therefore, the declaration of the rights of man in the French Revolution requires a second declaration of the rights of women and the radical reform of society that will allow for total sexual equality.

Wollstonecraft did more than anyone else to show that the personal is political and vice versa, and she led a turbulent personal life. Leaving England in 1792, she spent two years in France, and had a child out of wedlock in Paris with Gilbert Imlay, an American speculator. After being abandoned by Imlay, Wollstonecraft tried to commit suicide twice, once using laudanum and the second time throwing herself into the River Thames.

A couple of years later, Wollstonecraft became the lover of William Godwin, the first philosopher of anarchism. To the amusement of their friends, the couple got married and had a daughter, also called Mary, the future author of *Frankenstein* and wife of Percy Bysshe Shelley. Tragically, the placenta did not come away during childbirth and Wollstonecraft died of a fever eight days later.

### Marie-Jean-Antoine-Nicolas Caritat, marquis de Condorcet
(1743–94)

In the years after the French Revolution in 1789, political power was divided between the Girondins, a more moderate faction, and the radical Jacobins, whose leader was Robespierre.

Although an enthusiastic and active supporter of the French Revolution, becoming secretary to the Legislative Assembly and representative for Paris, Condorcet spoke against the execution of King Louis XVI. From that time, he was considered a Girondist. In October 1793, a warrant was issued for Condorcet's arrest and the great mathematician went into hiding for five months. It was during this clandestine existence that he wrote his most influential book, *Sketch for a Historical Picture of the Progress of the Human Mind*, which argued in classical Enlightenment fashion for the progress of human beings towards an ultimate perfection. However, Condorcet became convinced that the hiding place was imperfect and decided to flee Paris. Two days later, he was apprehended outside the city and two days after that he was found dead in his prison cell. Some people believe that Condorcet poisoned himself, while others insist that he was murdered by his Jacobin opponents.

### Jeremy Bentham
(1748–1832)

In the South Junction at the south end of the main building of University College London on Gower Street, the body of

Jeremy Bentham sits upright inside a wooden cabinet with glass windows, a little like an antique telephone box.

In a text called *Auto-Icon: or, Farther uses of the dead to the living*, Bentham gave careful instructions for the treatment of his corpse and its presentation after his demise. If an icon is an object of devotion employed in religious ritual, then Bentham's "Auto-Icon" was conceived in a spirit of irreligious jocularity. The "Auto-Icon" is a godless human being preserved in their own image for the small benefit of posterity. Bentham writes that he planned the "Auto-Icon"

to the intent and with the desire that mankind may reap some small benefit in and by my decease, having hitherto had small opportunities to contribute thereto while living.

As such, Bentham's body is a posthumous protest against the religious taboos surrounding the dead and embodies the founding spirit of University College London, which was established in 1828 as the first place of higher education in England free from the grip of the Anglican Church.

Bentham's body was dissected and his skeleton picked clean and stuffed with straw. He was dressed in a favourite suit of clothes, complete with his favorite stick, "Dapple," in his hand.

Bentham requested that his body be seated in a chair, "in the attitude in which I am sitting when engaged in thought." Bentham was greatly interested in the reports he had read from New Zealand about the islanders' way of mummifying heads and wished for his own head to be so treated. Indeed, in the last ten years of his life Bentham used to carry around the glass eyes that were to adorn his dead head. Sadly, the mummification process went badly wrong and a wax head was used as a replacement. The original, rotting and blackened head used to be kept on the floor of the wooden box between Bentham's feet. However, the head became a frequent target for student pranks, being used on one occasion for football practice in the front quadrangle. In 1975, some students stole the head and demanded that a ransom be paid to the charity Shelter. After the ransom demand was reduced from 100 pounds to 10, the head was discovered in a locker at Aberdeen railway station in Scotland. The original head is now refrigerated in the vaults of University College London.

It is reported that the "Auto-Icon" attends meetings of the College Council and that its presence is recorded with the words "Jeremy Bentham—present but not voting."

## Johann Wolfgang von Goethe
(1749–1832)

Goethe thought it

> entirely impossible for a thinking being to think of its own non-existence, of the termination of its thinking and life.

True enough, one might concur. However, the inference that Goethe drew from the inconceivability of death in the mind of the living was personal immortality. That is, if we cannot conceive of the end of our life, then our life has no end. This would seem to be confirmed by Goethe's famous last words, "*Mehr Licht*" ("More light").

However, there is another interpretation of Goethe's last words. Thomas Bernhard tells a story about a man from Augsburg in Germany who was committed to a lunatic asylum for insisting at every opportunity that Goethe's final words were not "*Mehr Licht*," but "*Mehr Nicht*" ("No more"). Although six doctors refused to commit the man to the madhouse, a seventh finally agreed under severe pressure from the good burghers of Augsburg. Some time later, the doctor was awarded the Goethe badge of the City of Frankfurt, the great poet's birthplace.

## Friedrich Schiller
### (1759–1805)

Apparently, in 1805 Goethe was filled with foreboding that either he or Schiller would die that year. By January, they were both struck down with a serious illness. Goethe eventually recovered, although convalescence took several months. Schiller, his body weakened by the effects of the pneumonia and pleurisy with which he had struggled since 1791, was not so lucky. On 1 May he contracted double pneumonia and drifted in and out of delirium.

His last words were full of doubt: "*Ist das euer Himmel, ist das euer Hölle?*" ("Is that your heaven, is that your hell?")

Goethe and Schiller were buried next to each other in Weimar.

## Johann Gottlieb Fichte
### (1762–1814)

The great philosopher of the Ego became Non-Ego at the age of fifty-two. Fichte contracted typhoid from his wife, who was tending wounded soldiers during the Wars of Liberation that raged from 1813 to 1815, when Prussia was trying to rid itself of the occupying French forces.

It was a suitably patriotic death for the philosopher whose last major work, *Addresses to the German Nation* (a book which has been through fifty editions in German alone), exhorted the German people to expel their Napoleonic invaders and restore national unity and moral purpose. He writes,

> All death in nature is birth, and in dying the intensification
> of life straightaway becomes visible. Death does not kill.
> On the contrary, behind the old obscurities, enlivening
> life begins and develops. Death and birth are only the

struggle of life with itself, in order that life may forever appear transfigured.

Fichte is buried next to Hegel in the Dorotheenkirche in Berlin.

## Georg Wilhelm Friedrich Hegel
### (1770–1831)

For Hegel, death is what he calls "the labour of the negative." In this light, it might appear that Hegel's entire work is a philosophy of death insofar as the method that he calls "dialectic" is a relentless movement of negation that spans all areas of existence.

Experience itself is understood by Hegel as the annulment of an old object and the emergence of a new object for consciousness, an object that itself will be negated. Experience, then, might seem like a long death march. However, crucially, the *via dolorosa* of negation does not lead to a dead end but to what Hegel calls "the negation of the negation," which is how he understands what he calls "Spirit." The latter is nothing other than the movement of life itself. So, what looks like a philosophy of death might more accurately be described as an attempt to understand life in its experiential and historical unfolding.

In this sense, what Hegel says about Christ's death is indicative and fascinating. Christianity, for Hegel, is the highest form of religion because in its central act the universal God takes on a particular human form in the incarnation. Christ is the God-man who is exposed to mortality in the painful death of crucifixion. In the language of the Trinity, the first person of God the Father becomes the second person of God the Son.

However, matters do not end there, for the consequence of the "death of God" (and Hegel anticipates Nietzsche's famous words by nearly a century, although his meaning is quite different) is the third person of the Trinity: Spirit. But the notion of Spirit tends to cause confusion. Hegel did not

believe in anything like disem-
bodied spirits or the immortality of the soul. For Hegel,
Spirit does not live narrowly in
the life of the Church, as in
Catholicism, but in the life of
the community itself. Spirit,
then, is simply a living community which knows itself and
determines itself freely. Interpreted in this way, and freed
from its mystical shell, one can
see how closely Hegel's idea of

Spirit resembles what might appear to be its materialist
inversion in Marx's communism. Although Marx famously
said that it was necessary to stand Hegel's philosophy on its
head in order to see its rational kernel, he always professed
himself "the pupil of that mighty thinker." But that, as they
say, is another story.

As for Hegel's own death, it was less than Christ-like. At
the end of August 1831, a cholera epidemic swept across Germany from the east. The so-called "Asiatic cholera" had first
been detected among British soldiers in India in 1817 and
had reached Russia by 1823. In 1832, 800 people died of the
disease in the impoverished East End of London. The cause
was usually bad drinking water.

In Berlin, between August and the end of the epidemic in
January 1832, there were 2,500 cases of cholera. It would
appear that Hegel was one of its victims. His body betrayed
signs of the infection, such as ice-cold blue face, hands and
feet. After his death, Hegel's wife protested that he had died
because of complications due to a stomach ailment from
which the philosopher had been suffering since a trip to
Paris in 1827.

Many of Hegel's biographers sympathize with his wife and
have accepted her version of events. However, the evidence
assembled by Dr. Helmut Döll in *"Hegels Tod"* seems to point
in the opposite direction. His wife's insistence that *"Mein*

*seliger, geliebter Mann"* ("my blessed and beloved husband," as she puts it in a letter written after Hegel's death) had not died from cholera was probably due to the stigma surrounding the burial of cholera victims. Like lepers, they were usually buried at night, without ceremony, and in a separate grave-yard.

What is the connection between Hegel and the Brooklyn Bridge? In the year of Hegel's death, favourite student and protégé Johann August Röbling—who was rumoured to have written a 2000-page thesis on Hegel's concept of the universe—left Prussia for the USA. After developing a revolutionary technique of bridge-building using wire rope and a truss system, Röbling was awarded the commission for the Brooklyn Bridge and began work in 1867. Sadly, his foot was badly damaged in a ferryboat accident and Röbling died from tetanus infection sixteen days later, even though his injured toes had been amputated.

Vast, heavy, gothic and incredibly solid, the Brooklyn Bridge spans and reconciles two opposed shores in a way that still appears to defy the laws of gravity. Like Hegel's system, at the time of its opening the Brooklyn Bridge was by far the largest and most impressive work of its kind in the world. Like the Brooklyn Bridge, the vast architecture of Hegel's system rests on sand.

## Friedrich Hölderlin
### (1770–1843)

In 1806, as Hegel was writing his monumental *Phenomenology of Spirit*, Hölderlin, his close friend and former fellow student, was forcibly sent to a clinic for the mentally ill in Tübingen, southern Germany. He was placed in the care of the celebrated Dr. Autenrieth, inventor of a face mask that he applied to his patients to stop them screaming. Medical articles on Hölderlin tend to agree that he was suffering from catatonic schizophrenia. Judged incurable and given a maximum of three years to live, Hölderlin was released from the clinic into the care of a humble artisan, Ernst Zimmer, with whom he stayed for the remaining thirty-one years of Zimmer's life. Hölderlin died from pleurisy some years later, aged seventy-three.

Shortly before his death, he was presented with a new edition of his poems by Christoph Schwab. After leafing through the pages, apparently Hölderlin said,

> Yes, the poems are genuine, they are from me, but the title is false; never in my life was I called Hölderlin, but rather Scardanelli or Salvator Rosa or the like.

"Hölderlin" also liked to call himself "Buonarroti" and "Killalusimeno."

## Friedrich Wilhelm Joseph von Schelling
### (1775–1854)

Schelling was a roommate with Hegel and Hölderlin at the Theological Seminary in Tübingen, to which he had been admitted at the unusually tender age of fifteen and a half. Unlike Hegel, whom Schelling called "the old man" and who had great difficulty in obtaining a university position, Schelling was appointed to a prestigious professorship at Jena when he was twenty-three.

Between 1795 and 1809, Schelling produced an astonishing range of philosophical work that seemed to keep changing year by year. There is a story of an English student of his from the early 1800s called Henry Crabb Robinson. Apparently, Schelling asked Robinson whether the serpent was not characteristic of English philosophy. Robinson replied that he thought it emblematically German, as, like Schelling, it shed its skin every year. Schelling riposted that the English only see the skin and not what lies beneath.

In 1841, the elderly Schelling was appointed Professor of Philosophy at the University of Berlin. He was brought in by the authorities to try to eradicate the fever of Hegelianism that some people thought was sweeping across German intellectual life like cholera. His eagerly awaited inaugural lecture was attended by a vast crowd, including Kierkegaard, Engels and Bakunin. Although the cure for Hegelianism was not discovered, Schelling died peacefully in Switzerland in his eightieth year.

## Novalis, Friedrich Leopold Freiherr von Hardenberg
### (1772–1801)

Along with Friedrich Schlegel, Novalis is the quintessential Romantic philosopher. Deeply influenced by Fichte's concept of the Ego defined by the activity of endless striving, Novalis writes,

> Inward goes the mysterious path. In us or nowhere is eternity with its worlds, the past and future.

He espoused what he called "magic idealism," which begins from the premise that "the world is animated by me," and claims that language is that magical medium for shaping the world. However, in a move that would influence contemporary deconstructive thinking, Novalis did not believe that language was adequate as a way of giving voice to the eternity within us. To put this in other terms, because the human being is finite, the infinite will always escape us. The name that the Romantics gave to this gap between the finite and the infinite was *irony*, and Friedrich Schlegel writes that "Philosophy is the real homeland of irony." For the German Romantics, the most appropriate medium for the expression of this ironic failure is the fragment or the witty aphorism. To this end, in the late 1790s, Novalis and Schlegel published collections of fragments in their hugely influential journal, the *Athenaeum*. They famously compare the fragment to a hedgehog:

> A fragment, like a miniature work of art, has to be entirely isolated from the surrounding world and be complete in itself like a hedgehog.

Against a systematic philosopher like Hegel, they write,

> It is equally fatal to the spirit to have a system and not to have a system. It will simply have to combine the two.

In the condition that the Romantics saw as the homelessness of modern human beings, it is only the poet who can lead humanity home, a theme that is reiterated in much English Romanticism.

Novalis is the only thinker in this book who studied mining (apart from Leibniz). He worked in the administration of the Saxon salt works in Weissenfels until his premature death in his twenty-ninth year. After a period of deteriorating health and having suffered a stroke, Novalis sent for his friends. On 25 March 1801 he fell asleep as Friedrich Schlegel sat beside him, listening to his brother Karl playing the piano. He never woke up.

## Heinrich von Kleist
### (1777–1811)

At the end of his peculiar yet powerful short essay, "On the Puppet Theatre," Kleist ponders the nature of grace. Given the restless nature of human consciousness, Kleist concludes that grace will only appear in bodily form in a being that

> has either no consciousness at all or an infinite one, which is to say, either in the puppet or a god.

On the afternoon of 21 November 1811, in a suicide pact, Kleist shot his friend Henriette Vogel through the chest and then emptied the pistol in his mouth. Apparently they had a table and some coffee brought from a nearby café to enjoy the view before they topped themselves. Both were buried the following day at the precise spot where they had died. Suicide is therefore a return to a state of grace. The essay on the puppet theatre concludes, "This is the final chapter in the history of the world."

With savage historical irony, the location of Kleist's and Henriette's suicide—on the shore of the Wahnsee in south-west Berlin—was the place where the murder of the European Jews was decided some 130 years later.

## Arthur Schopenhauer
(1788–1860)

Schopenhauer is perhaps the modern philosopher who said most about death and whose unrelenting pessimism exerted a vast influence that can be felt in Freud and existentialism, and continues to be felt in writers such as John Gray.

Schopenhauer is the Eeyore of Continental philosophy, insisting that existence is really some sort of mistake and "life is an expiation of the crime of being born." That said, Schopenhauer does have a point: if the purpose of human life is *not* suffering, then human beings are ill adapted to its true purpose. Affliction, pain, illness and woe are every-where. Human life is a sheer restlessness for Schopenhauer, a constant inconstancy that shows itself most clearly in the tragi-comedy of sexual desire. He writes,

We begin in the madness of carnal desire and the transport of voluptuousness, we end in the dissolution of all our parts and the musty stench of corpses.

Schopenhauer was a notorious misogynist. He wrote that "marrying means, to grasp blindfold into a sack hoping to find out an eel in an assembly of snakes." In 1820, he was found guilty of a charge of battery brought against him by a seamstress. The philosopher was particularly sensitive to noise and had become so enraged by the loud talking of the seamstress on the landing outside his room that he pushed her down a flight of stairs. He was obliged to pay her a monthly allowance until her death. When she finally expired, some twenty years later, Schopenhauer wrote, "*Obit anus, abit onus*" ("The old woman dies, the burden is lifted").

For Schopenhauer, death is the reason for philosophizing and life is a constant dying in a state of suffering. The human being is an *animal metaphysicum* and our metaphysical need has its root in trying to stand face-to-face with mortality. Life, then, is literally a *mortgage*, a contract with death:

> Life is to be regarded as a loan received from death, with sleep as the daily interest on this loan.

The problem of suicide haunts Schopenhauer. His father killed himself in 1805. But if life is as imperfect as Schopenhauer insists, then why not kill oneself? What possible reason can there be to live? As Dale Jacquette rightly argues, it would appear that Schopenhauer positions himself for an enthusiastic defence of suicide. However, he insists that suicide is a cowardly act. Why?

The answer lies in his metaphysics. The basic argument of Schopenhauer's greatest philosophical work, *The World as Will and Representation*, is that the world is simply a series of fleeting appearances. Behind these appearances there lies a vast, irrational, impenetrable and merciless Will. Therefore, and this thought finds its home in Freud, we do not really will but are willed by an unconscious agency over which we have no power. The problem with suicide, then, is that it maintains the illusion of wilfulness. For Schopenhauer, the only permissible suicide is the self-starvation of the ascetic, which we will see below with the example of Simone Weil.

Schopenhauer's view of the Will has a peculiar corollary: the possibility of an afterlife. If it is true that we are willed by an implacable and immortal Will, if all material things, ourselves included, are but effects of such a Will, then the life of that Will cannot be said to end with our death. Thus, death is not total annihilation, but the decomposition and reconstruction of individual beings into new forms.

This is what Schopenhauer calls—in a way that echoes the Stoics and Daoists—*palingenesis* (rebirth). Therefore, little bits of Schopenhauer or anybody else (even the loathed seamstress) might be lurking in your pencil, your jacket or your breakfast cereal. Schopenhauer's material appearance underwent palingenesis after a second heart attack and lung infection. He was found dead sitting in his chair on 21 September 1860.

## Heinrich Heine
### (1797–1856)

Heine's writing and wit were always closer to Diderot or Laurence Sterne than his German contemporaries. He once remarked that if a fish in water were asked how it felt, it would reply, "Like Heine in Paris." Appropriately, he died there, probably from syphilis. His final words were, "God will pardon me. It's his *métier*."

## Ludwig Feuerbach
### (1804–72)

The young Karl Marx wrote in a note to himself,

> There is no other road for you to *truth* and *freedom* except that leading *through* the brook of fire [ *Feuerbach* ]. Feuerbach is the *purgatory* of the present times.

Although now best known as a precursor to Marx, Feuerbach was the most widely read and controversial philosopher in Germany in the late 1830s and 1840s. Because of his radical views, he never received a university professorship and was obliged to live on the profits of his wife's share in a porcelain factory in Bruckberg, Germany. When the porcelain business cracked and went bankrupt in 1859, Feuerbach and his wife lived in straitened circumstances. The money for Feuerbach's medical care after the stroke that led to his death had to be raised by contributions from supporters of the newly founded German Social Democratic Party.

After having simply denied the possibility of personal immortality in "Thoughts on Death and Immortality," written when he was only twenty-six, Feuerbach radicalized his critique of Christianity in his later work. Christianity is essentially the elevation and objectification of an ideal of human perfection into divine form: the person of Christ. Human beings then proceed to alienate themselves from this perfection. What Christians worship when they kneel is nothing other than themselves in an alienated, idealized form. The philosophical cure consists in overcoming alienation, demystifying Christianity and bringing human beings towards a true self-understanding. For Feuerbach, this means that philosophy becomes anthropology, the science of humanity. In a diary entry from 1836, he writes,

> Away with lamentations over the brevity of life! It is a trick of the deity to make an inroad into our mind and heart in order to tap the best of our sap for the benefit of others.

## Max Stirner, born Johann Kaspar Schmidt
### (1806–56)

Stirner didn't think that Feuerbach was nearly radical enough in his critique of religion. In *The Ego and Its Own* (1845), he rejects all religious concepts, moral norms and social conventions. It remains the classic statement of individualistic anarchic egotism and is a terrific read. Stirner writes,

> The divine is God's concern; the human, man's. My concern is neither the divine nor the human, not the true,

good, just, free, etc., but solely what is *mine*, and it is not a general one, but is unique, as I am unique. Nothing is more to me than myself.

*The Ego and Its Own* attracted a great deal of critical attention, and evidence of its influence can be found in the fact that Marx and Engels spend several hundred pages of *The German Ideology* picking apart "Saint Max" line by line.

But Stirner's success was short-lived and the remainder of his life was dismal. His later books had no success, and his second wife left him, saying later that he was a sly and unpleasant man. He fell into severe poverty and was imprisoned on two occasions.

On 25 June 1856, Stirner was stung on the neck by a flying insect and died a month later from the resulting fever.

# The Masters of Suspicion and
# Some Unsuspicious Americans

## Ralph Waldo Emerson
### (1803–82)

Emerson is the first American philosopher in this book. He was enthusiastically admired by someone as difficult to please as Nietzsche, although the latter does describe Emerson as "German philosophy that had taken on quite a lot of water on the trans-Atlantic passage." That said, Emerson is still far too little read in Europe and not taken philosophically seriously enough anywhere else. Most Americans might have read a couple of essays in high school and then he is quickly forgotten. Most non-Americans don't even get that far.

The dense, compact and oracular style of Emerson, combined with the extraordinary meditative voice which defines his prose, can be seen in "Experience" (1844), an essay prompted by the death of his son two years earlier. But this death does not yield the usual ritual lamentation. On the contrary, Emerson writes that the calamity of his son's death "does not touch me." Something that he thought part of him and which could not be torn away without tearing him apart "falls off from me and leaves no scar." Emerson goes on, "I grieve that grief can teach me nothing." He concludes, in utter darkness,

> Nothing is left us now but death. We look to that with a grim satisfaction, saying, There at least is reality that will not dodge us.

What is being faced here is not the refusal to mourn, but the inability to do so. What, then, is the good of thought? As Emerson quips, against Hegel, "Life is no dialectics." On the contrary, life is a "bubble and a scepticism, a sleep within a sleep."

And yet, all is not quite lost. Happiness consists in living "the greatest number of good hours" and this requires the cultivation of the practice of patience. Emerson writes,

> Patience and patience, we shall win at the last [. . .] Never mind the ridicule, never the defeat; up again, old heart!— it seems to say,—there is victory yet for all justice.

Emerson died patiently of pneumonia.

## Henry David Thoreau
### (1817–62)

A disciple of Emerson, Thoreau's meditations on nature in *Walden* and defence of individual conscience against an unjust government combine the romanticism and reform at the heart of the movement known as New England Transcendentalism.

Following a typical late-night excursion to count the rings on tree stumps during a rainy night, Thoreau contracted bronchitis. His health declined over the next three years and he seems to have been fully aware that his end was nigh and calmly accepted death.

When asked if he had made his peace with God, he replied, "I did not know we had ever quarreled." He died at the age of forty-four and there is but one word written on his· grave in Sleepy Hollow Cemetery, Concord, Massachusetts: "Henry."

## John Stuart Mill
### (1806–73)

In Room 26 of the National Portrait Gallery in London, there is a portrait of Mill by G. F. Watts painted a couple of months before the philosopher's death. Eyes downcast in meditation, lips sealed, face poised and half in shadow, Mill's Atlantean brow is surrounded by almost total funereal blackness.

Happily, Mill's demise was less gloomy. He had retired to his villa at Saint-Véran in Avignon, France, with his step-daughter, Helen Taylor, who was Mill's constant companion after his wife's death fifteen years earlier. Like the aged Rousseau, Mill took enormous pleasure in botany. On the night of Saturday 3 May, Mill caught a chill after a fifteen-mile walk. His condition deteriorated and he died calmly in his sleep four days later.

Mill's favourite motto was from Thomas Carlyle's wonder-fully witty satire on German philosophy, *Sartor Resartus*: "Work while it is called Today; for the Night cometh, wherein no man can work." Before he died, Mill is reported to have said to Helen, "You know that I have done my work." He was buried beside his wife in the cemetery of Saint-Véran.

## Charles Darwin
### (1809–82)

Darwin's final book, published in the year before his death, was *The Formation of Vegetable Mould, through the Action of Worms, with Observations on Their Habits*. Although hardly a catchy title, the book was—to Darwin's surprise and delight—enthusiasti-cally received and outsold *On the Origin of Species*. As John

Bowlby points out, with Darwin's eye for small detail, immense perseverance and the theoretical cast of mind that characterized all of his work, he showed how our entire ecosystem was dependent on the activity of the earth's humblest creatures.

Of course, it is poignant that Darwin should interest himself in worms on the way to becoming wormfood. He seems to have longed for death towards the end, viewing the graveyard near his house in Downe, Kent, "as the sweetest place on earth." In his last year, Darwin felt increasingly tired and complained that

> I have not the heart of strength at my age to begin any investigation lasting years, which is the only thing which I enjoy.

Life had become wearisome for Darwin and after a heart attack and almost daily anginal attacks, he confessed, "I am not in the least afraid to die." Against his wishes, Darwin was not allowed to submit to the action of worms in Downe Churchyard. The famous agnostic (Thomas Huxley's neologism to describe Darwin's attitude towards religious belief) was buried with great ecclesiastical ceremony and now rests a few feet from Isaac Newton in Westminster Abbey.

## Søren Kierkegaard
### (1813–55)

Apart from a long period of constipation, Kierkegaard seems to have enjoyed reasonable health. However, he became ill in late September 1855 and collapsed in the street on 2 October. At his own request, he was taken to Fredrik's Hospital in Copenhagen, where his condition deteriorated. Kierkegaard's niece reports that when brought to the hospital, he said that he had come there to die. He died six weeks later on 11 November, aged forty-two. The cause of death is unclear and the tentative diagnosis was tuberculosis.

It seems that Kierkegaard had simply lost the will to live,

exhausted by his voluminous and brilliant literary work and depressed by the sorry state of his personal life and the state of Christianity in Denmark. His lifelong friend Emil Boesen visited him as he was dying and kindly suggested to Kierkegaard that much in his life had worked out well. He replied, "That is why I am very happy and very sad, because I cannot share my happiness with anyone." He continued, "I pray to be free of despair at the time of my death."

This last remark is significant and poignant because six years earlier, under the pseudonym "Anti-Climacus," Kierkegaard had published *The Sickness Unto Death* (1849). This fatal sickness is despair, which is understood by Kierkegaard as the conscious-ness of sin. The only cure for the sickness unto death is faith, specifically faith in Christ's forgiveness for our sins. For Kierkegaard, following Saint Paul and Luther, the overcoming of despair requires dying to the world through faith in Christ, who is the death of death. Faith is the opposite of sin and is that state where the self wills to be itself and "rests transparently in the power that established it."

Sadly, Kierkegaard's peaceful rest was short-lived. None other than Hans Christian Andersen reports a scandal that took place at Kierkegaard's *kierkegaard* ("churchyard" in Danish). Despite his tireless tirades against the degraded Christianity of the Danish pastors, Kierkegaard was buried with a full religious service and the eulogy was delivered by his brother Peter, the Bishop of Aalborg. Outraged by such hypocrisy, Kierkegaard's nephew, Henrik Lund, made a protest speech at the graveside. He ridiculed the clergy, and in particular Bishop Peter, for burying someone who had renounced all connection to what Henrik called the "plaything Christianity of the pastors."

In the years following his brother's death, Peter Kierkegaard resigned his bishopric and renounced his legal right to
take care of his affairs. He ended his days insane in 1888.

## Karl Marx
### (1818–83)

Marx seems to have had a long, painful affair with illness.
During the writing of *Das Kapital* (1860–6), he suffered from
what he describes in various letters as "abominable catarrh,
eye inflammation, bile-vomiting, rheumatism, acute liver
pains, sneezing, dizziness, persistent coughing, and dangerous
carbuncles." The carbuncles caused the most "frightful pains"
and for periods covered his "whole cadaver." They were particularly virulent on his genitals, which caused him obvious
distress. This is without mentioning pleurisy and the lung
tumour that eventually killed him.

The last decade of Marx's life was one of constant illness
and endless travel in search of a cure for his many ailments.
This took him for long periods to various resorts in Austria,
Germany, Switzerland, France, Algiers and the less exotic des-
tinations of Ventnor on the Isle of Wight, the Channel Islands,
Eastbourne and Ramsgate. Marx seems to have been followed
by rain wherever he went, even in Algiers and Monte Carlo.

In his last years, he was increasingly politically crotchety
and too depressed to engage in serious work. Marx was broken by the deaths of his beloved wife, Jenny, in 1881, and his
first and favourite child, whom he nicknamed "Jennychen,"
two months before him. However, his end was peaceful
enough, falling asleep in an easy chair. As Engels puts it in
his funeral oration, with unintended bathos,

On the 14th of March, at a quarter to three in the afternoon, the greatest living thinker ceased to think.

Marx was buried in the same grave as his wife in Highgate
Cemetery in north London. His tomb, which has long been a

place of pilgrimage, is adorned in gold with the famous eleventh thesis on Feuerbach,

The philosophers have only interpreted the world in various ways. The point however is to change it.

Marx was voted the world's greatest philosopher by a huge margin on BBC Radio 4 in July 2005.

# William James
## (1842–1910)

Although a pragmatist, an empiricist and one of the founders of scientific psychology, James had a lifelong fascination with psychical research and mystical experience. This led him to experiment with various drugs; he claimed, for instance, that it was only under the influence of nitrous oxide that he was able to understand Hegel.

In his late essays, James develops the idea of what he calls "pure experience." Disregarding the idea of consciousness as a fiction, pure experience is an apprehension of the present as it simply is, without regard for divisions of past and future or subject and object. In pure experience, the present is simply there to be lived.

James had an agnostic position on issues like the immortality of the soul and the existence of God. In his *Varieties of Religious Experience*, he is willing to accept the possibility of "something larger than ourselves," in which we might "find our greatest peace." As someone who had suffered from what he called "anhedonia" in earlier life, which included long periods of depression and even attempted suicide, it is clear that James's curiosity about such realms of experience was not simply theoretical.

James died of an enlarged heart, which was brought on by vigorous hiking in the mountains, his favourite means of relaxation. It is characteristic of James's boundless intellectual energy that he was writing an introduction to philosophy until very shortly before his death. In its opening pages, he writes,

Philosophy, beginning in wonder, as Plato and Aristotle said, is able to imagine everything different from what it is. It sees the familiar as if it were strange, and the strange as if it were familiar.

In the year before his death, James went to hear Freud lecture on his first visit to the USA. Freud recalls walking and talking with James, when suddenly James handed him his bag and asked him to walk on until he got through his attack of angina. Freud continues,

He died of that disease a year later; and I have always wished that I might be as fearless as he was in the face of approaching death.

James died cradled in the arms of his wife, Alice, at the family home in Chocorua, New Hampshire. He told his wife that he longed to die and asked her to rejoice for him. She notes in her diary, "William died just before 2:30 in my arms . . . No pain at the last and no consciousness." His son Billy photographed his father's corpse lying in rumpled white sheets on his iron bed and made a death mask.

William's brother, the novelist Henry, died six years later in 1916. For the pained and utterly honest beauty of her prose, I'd like to cite Edith Wharton's testimony of the death of Henry James from *A Backward Glance* (1934):

His dying was slow and harrowing. The final stroke had been preceded by one or two premonitory ones, each causing a diminution just marked enough for the still conscious mind to register it, and the sense of disintegration must have been tragically intensified to a man like James, who had so often and deeply pondered on it, so intently watched for its first symptoms. He is said to have told his old friend Lady Prothero, when she saw him after the first stroke, that in the very act of falling (he was dressing at the time) he heard in the room a voice which was distinctly, it seemed, not his own, saying: "So here it is at last, the dis-

tinguished thing!" The phrase is too beautifully characteristic not to be recorded. He saw the distinguished thing
coming, faced it, and received it with words worthy of all
his dealings with life.

## Friedrich Nietzsche
### (1844–1900)

Much—perhaps too much—has been written about Nietzsche's collapse in Turin in early January 1889, his subsequent
"madness" and his death eleven years later. A good deal of the
speculation about Nietzsche's madness turns on the role of
his sister, Elisabeth Förster-Nietzsche. She returned to
Germany after trying to establish a colony of Aryans in
Paraguay called *Nueva Germania*. Elisabeth's husband com-

mitted suicide in 1889 and the
colony foundered financially.

A passionate anti-Semite,
Elisabeth was clearly not a
pleasant person and her role
in the editing and distortion
of Nietzsche's work and the
concealment of her brother's
medical history is revealing.
She always insisted that her
brother's madness was due to
mental exhaustion brought
about by excessive intellectual labour. Elisabeth never
accepted that Nietzsche's collapse was the consequence of
the syphilitic infection that he contracted as a student in a
brothel in Cologne in 1865, for which he was treated in
Leipzig in 1867. However, the course of Nietzsche's syphilis
is entirely typical, from his first incapacitations in 1871 to his
collapse in 1889 (tertiary syphilis was the AIDS of the late
nineteenth century).

The only peculiarity is the length of time between Nietzsche's collapse and death. (Incidentally, Richard Wagner
thought that the cause of Nietzsche's sickness was excessive

masturbation, and the great composer was kind enough to communicate his diagnosis to Nietzsche's doctor.)

After his return to Germany, Nietzsche was delivered into the care of Otto Binswanger, uncle of the famous existential psychologist Ludwig Binswanger, who would be greatly influenced by Heidegger. Otto Binswanger was clearly a remarkably assiduous doctor and, although Nietzsche was virtually unrecognized as a philosopher at the time, he studied Nietzsche's work in order to better understand his patient.

Binswanger diagnosed Nietzsche's condition diplomatically as "progressive paralysis." The contents of Nietzsche's medical file reveal some rather nastier details. Nietzsche seems to have been coprophagic, that is, to have been partial to eating his own faeces and drinking his own urine.

On one occasion, there is a deeply poignant exchange between Nietzsche and Binswanger, where the former smiles at the latter and asks him, "Please, give me some health."

Such was Elisabeth's obsession with concealing the nasty truth about her brother that it would appear that she arranged to have Nietzsche's medical file stolen and its contents only became known in the years after her death in 1935 (Hitler attended her funeral).

What is often underestimated in the works of Nietzsche's "madness" is their lacerating irony and self-parody. Is one meant to take seriously the title of Nietzsche's pseudo-autobiography, *Ecce Homo*, the words that Pontius Pilate said to the flogged and humiliated Christ? Is there not the slightest levity in chapter titles like "Why I am So Wise," "Why I am So Clever," "Why I Write Such Excellent Books," and "Why I am a Destiny"? When Nietzsche writes, "One pays dearly for being immortal: one has to die several times while alive," is one not meant to smile, just a little?

In the letter of 6 January 1889 that led to his friend and former colleague at Basel, Franz Overbeck, coming to fetch him from Turin, Nietzsche writes to the historian Jakob Burckhardt,

Dear Professor, ultimately I would much rather be a Basel professor than God, but I did not dare to push my private egoism so far as to neglect the creation of the world.

Something similar might be speculated about Nietzsche's attitude towards Christianity. *Ecce Homo* ends with the seemingly dramatic words, "Have I been understood?—*Dionysos against the Crucified.*" But Nietzsche's long war on Christianity should not lead Christians to see him as some sort of satanic apostate. On the contrary, he notes, "The most serious Christians have always been well-disposed towards me." As if to prove his point, the present Archbishop of Canterbury, Rowan Williams—a very serious Christian—has written a poem on Nietzsche's "madness" and death. It ends with the following words:

> At night he roared; during the day, My voice
> Is not nice, he would whisper. White,
> Swollen, his skull drowned him like a stone,
> His breath, at the end, the sound
> Of footsteps on broken glass.

Like Nietzsche said, with his tongue firmly in his cheek, "Some men are born posthumously."

## Sigmund Freud
### (1856–1939)

In a letter written in his final year, Freud speaks of "a new recurrence of my dear old cancer with which I have been sharing my existence for sixteen years." Between April 1923 and his death, Freud had numerous operations for cancer of the mouth, jaw and palate. Estimates vary from twenty-two to thirty-three operations. The cause was his prolific cigar smoking, up to twenty a day, without which he was unable to think and write and which he never gave up.

Freud lived in constant pain, but the only drug he ever took prior to the very end was a little aspirin. He wrote to Stefan Zweig, who also spoke at his funeral, "I prefer to think in torment than not to be able to think at all." In his last months, Freud developed a cancerous growth on his cheek that created such an unpleasant odour that his favourite dog, a chow (and Freud was unusually fond of dogs), refused to stay with him and cowered instead in the corner of the room. After the growth had eaten through his cheek and his body had atrophied because of his inability to eat, he said to his trusted physician, Max Schur,

> My dear Schur, you remember our first talk. You promised me then you would help me when I could no longer carry on. It is only torture now and it has no longer any sense.

Schur gave Freud morphine and he fell into peaceful sleep, dying the following day.

Freud had a rather morbid disposition and said that he thought of death every day. He also had the disturbing habit of saying to departing friends, "Goodbye; you may never see me again." Without entering into discussions of the death drive, where Freud claims, in a way that is explicitly indebted to Schopenhauer, that the goal of human striving is an inert state where all activity ceases, there is also evidence of a longing for death on Freud's part. After a fainting attack in Munich in 1912, Freud's first words after regaining consciousness were "How sweet it must be to die."

However, Freud's response to his physical suffering shows a complete absence of self-pity and an acceptance of reality. Freud showed no sign of complaint or irritability with his painful condition, but accepted it and was resigned to his fate. Much closer to Epicurus or Montaigne than Schopenhauer, there is no celebration or evasion of suffering in Freud. There is simply a lucid acceptance of reality and the pain that can accompany it. As Ernest Jones put it in his funeral oration in Golders Green Crematorium in north London, a few weeks after the outbreak of the Second World War,

> If ever man can be said to have conquered death itself, to live on in spite of the King of Terrors, who held no terror for him, that man was Freud.

## Henri Bergson
### (1859–1941)

Bergson died a genuinely heroic philosophical death. Under the racist laws implemented by the collaborationist Vichy government after France's defeat by Nazi Germany in 1940, Jews were required to line up to register with the authorities. Although an exemption had been granted to Bergson because of his fame, on 3 January he chose to stand in line with the other Jews and died from the ensuing chill. Although he was spiritually attracted to Christianity, Bergson refused to convert, saying,

> I would have become a convert, had I not foreseen for years a formidable wave of anti-Semitism about to break upon the world. I wanted to remain among those who tomorrow were to be persecuted.

Bergson was a widely read and hugely influential philosopher during his lifetime, who received every conceivable literary and academic honour. His fame was such that the French spoke of "*le Bergson boom*" after the appearance of *Creative Evolution* in 1907. The first recorded traffic jam on Broadway in Manhattan was caused by Bergson's inaugural public lecture in 1913 and he was the first of the very few philosophers to receive the Nobel Prize for Literature, in 1928. However, after his death Bergson disappeared from the philosophical scene until the recent renewal of interest in his work, which is largely due to the influence that Bergson exerted on Gilles Deleuze.

# John Dewey
(1859–1952)

Dewey is an unjustly under-appreciated figure in contemporary philosophy. The influence of the huge body of work written during his long life was eclipsed, after his death, by two factors: the emergence of an increasingly scientistic trend in Anglo-American philosophy in the 1950s and a compensating tendency towards phenomenology and Marxism in Continental thought during the same period.

Dewey's work belongs to neither of these philosophical tendencies, but embraces both of their concerns. It is open to the influence of Continental thought, particularly Hegel, and Dewey did important work in logic and the philosophy of science, particularly on the influence of Darwinism on philosophy. There is much, sometimes flatulent, discussion of pluralism in philosophy. Dewey got there first and a long time ago.

Philosophy has arguably always had an allergic reaction to democracy, from Plato's ridiculing of a politics based on opinion and not knowledge to Nietzsche's lampooning of egalitarianism. Dewey shows the contribution that philosophy can make to democratic life. This doesn't mean that philosophers will be Platonic kings, but neither are they simply Lockean "under-labourers" or janitors in the Crystal Palace of the sciences. All turns here on the relation between democracy and education. Dewey sees education as the dynamic and continuous development of democratic life, what he called "reconstruction," and rightly believed that society cannot transform itself without paying scrupulous attention to pedagogy. Dewey saw learning as more important than knowing and defined philosophy as "the general theory of education." He set his influential views on education to work at the newly established University of Chicago after 1894 and later at Columbia University in New York.

He died from pneumonia after suffering a fractured hip in 1951 from which he was not able to recover.

# The Long Twentieth Century I:
## Philosophy in Wartime

## Edmund Husserl
### (1859–1938)

Although he converted to Lutheran Protestantism as a young man, Husserl's Jewish origins led to his exclusion from the University of Freiburg after Hitler's seizure of power in 1933. The behaviour of Heidegger—Husserl's former student and successor to his Chair of Philosophy at the university—was particularly shameful; he even denied his former mentor library privileges.

In 1935 and 1936, as the lights were going out all over Europe, the elderly Husserl travelled to Vienna and Prague to give the lectures that were developed into his final, unfinished book, *The Crisis of the European Sciences and Transcendental Phenomenology.* For Husserl, philosophy is the freedom of absolute self-responsibility and the philosopher is "the civil servant of humanity." He concludes by asserting that the duty of the philosopher is to confront "the barbarian hatred of spirit" and renew philosophy through "a heroism of reason." At a time of crisis, then as now, the greatest danger facing "good Europeans" is weariness, the refusal to take up the philosophical battle of reason against barbarism.

According to his former assistant and devoted disciple

Ludwig Landgrebe, when Husserl was assailed by the illness that would eventually kill him, he had only one wish: to be able to die in a way worthy of a philosopher. Refusing the intercession of his church, Husserl said, "I have lived as a philosopher and I want to die as a philosopher."

## George Santayana
(1863–1952)

After the death of his mother in 1912, Santayana—already a celebrated and influential philosopher—resigned his position at Harvard and travelled to Europe, never to return to the USA. Rome became his adopted home. He lived monkishly in the Convent of the Blue Nuns off the Capitoline Hill, though he never converted to Catholicism. When he was asked by a friend why he had never married, Santayana replied, "I don't know whether to get married or buy a dog." His conservator and former assistant, Daniel Cory, writes of a typical scene with Santayana in the last years.

> Unless it was raining heavily, we would walk to a nearby restaurant for luncheon, and here Santayana would order a dish that struck me as being rather rich, such as a spicy Indian curry or an elaborate *dolce* to cap the feast. And he drank three glasses of wine—nearly a *mezzo-litro*—with his food. (It always astonished me the way he poured any leftover wine on his cake.)

As if such wanton hedonism was not enough to infuriate American Puritan good taste, his views on politics were wonderfully non-committal. According to Todd Cronan, an article on Santayana appeared in *Life* magazine after U.S. soldiers discovered him in Rome during the liberation of Italy in 1944. Asked his opinion of the Second World War, Santayana said, "I know nothing, I live in the Eternal." Santayana had little patience for what did not give pleasure. If we accept that the spirit is rooted in the flesh, then, as he writes in a letter,

The solution would be a sort of Epicureanism, that is, the enjoyment of life from moment to moment in its purity, beyond care and regret.

Santayana counted among his Harvard students such important poets as Robert Frost, T. S. Eliot and Wallace Stevens, and the latter's verse is particularly pregnant with the philosopher's influence. Stevens wrote one of his final poems after the death of Santayana, "To an Old Philosopher in Rome," where he is pictured "On the threshold of heaven." The dying Stevens's identification with the dead philosopher is obvious and he writes, with obvious warmth but not without ambivalence,

> *Your dozing in the depths of wakefulness,*
> *In the warmth of your bed, at the edge of your chair, alive*
> *Yet living in two worlds, impenitent*
> *As to one, and, as to one, most penitent,*
> *Impatient for the grandeur that you need.*

Santayana died after a painful struggle with cancer. A couple of days before his death, he was asked by Cory whether he was suffering. "Yes, my friend. But my anguish is entirely physical; there are no moral difficulties whatsoever."

Santayana was not the only philosopher to choose to die in the Eternal City. Dying of terminal cancer, Bernard Williams ended his days in Rome in 2003.

## Benedetto Croce
### (1866–1952)

Croce was the most important Italian philosopher of the first half of the twentieth century and a symbol for opposition to Mussolini's Fascism. After having been orphaned by the earthquake of Casamicciola in 1883, his life became his work. Shortly before his death at the age of eighty-six, Croce was asked about his health. He replied, appropriately, "I am dying at my work."

## Giovanni Gentile
(1875–1944)

Although Croce was a friend of Gentile and they edited the highly influential periodical *La Critica* between 1903 and 1922, a lasting disagreement arose between them over Gentile's embrace of Fascism. Described by himself and Mussolini as "the philosopher of Fascism," Gentile became minister of education and held several influential political posts in the 1920s and 1930s. On 15 April 1944, after the liberation of Italy, Gentile was assassinated by partisans on the outskirts of Florence, probably under orders from the Italian Communist Party.

## Antonio Gramsci
(1891–1937)

Which brings us to the greatest communist philosopher in Italy or arguably anywhere else. In 1926, in breach of parliamentary immunity, Gramsci was imprisoned by the Fascists after he had been elected a parliamentary deputy in 1924. Following a special tribunal in 1928, Gramsci was sentenced to twenty years and eight months in prison. Apparently, the prosecuting attorney said of Gramsci, "For twenty years we must stop this brain from working."

Although in very poor health and initially forced to share a cell with five other prisoners, Gramsci's brain kept working and he produced the posthumously published *Prison Notebooks* which offer a powerfully consequent critique and reconstruction of the basic concepts of Marxism. Gramsci described his position as a "philosophy of praxis," which meant the unity of theoretical reflection with practical life in the way described above in Marx's eleventh thesis on Feuerbach.

In Gramsci's hands, Marxism is not reduced to some sort of historical determinism where all aspects of life have to be explained in terms of their economic causes. On the contrary, conceived as a philosophy of praxis, Gramsci's Marxism expands to take into consideration the spheres of politics, ideology, religion and culture in the broadest sense.

After his health was broken in prison, Gramsci became legally free in 1937, but was too ill to move. He died on 27 April following a cerebral haemorrhage.

## Bertrand Russell
(1872–1970)

The first hardback book that I remember buying was a first edition of Russell's *Why I Am Not a Christian* (1957). On the rather tattered blue cover, Russell writes, in words that echo Epicurus and Lucretius,

I believe that when I die I shall rot, and nothing of my ego will survive. I am not young and I love life. But I should scorn to shiver with terror at the thought of annihilation. Happiness is nonetheless true happiness because it must come to an end, nor do thought and love lose their value because they are not everlasting.

Any conception of the immortality of the soul is therefore both iniquitous, because it is untrue, and destructive of the possibility of happiness, which requires that we accept our finitude. As such, Russell thought that all the great religions of the world were both fallacious and morally harmful. The world that we inhabit is not shaped by some divine plan, but is a mixture of muddle and accident. What the world needs, then, is not religious dogma but an attitude of scientific inquiry that may enable us to make a little sense of the muddle and accident.

Russell died after suffering from acute bronchitis in the company of his fourth wife, Edith. He insisted that there

should be no funeral service and the place of his crema-
tion should not be made public. It was also stipulated that
there should be no music. Russell's ashes were scattered over
the Welsh hills and his granddaughter Lucy wrote to Russell's somewhat resentful second wife, Dora, "If there are
ghosts to lay, let them be laid, along with our childhoods,
among the magnificent mountains." As Russell's biographer,
Ray Monk, has shown, his life was defined by the ghost of
madness and these ghosts survived his death. Monk writes,

> At his death Russell left two embittered ex-wives, an
> estranged schizophrenic son and three granddaughters
> who felt themselves haunted by the "ghosts of maniacs," as
> Russell had described his family back in 1893.

Five years after Russell's death, Lucy got off the bus in St.
Buryan in Cornwall, doused herself in paraffin and set herself alight like a Buddhist monk in Vietnam during the
American occupation. The pain was too intense and she ran
screaming to the blacksmith's shop, where they wrapped her
in blankets and sacks to put out the flames. She lost consciousness and died before reaching hospital.

## Moritz Schlick
### (1882–1936)

In the history of philosophy, there are happy and unhappy acci-
dents. Happily, Moritz Schlick took a chair in philosophy at the
University of Vienna in 1921, the same year as the publication of
a short and difficult book by a young Viennese philosopher,
Ludwig Wittgenstein, the *Tractatus Logico-Philosophicus*.

Schlick became the figurehead for a hugely influential
intellectual group that became known in 1929 as the Vienna
Circle. Roughly and readily, Viennese logical positivism
believed that all truth was either logically valid or empirically verifiable. In this way, all traces of metaphysics could
be eliminated from philosophy.

Unhappily, the Vienna Circle dispersed after Schlick was

murdered by a mentally deranged student on the steps of the University of Vienna. Austria drifted towards the *Anschluss* with Germany in 1938 and the remaining members of the Vienna Circle gradually left for England and the USA, where they had an enormous influence on the development of professional philosophy.

Although the student became a member of the Nazi Party, the murder seems to have been the consequence of a personal grudge because Schlick had rejected his doctoral thesis. Apparently, the student had been stalking Schlick for several weeks before he killed him. The student would follow Schlick and his wife into the cinema, take a seat in the aisle immediately in front of the Schlicks and spend the whole time turned around in his seat, looking Schlick straight in the face. Schlick's other students and friends advised him to get the police to put a stop to the stalking, but Schlick—a devoted liberal—refused to get the police to intervene.

In a paper from the *Philosophical Review* in the year of his death, Schlick writes,

> I can easily imagine witnessing the funeral of my own body, for nothing is easier than to describe a world which differs from our ordinary world only in the complete absence of all data which I would call parts of my body.

It is not known whether Schlick was able to empirically verify this remark.

## György Lukács
### (1885–1971)

Lukács was buried in Budapest with Communist Party honours after regaining political favour in Hungary in the 1960s. However, he had narrowly escaped execution in 1956 when he was minister of culture in the government of Imre Nagy. Thereby hangs a darkly funny story.

Lukács was not a great admirer of the work of Franz Kafka,

whom he declared to be "idealist" and a bad example of decadent aesthetic modernism. Lukács advocated an aesthetic realism that rejected the Kafkaesque world of *Angst* and alienation where isolated individuals were arrested for unknown crimes, submitted to absurd trials and condemned without reason.

After the Soviet tanks moved into Budapest to crush the Hungarian uprising, Nagy was executed and Lukács was arrested in the middle of the night and thrown into a military lorry along with other government officials. The lorry then disappeared into the obscurity of the countryside for an appointment with an unknown but probably unsavoury fate.

Lukács was taken to a vast castle in Transylvania and wasn't told whether he was going to be freed or permanently detained. So the story goes, Lukács turned to one of the other detained ministers and said, "So, Kafka was a realist after all."

The bleak beauty of this joke is that in this perilous situation, Lukács ironizes himself. The humour consists in the fact that Lukács finds himself ridiculous because reality has conspired to bring about a situation that directly contradicts his aesthetic judgement, something which he admits willingly. True humour consists in laughing at oneself.

## Franz Rosenzweig
### (1886–1929)

In 1919, Lukács experienced something close to a religious conversion to Bolshevism and participated in the short-lived communist government of Béla Kun in Hungary. Six years earlier, in 1913, Rosenzweig had experienced a conversion of a rather different kind. During the night of 7 July, during intense discussion with his friend Rosenstock, Rosenzweig decided to convert to Christianity. However, he declared that he "could turn Christian only *qua* Jew" and attended synagogue in Berlin until the time of baptism. During the Yom Kippur service on 11 October, however, he underwent a religious experience that led him to recommit to Judaism. The

precise nature of this experience is not known, although
Rosenzweig said some years later that if he had become
Christian he would have left himself behind. "The life of the
Jew," he writes,

> must precisely not lead him out of himself, he must rather
> live his way even deeper into himself.

After serving in an anti-aircraft gun unit in the German
army on the Balkan front during the First World War, Rosenzweig began to write his masterpiece, *The Star of Redemption*,
on army postcards (it should be remembered that Wittgenstein wrote the first draft of the *Tractatus Logico-Philosophicus* on
the Russian and Italian fronts in 1917–18).

Violently rejecting his earlier attachment to Hegel,
Rosenzweig begins *The Star of Redemption* by claiming that

> Philosophy takes it upon itself to throw off the fear of
> things earthly, to rob death of its poisonous sting.

From Thales' attempt to grasp the principle behind the whole
of reality ("all is water"), through to Hegel's idea of Absolute
Knowing, philosophy has attempted to know the whole and
thereby deny the singular reality of death. For the philosopher, death is nothing because we have an understanding of
reality in its entirety. As such, for Rosenzweig, philosophy is a
disavowal of death and "it plugs up its ears before the cry of
terrorized humanity." By contrast, Rosenzweig argues that we
have to learn to walk humbly with God and look at all things
from the standpoint of redemption. "Life becomes immortal,"
Rosenzweig writes, "in redemption's eternal hymn of praise."
It is only in this way that we are able to walk, in the final
words of *The Star of Redemption*, "INTO LIFE."

Rosenzweig was diagnosed with amyotrophic lateral scle-
rosis in 1922 (the same degenerative disease that afflicts
Stephen Hawking). In his final years, Rosenzweig could only
communicate by his wife reciting letters of the alphabet until

he asked her to stop and she would guess at the intended word. His final words, written in this laborious manner, were an unfinished sentence that reads,

> And now it comes, the point of all points, which the Lord has truly revealed to me in my sleep, the point of all points for which there . . .

Apparently, the writing was interrupted by a doctor's visit. Rosenzweig died during the night.

## Ludwig Wittgenstein
### (1889–1951)

Wittgenstein's ignorance of significant stretches of the history of philosophy was legendary. Sadly, it has licensed a similar ignorance amongst many of his followers, who lack his brilliance. In the *Tractatus Logico-Philosophicus*, we find a possibly unwitting echo of Epicurus' view of death:

> Death is not an event in life: we do not live to experience death. If we take eternity to mean not infinite temporal duration but timelessness, then eternal life belongs to those who live in the present. Our life has no end in just the same way in which our visual field has no limits.

In the next proposition, slightly closer to Lucretius, Wittgenstein adds, "Is some riddle solved by my surviving for ever?"

A few days before his death, just after his sixty-second birthday, Wittgenstein amplified this remark in a comment to his friend Maurice Drury:

Isn't it curious that, although I know I have not long to live, I never find myself thinking about a "future life." All my interest is still on this life and the writing I am still able to do.

Wittgenstein was writing philosophy until the end and experiencing an eternity that was not haunted by the prospect of annihilation or the afterlife. After he had been diagnosed with terminal cancer, news that he apparently greeted with much relief, Wittgenstein moved in with Dr. and Mrs. Bevan. He remarked to the latter that "I am going to work now as I have never worked before." In the remaining two months of his life he wrote the entire second half of the manuscript that was published as *On Certainty*. The last fragment of *On Certainty* is dated 27 April, the day before his death.

There is a story of Wittgenstein visiting the philosopher G. E. Moore in 1944 after Moore had suffered a stroke during a trip to the USA. Under instructions from his doctor, Moore's wife insisted that his friends limit their visits to an hour and a half. Wittgenstein was the only person to resent this rule, claiming that a discussion should not be broken off until it had reached its proper end. Furthermore, Wittgenstein added, if Moore did expire during such discussion, then that would be a very decent way to die, "with his boots on."

Wittgenstein died with *his* boots on. He had developed a friendship with Mrs. Bevan; they would go to the pub together every evening at six o'clock where she would drink port and Wittgenstein would empty his glass into an aspidistra plant. She presented him with an electric blanket on his birthday and said, "Many happy returns." Wittgenstein replied, staring back at her, "There will be no returns."

Mrs. Bevan stayed with Wittgenstein during the last night and when she told him that his friends would be visiting the next day, he said to her, "Tell them I've had a wonderful life."

Peculiarly, Wittgenstein was given a Catholic funeral in Cambridge. Although very far from being Catholic, there is no doubt that, as Ray Monk claims, Wittgenstein led a devoutly religious life. Wittgenstein's life and death resemble those of a saint for our time. It is defined by austerity, frugality, inner torment, a deeply troubled relation to sexuality, and utter ethical earnestness.

## Martin Heidegger
(1889–1976)

Wittgenstein put himself into situations of reckless danger during the First World War, and was delighted when he was assigned to a fighting unit on the Russian front, volunteering for the most dangerous job of occupying the observation post. He showed remarkable courage in combat and was rapidly promoted. When Wittgenstein was first shot at by Russian soldiers in the Carpathian Mountains, he declared,

> Yesterday I was shot at. I was scared! I was afraid of death. I now have such a desire to live.

By contrast, Heidegger served during the final year of the war in a meteorological unit, first in Berlin and later on the Marne, engaged in the dangerous business of weather forecasting. However, like Lukács and Rosenzweig, Heidegger also underwent some sort of conversion through the events of the First World War, breaking with what he called "the dogmatic system of Catholicism." After 1919, when appointed Husserl's assistant at the University of Freiburg in south-west Germany, he began a stunningly original series of lectures and seminars that culminated in the completion of *Being and Time* in 1926. At the centre of this book is a highly influential meditation on death.

Despite its length and legendary difficulty, the basic idea of *Being and Time* is extremely simple: being *is* time. That is, what it means for a human being to be is to exist temporally in the stretch between birth and death. Being is time and time is finite; it comes to an end with our death. Therefore, if we want to understand what it means to be an authentic human being, then it is essential that we constantly project our lives onto the horizon of our death, what Heidegger calls "being-towards-death." Crudely stated, for thinkers like Paul, Augustine, Luther and Kierkegaard, it is through the relation to God that the self finds itself. For Heidegger, the question of God's existence or non-existence has no philosophical relevance. The self can only become what it truly is through the confrontation with death, by making a meaning out of our finitude. If our being is finite, then what it means to be human consists in grasping this finitude, in "becoming who one is" in a phrase of Nietzsche's that Heidegger liked to cite.

Despite its baroque linguistic garb, Heidegger's analysis of being-towards-death is exceptionally direct and powerful. However, it is open to the following objection. Heidegger argues that the only authentic death is one's own. To die for another person, he writes, would simply be to "sacrifice oneself." To that extent, for Heidegger, the deaths of others are secondary to my death, which is primary. In my view (this criticism is first advanced by Edith Stein and Emmanuel Levinas), such a conception of death is both false and morally pernicious. On the contrary, I think that death comes into our world through the deaths of others, whether as close as a parent, partner or child or as far as the unknown victim of a distant famine or war. The relation to death is not first and foremost my own fear for my own demise, but my sense of being undone by the experience of grief and mourning.

Also, there is a surprisingly traditional humanism at work in Heidegger's approach to death. In his view, only human beings die, whereas plants and animals simply perish. I can't speak with any expertise about the death of plants, but empirical research would certainly seem to show that the higher mammals—dolphins, elephants, but also cats and dogs—also have an experience of mortality, of both their own and of those around them. We are not the only creatures in the universe who are touched by the sentiment of mortality.

In the winter of 1975, when Heidegger had turned eighty-six, his friend Heinrich Petzet visited him for the last time. As Petzet was about to leave, Heidegger raised his hand and

said, "Yes, Petzet, the end is now drawing near." After a
refreshing night's sleep on 26 May 1976, Heidegger fell
asleep again and died.

## Rudolf Carnap
(1891–1970)

What is the world's shortest book? Answer: *What I Learned from
Heidegger,* by Rudolf Carnap. Don't worry, I'm only joking. In
1932, Carnap wrote an infamous and influential critique of
Heidegger, called "The Overcoming of Metaphysics through
Logical Analysis of Language." He claimed that Heidegger's
propositions were nonsensical because they were neither
logically valid, nor empirically verifiable. Views such as
Heidegger's may well give expression to an attitude towards
life but, in Carnap's view, they are shot through with pseudo-
philosophy and metaphysical mumbo-jumbo. The expression
of such an attitude towards life has no right to a home in philosophy, but is better expressed in literature or music. Carnap
writes, sarcastically, "Metaphysicians are musicians without
musical ability."

For Carnap, science can say all that can be said and
potentially leaves no question unanswered. Science is also
cumulative and there is progress in knowledge. Carnap
thought that philosophy could and should be modelled on
this idea of science and therefore although the history of
philosophy (let alone the history of philosophers) might be
an interesting curiosity, it is entirely secondary to the scientific activity of philosophy. Wittgenstein can be said to have
exerted a vast influence on philosophy in Britain after his
death. But through the agency of students like Quine, Carnap can be said to have been a massive force in shaping professional philosophy in the USA after the Second World
War. Perhaps this is what accounts for American philosophy's infatuation with science and its isolation from the arts
and humanities.

Although this is not widely known, as well as being a
philosopher of logic and science, Carnap was a lifelong

socialist humanist. He initially turned down the offer of a chair at UCLA because it would have obliged him to sign a McCarthyite loyalty oath.

Shortly before his death, Carnap visited imprisoned Mexican philosophers in Mexico City in a show of solidarity and he was very active in anti-racist politics. The last photograph of Carnap shows him attending the discussion of a black peace organization in Los Angeles. His was the only white face in the group. Carnap lived just below where I am writing, in a secluded home in the Santa Monica hills. His wife, Ina, committed suicide in 1964 and Carnap died at the age of seventy-nine after a brief but severe illness.

### Edith Stein,
### Saint Teresa Benedicta of the Cross
(1891–1942)

Another story of conversion, this time with a tragic ending. Edith Stein was born into an orthodox Jewish family before becoming an atheist in 1904. She was a brilliant student of philosophy and Husserl appointed her as his assistant when he took the chair in Freiburg in 1916. This was no easy task as Husserl was a particularly chaotic thinker and wrote in Gabelsberger shorthand, which was hard to decipher and even harder to edit.

Stein took the opposite path to Heidegger: he began as a Catholic and a Thomist before losing his faith; she began as an atheist and converted to Catholicism and even translated Aquinas. In an appendix to her posthumously published major philosophical work, *Finite and Eternal Being,* she criticizes Heidegger's conception of being-towards-death. As Alasdair MacIntyre puts it in his book on Stein,

We learn what it is to anticipate our own deaths from those others whose anticipation of their deaths we have in some significant way shared.

One evening, when staying with friends in the summer of 1921, Stein was left alone in the house. She took down the autobiography of St. Theresa of Avila and was unable to stop reading until the end. She immediately decided that she had to convert to Catholicism and enter Theresa's Carmelite order in Cologne. On 31 December 1938, Stein crossed the border into Holland to escape Nazi persecution of so-called "non-Aryans." However, in 1942, after the Dutch bishops published a condemnation of Nazi anti-Semitism, Hitler ordered that all non-Aryan Roman Catholics be arrested. She was sent to Auschwitz-Birkenau, where she died in the gas chamber with her sister, Rosa, who was also a convert. Survivors of the death camp testified that Stein acted with great compassion to other sufferers.

Pope John Paul II (who was also, lest it be forgotten, a phenomenologist) canonized her on 11 October 1998.

### Walter Benjamin
(1892–1940)

After the Nazis came to power in 1933, Benjamin left Berlin for Paris, where he worked on his massive and unfinished *Arcades Project*. This was a study of the commodification of nineteenth-century bourgeois life seen through the lens of the Paris arcades of glass-roofed shops.

When France fell to the Germans in 1940, Benjamin headed south in the hope of leaving for the USA via Spain. Having crossed a wild part of the Pyrenees with a group of refugees, Benjamin arrived at Portbou on the French–Spanish border. The exact order of events after this point is unclear, but Benjamin appears to have committed suicide with morphine pills at the Hotel de Francia on the night of 27–28 September. Some say that the chief of police told Benjamin that he would be handed over to the Gestapo. As a

Jew, a friend of Brecht and Adorno and a public critic of Nazism, it was clear that he would not be treated with mercy.

Hannah Arendt crossed the French–Spanish border a few weeks later at exactly the same spot, and when in New York she gave Adorno a copy of what might be the last text that Benjamin wrote, "Theses on the Philosophy of History." This extraordinarily powerful, if enigmatic, text finishes with the following words:

> We know that the Jews were prohibited from investigating the future. The Torah and prayers instruct them in remembrance, however. This stripped the future of its magic, to which all those succumb who turn to the sooth-sayers for enlightenment. This does not imply, however, that for the Jews the future was turned into homogenous, empty time. For every second of time was the strait gate through which the Messiah might enter.

It is only by cultivating remembrance that one might turn away from the illusory and finally ideological obsession with the future, which is always a brighter future made possible by scientific and technological progress and ensuring eternal human happiness. On the contrary, Benjamin insists that the angel of history faces backwards. It is only looking at the past, by brushing history against the grain, that we can keep alive what Benjamin calls "a *weak* messianic power." This weak power, this hope against hope, is the possibility that at each and every moment of time a revolutionary transformation might be brought about. In Benjamin, messianic Judaism and a revolutionary Marxism fuse together in a desperately apocalyptic vision.

# The Long Twentieth Century II:
## Analytics, Continentals,
## a Few Moribunds and a
## Near-death Experience

### Hans-Georg Gadamer
(1900–2002)

Gadamer is the only philosopher in this book whom I saw nearly die. It was in Perugia, Italy, at a summer school on Heidegger in 1986 when I was a PhD student. Gadamer was due to give a talk on his former teacher and a crowd of about forty people were eagerly waiting to hear what he had to say about the recently published Heidegger lectures that he had himself attended in Marburg in the 1920s.

Already frail with age and walking with sticks because of the polio that had afflicted him when he was twenty-two, Gadamer descended the high staircase to the seminar room. Suddenly he fell, and the sound of sticks clattering and his body bumping against each of the twenty-five Italian marble steps reverberated externally and internally in all of us.

We feared the worst. An ambulance was called and he was taken to hospital. Remarkably, Gadamer made a speedy recovery, and gave his talk a few days later with some bandages to cover his bruised head.

The story is typical of the tenacity of the man and the humanism that he defended philosophically. Gadamer was a very impressive human being. I remember another evening from the same period in Italy when a few students were sitting outside with Gadamer, enjoying the Umbrian night and discussing Plato, Gadamer's constant philosophical passion. We were drinking red wine—in fact, rather a lot of red wine—and Gadamer said, "Plato thought wine was very important. It moves the blood." Happily, medical science has recently confirmed Platonic wisdom.

In his 102nd year, Gadamer was asked for his reaction to the attack on the World Trade Center in New York. He answered in German, "*Es ist mir recht unheimlich geworden,*" meaning that the world had become strange, even uncanny, to him. He went on to add that "people cannot live without hope; that is the only thesis I would defend without any restriction." Yet, when his pupil and successor Dieter Henrich visited him for the last time in Heidelberg, he repeated that one cannot live without hope, but added that this hope had become this small, and he raised his hand and showed the tiny gap of light between his thumb and index finger.

When Gadamer was asked about death, he replied sardonically that it is "one of the most unpleasant things that are part of life." And when journalists asked him whether he felt anguish, he said, "No, not really, everything has just become so difficult." Gadamer's mobility had been restricted for some time in the last years. "Thank God, one does not have to think with one's legs," he used to quip.

Shortly before his death, Gadamer complained of stomach pains and had an operation from which he seemed to recover fully, which was remarkable for a man of his age. On the evening of the day when he was given a clean bill of health, Gadamer celebrated with a bowl of soup and a glass of red wine. The next morning he had a heart attack, lost consciousness and died in the evening.

## Jacques Lacan
### (1901–81)

There is perhaps no more divisive figure in recent Continental thought than Lacan. To some, he is an obscurantist charlatan with the colourful dress sense of a Sophist; to others, he is a venerated authority whose often oracular words are invested with the authority of Scripture. .

In my view, he must be approached as a teacher. First and foremost, Lacan was a teacher of psychoanalysts who provided a philosophical framework for psychoanalysis of great originality and significant clinical import. As a teacher, Lacan's medium was his seminar, which ran from 1953 until 1979. Here, Lacan would speak without notes, often to hundreds of people, with enormous erudition, originality and considerable wit.

At the opening session of his twenty-sixth and final seminar, on 21 November 1978, Lacan opened his mouth and found himself unable to speak. His audience, disbelieving, was as silent as he was. He had lost the voice that had captivated French intellectual life for the previous quarter of a century. He turned to the board and began to draw the knots, plaids and other topological features that had increasingly come to fascinate him in his later years. He became confused, turned to his public, made reference to his mistake and left the room. According to his faithful, though often acerbic, biographer, Elizabeth Roudinesco, someone was reported to have said, "It doesn't matter. We love you just the same."

Silences had increasingly come to mark Lacan's teaching in his last years. Some have attributed this to sagacity and profundity, others to local paralysis and vascular distur-bances to the brain. Whatever the cause, and quite sepa-rately, some time later Lacan seems to have accurately diagnosed himself with colon cancer, but refused to have the operation because of a phobia of surgery.

In his last year, Lacan seemed to be an increasingly iso-lated and confused man surrounded by a family entourage who supervised the dissolution of his psychoanalytic training school and the hurried founding of another school with his daughter and son-in-law in charge. The colon cancer took its inexorable course and Lacan submitted to an operation where a mechanical suture was fitted. The suture unexpect-edly burst and Lacan suffered from peritonitis and then sep-ticaemia and was in terrible pain.

As for his great hero, Freud, morphine was administered and before it did its work, Lacan uttered his last words, "I'm obstinate . . . I'm dying."

## Theodor W. Adorno
### (1903–69)

I have thought of Adorno, Teddie to his friends—"Your Old Teddie" to his more intimate correspondents—often during the writing of this book. During his exile from his native Frankfurt during the Second World War, Adorno lived for nearly eight years in Brentwood, West Los Angeles, five blocks from where I am writing these words. Between December 1941 and October 1949, the Adornos lived in a comfortable house on South Kenter Avenue, just a knife-throw from where O. J. Simpson "allegedly" murdered his ex-wife.

Adorno's Los Angeles years were hugely productive. He wrote *Dialectic of Enlightenment* with Max Horkheimer, finished the *Philosophy of Modern Music*, collaborated on the research project published as *The Authoritarian Personality* and sketched the wonderfully pithy fragments in what remains his most readable book, *Minima Moralia*. Indeed, it is difficult to think of Adorno's reflections on the culture industry and commodity capitalism without thinking of the affluent sunlit emptiness of West Los Angeles. That sunlight casts sharp and dark shadows that are refracted in the best Hollywood film noir of the period.

Although one would never guess it from the purgatorial tone that defines Adorno's prose of the period (he writes that every trip to the cinema left him "stupider and worse"), Teddie and his much-sinned-against wife, Gretel, were happy in Brentwood. They spent much time with the Horkheimers and Thomas Mann, who lived very close by. They were active in Hollywood society, met figures like Greta Garbo, and Teddie had his usual series of love affairs. Indeed, Charlie Chaplin invited Adorno to a private screening of his 1947 movie, *Monsieur Verdoux*. After dinner, Adorno played the piano while Chaplin accompanied him in parodic mimicry.

It was perhaps the "No" in "AdorNo" that precipitates his demise (Teddie Wiesengrund only took on his mother's Corsican Catholic name when he applied for U.S. citizenship in California). During the political drama of the student movement in Frankfurt in 1968, Adorno was singled out for criticism by radical leftist students. His critical "No!" was seen as a reactionary denial of the positivity of the revolutionary politics of direct action. In a letter to Samuel Beckett, Adorno wrote, "The feeling of suddenly being attacked as a reactionary at least has a surprising note."

On 22 April 1969, at the beginning of his last lecture course, matters came to a head with an incident that profoundly shook Adorno. Two male students mounted the platform and insisted that Adorno publicly criticize himself for calling the police to clear the students from an occupation of the Institute for Social Research and for participating in legal proceedings against a former student, Hans-Jürgen Krahl, who was a cause célèbre of the radical left at the time.

A student wrote on the blackboard, "If Adorno is left in peace, capitalism will never cease." He was then surrounded by three women students who covered him in flower petals and bared their breasts while acting out some sort of erotic performance. Very far from being a sexual prude, in other circumstances Teddie might have quite appreciated this, but instead escaped the lecture hall in a state of desperate anxiety. Adorno was never able to resume his lectures.

Physically and mentally exhausted, he left with Gretel for a holiday in Switzerland. After making a vigorous ascent to a 3,000-metre peak, Adorno suffered heart palpitations. As a precaution, Gretel took him to the nearby hospital and returned later to their hotel. The next day she learnt that Adorno had died suddenly that morning of a heart attack.

For those familiar with the relentless critical negativity of Adorno's work, it does raise a wry smile to know he was born on 11 September and died on 6 August, the anniversary of the bombing of Hiroshima.

In 1970, shortly after the publication of her husband's

final, unfinished work, which he valued so much, *Aesthetic Theory*, Gretel attempted suicide with sleeping pills. She failed, but required constant attention until her death in 1993.

## Emmanuel Levinas
### (1905–95)

In a brief, laconic inventory of autobiographical remarks, called "Signature," Levinas says that his life had been "dominated by the memory of the Nazi horror." Originally from Lithuania and naturalized as a French citizen in 1930, Levinas lost most of his immediate and extended family in the Second World War. In all likelihood the Nazis murdered them during the bloody pogroms that began in June 1940 with the active and enthusiastic collaboration of Lithuanian nationalists.

Following the fall of Paris, Levinas was captured by the Germans in Rennes in June 1940 and transferred to a camp in Magdeburg, northern Germany. Because Levinas was an officer in the French army, he was not sent to a concentration camp, but to a military prisoners' camp, where he did forced labour in the forest for five years. Levinas's wife and daughter changed their names and were concealed in a Catholic convent outside Orléans. After the war, Levinas vowed never to set foot on German soil again.

Levinas lists the names of his murdered family members in the Hebrew dedication to his second major philosophical work, *Otherwise than Being or Beyond Essence* (1974). However, he goes on to write in a second French dedication—and Levinas is thinking specifically of the war in Vietnam—to recall all those killed by "the same anti-Semitism, the same hatred of the other man." For Levinas, anti-Semitism is anti-humanism and the moral lesson of the Holocaust is to learn to assume responsibility for the other human being. It is this responsibility that suffered a total eclipse during the Second World War and in so many other wars.

If Levinas's personal life was dominated by the memory of the Nazi horror, then so was his philosophical life. In 1928,

Levinas studied in Freiburg where he gave a presentation in Husserl's last seminar and attended the first seminar of Husserl's successor, Heidegger. His time in Freiburg was marked by an intense reading of Heidegger's *Being and Time*. As Levinas said many years later, "I went to Freiburg because of Husserl, but discovered Heidegger."

In the years that followed, when Levinas had returned to France, he planned to write an introductory book on Heidegger, which would have been the first in any language. Imagine, then, Levinas's utter shock when he discovered that Heidegger had joined the Nazi Party in 1933. Years later, he wrote, "One can forgive many Germans, but there are Germans it is difficult to forgive. It is difficult to forgive Heidegger." Levinas abandoned the book on Heidegger and spent the next years beginning to rethink his approach to philosophy and to Judaism.

Accepting that there is indeed a fatal connection between Heidegger's philosophy and his politics, the question for Levinas is how philosophy might be possible without suffering the same fate. As we have already seen in Edith Stein, death is the central concept that needs to be rethought. In *Being and Time*, Heidegger writes that death is "the possibility of impossibility." That is, my death is that limit to my life that I must seize hold of and understand in order to become authentically who I am.

Levinas simply reverses this dictum and claims that death is "the impossibility of possibility." That is, death is something that cannot be predicted, represented or even understood. Death is not that by virtue of which the self becomes authentic, but is rather that ever-unknowable event that shatters the framework of my life and leaves me in a position of powerlessness and passivity. In other words, for Levinas, death is not mine, but something other. On this basis, he tries to construct an ethics that is endlessly open to the surprise of an otherness whose most eloquent expression is that of the other person.

With unintended irony, the great Jewish philosopher died on Christmas Eve, 1995. The funeral oration, "Adieu," was given by Jacques Derrida at the interment four days later. The cause was probably Alzheimer's disease, although it has not been confirmed because of a long and disappointingly fractious dispute between Levinas's son and daughter over the rights to his estate.

## Jean-Paul Sartre
(1905–80)

A couple of years before his death, Sartre said,

> Death? I don't think about it. It has no place in my life, it will always be outside. One day, my life will end, but I don't want it to be burdened by death. I want my death never to enter my life, nor define it, I want always to be a call to life.

Blind, toothless, barely able to work, his body devastated by years of abuse of alcohol, tobacco and drugs, the story of Sartre's last years does not make pleasant reading. Sartre seemed to have an uncanny ability—more truly a desire—to surround himself with a crowd of beautiful, fragile women who became financially dependent upon him. Simone de Beauvoir, the "Beaver" as Sartre always called her, remained loyal and devoted throughout his life. In the last of the many medical emergencies that punctuated the last decade of his life, he anxiously asked Beauvoir, "How are we going to manage the funeral expenses?" Before he slipped into his final coma, his eyes closed, Sartre took Beauvoir by the wrist and said, "I love you very much, my dear Beaver."

After he died, Beauvoir and a group of close friends stayed with Sartre's corpse, reminiscing, weeping and drinking whisky. Beauvoir then wanted to be left alone with Sartre. The others left and, in Hazel Rowley's words,

> She pulled back the sheet and went to lie down beside him. "No, don't do that!" an orderly shouted at her. A nurse explained: "It's the gangrene, Madame." Beauvoir

had not realized that Sartre's sores were gangrenous. The nurse let Beauvoir lie on top of the sheet beside Sartre. She was so drugged she even fell asleep for a short time. At five in the morning, the orderlies came and took Sartre away.

The President of France, Valéry Giscard d'Estaing, came in person to the hospital and spent an hour beside Sartre's coffin. Giscard recalls the event in a darkly humorous anecdote:

> At the hospital, the director was waiting for me. Then I turned left and saw two coffins. Nobody else showed up. Outside, there was a great commotion, everybody was talking about the funeral that was supposed to take place two days later, but there I was, alone, next to Sartre's coffin, in an anonymous hospital room. Leaving, I told myself that Sartre would probably have appreciated the starkness of my homage.

Giscard even told Sartre's friends that the French government would pay the funeral costs. They declined and 50,000 people attended Sartre's funeral in what Claude Lanzmann described as "the last of the 1968 demonstrations." Sartre's friends had refused to allow any police presence at the funeral and there were chaotic scenes, with one man falling into the hole on top of Sartre's coffin and masses of flowers passing from hand to hand to be tossed onto the coffin.

Despite the atheism which was axiomatic for his approach to philosophy and life itself, in an interview with Simone de Beauvoir from 1974, Sartre made the following curious remark:

> I do not feel that I am the product of chance, a speck of dust in the universe, but someone who was expected, pre-

pared, prefigured. In short, a being whom only a Creator could put here; and this idea of a creating hand refers to God.

Then again, as a student of mine once said to me during a class I was teaching on Hegel, people say all sorts of things when they are drunk.

## Simone de Beauvoir
### (1908–86)

Beauvoir began *Adieux—A Farewell to Sartre*, the last book she published in her lifetime, with the words:

> This is the first of my books—the only one no doubt—that you will not have read before it is printed.

Beauvoir died, like Sartre, of a pulmonary œdema and over 5,000 people followed her funeral cortège to Montparnasse Cemetery, where her ashes were placed beside those of Sartre. They share an elegantly simple grave, which bears no inscription or decoration apart from their names and dates of birth and death.

But Beauvoir's philosophical importance must not always be viewed through the lens of her lifetime companion. In her insightful, if depressing, 1970 book, *Old Age*, she brings the existential analysis begun in the groundbreaking *The Second Sex* (1949) to the topic of ageing. She writes that society sees old age as a "shameful secret that it is unseemly to mention." Beauvoir argues that we do not experience old age from within but without. Old age is not discovered, it is imposed from the outside. As Stella Sandford writes,

> It also reveals the fundamental mistake—the pathetic delusion—in the claim that "you are only as old as you feel." You are, on the contrary, as old as the others say you are.

Ageing opens up a gap between one's subjective existence and how that existence is viewed objectively. In old age, one's being is defined by the way in which one is seen by others, regardless of how one might feel subjectively. This gap between the subjective and the objective cannot be filled by cosmetic surgery. On the contrary, such surgical interventions transform that gap into the grotesque abyss of manufactured youthfulness that one sees in the bars and restaurants of Los Angeles and elsewhere. Of course, one can always lie about one's age, but isn't this truly the saddest thing in the world, as it is a denial of the fact of one's life, of one's past and memory? I think it is in the stigma attached to old age that our society stands most condemned. As Beauvoir writes,

> It is the whole system that is at issue and our claim cannot be otherwise than radical — change life itself.

## Hannah Arendt
### (1906–75)

In her unfinished final book, *The Life of the Mind*, Arendt gives an erudite and nicely sceptical account of the relation between philosophy and death. She ponders at length the classical view that to philosophize is to learn how to die and cites Zeno of Citium's words that the philosopher must "take on the colour of the dead." For Plato, but also for Montaigne, Schopenhauer, and Arendt's teacher and former lover Heidegger, death is the "inspiring genius of philosophy."

Arendt is critical of the priority of contemplation over action that defines the highest level of philosophizing in antiquity, what she calls the *vita contemplativa* (the contemplative life). The philosopher is a spectator or sightseer in the world of human affairs but not a full participant in them. In this sense, the philosopher's notorious absent-mindedness is a disappearance from what Arendt called the *vita activa*, the life of action in concert with others. The contemplative life is a kind of death within life and a living death.

Although Arendt recognizes and accepts that the activity of contemplative thinking is essential to the life of the mind, what counts for her is action in the world, and the concrete analysis of that world. This is what Arendt achieved with such intellectual power in the books that precede *The Life of the Mind*, from *The Origins of Totalitarianism* (1951), through *Eichmann in Jerusalem* (1963), to *On Violence* (1970). She recounts the story with which this book began, where the Thracian peasant girl bursts out laughing when she sees Thales, the professional thinker, fall into a well because he was watching the stars.

This is clearly an autobiographical parable on Arendt's part: she is the Thracian girl, Heidegger the professional thinker. The moral of the tale is that if one views political life from a contemplative philosophical distance, one inevitably sees the people as a rabble to be controlled by one form or other of authoritarianism, rather than a human plurality to be participated in and celebrated. In other words, the philosopher might be an expert in thinking, but not in judging, especially political judgement.

Although she had problems with angina from 1971, and suffered a near-fatal heart attack in the year before her death, Arendt declared to Mary McCarthy, "I am certainly not going to live for my health." She continued to be a committed smoker and took on far too many speaking engagements.

The day after Thanksgiving in 1975, as she was returning to her apartment in Manhattan, Arendt tripped over a pothole as she stepped out of a taxi. She was in a little pain and made an appointment for the doctor, but cancelled it because of the foul New York weather. Her friends Salo and Jeanette Baron came round to dinner a couple of days later. As she was serving after-dinner coffee, Arendt had a brief coughing fit and lost consciousness. She had died from a heart attack.

After her death, a sheet of paper was found in her typewriter. It was bare except for a single word, "Judging," which was going to be the topic of the third and final part of *The Life of the Mind*. She finished the second part on "Willing" on the

Saturday prior to her death. It is extremely poignant that the last two paragraphs that Arendt wrote were a paean to Augustine, the subject of her PhD dissertation in 1929. She wrily notes that Augustine was "the only philosopher the Romans ever had."

This leads her into a discussion of *natality*, which is a vital theme in her work. She writes, "The purpose of the creation of man was to make possible a beginning." Arendt was suspicious—and perhaps rightly so—of the constant emphasis on mortality that one finds in ancient and modern philosophy. Philosophical meditations on death are all very well, but what justice do they bring to the phenomenon of life if they leave no room for the question of birth, the power of beginning? Perhaps this might inspire someone to write a counterpart to this book on the births of philosophers.

## Maurice Merleau-Ponty
### (1908–61)

There is a story of the last meeting between Lacan and Merleau-Ponty, who were close friends. They met at Lacan's country house outside Paris two days before Merleau-Ponty's untimely death aged fifty-three. The two of them had been picking lilies of the valley for May Day. Of course, lilies are the traditional death flower and their presence at funerals is meant to symbolize the restored innocence of the departed. Madelaine Chapsal said of Merleau-Ponty,

> In the last image I have of him he's standing on the open platform at the back of a no. 63 bus. In his buttonhole he was wearing a sprig of lily-of-the-valley that Lacan had given him, and he was waving me goodbye.

Merleau-Ponty died suddenly of a coronary thrombosis two days later. Paul Ricoeur described his death "as the most improbable of all, which *avait coupé la parole* [it cut off his speech]." It left us with the bare trunk of a manuscript called

*The Visible and the Invisible*, which promised to be his most original and challenging work.

In Merleau-Ponty's view, true philosophy consists in relearning to see the world. What this might mean is indicated in a wonderful essay on Cézanne that appeared in the year of his death. Merleau-Ponty shows that the paintings of Cezanne—think of his repeated renderings of Mont Ste.-Victoire in Provence—do not lead us to some transcendent realm beyond appearance or behind the scenes. On the contrary, Cezanne's art returns us to the world in which we live, but momentarily freed from the weight of habit and the blindness of everyday routine. Philosophy must attempt to do something similar, to return us to what Merleau-Ponty called "the perceptual faith" of our openness to the world.

It is said that Merleau-Ponty was found dead in his study with his face in a book by Descartes. To go back to Ricoeur's word, this is also slightly improbable. Merleau-Ponty's philosophical taste was much closer to Montaigne than Descartes. In a paper on Montaigne that was also published in the year before Merleau-Ponty's death, he writes that the purpose of a meditation on death is not moroseness. On the contrary, "To know death in all its nakedness, life is laid wholly bare." Paradoxically, intimations of mortality allow us to seize hold of that accidental but precious portion of existence that is our life. The remedy for death is not to turn away in fright, but to move through it and back to our elemental vitality.

## Willard van Orman Quine
### (1908–2000)

Quine was a philosopher of enormous professional influence and considerable linguistic wit (see his amusing *Quiddities* from 1987). Philosophically Quine was a naturalist, which means he believed that it is the role of science to explain what exists and how it exists. As such, he rejected any idea of metaphysics or the attempt to ground scientific activity on something other than itself. On this view, the scope of philosophy is dramatically reduced: philosophy, done well, is simply science.

Perhaps wisely, Quine seems to have offered no opinion about death, although he did have the question mark character removed from his typewriter and replaced with a mathematical symbol.

He died after a brief illness on Christmas Day 2000. During a memorial talk given at Harvard in 2001 his daughter, Norma, cites the following jotting by her father, "Famous last words: To be continued."

## Simone Weil
### (1909–43)

For Schopenhauer, the only permissible form of suicide is the self-starvation of the ascetic. He writes,

> The highest degree of asceticism, the total denial of the temporal consciousness, is the *voluntary death through starvation*.

To achieve such a death—which is truly the death of a saint—two conditions have to be met. First, there has to be a complete renunciation of the will. If suicide is an act of the will, then it remains imprisoned within the illusions of wilful life in the world of representation, according to Schopenhauer's metaphysics. Second, the starving ascetic has to have attained the highest degree of philosophical wisdom before he or she can die. The saint must also be a philosopher. Without doubt, Simone Weil more than meets both these conditions.

After teaching philosophy in a girls' school, working in a car factory, serving in an anarchist unit in the Spanish Civil War, and working as a farm servant after fleeing Paris in 1940, Weil left Marseille for New York in 1942 on one of the last convoys to leave France. After studying intensively at the New York Public Library, she yearned to go to London and work for the Resistance. When in London, Weil refused to

eat more than the official ration in occupied France. Due to
malnutrition and overwork, she suffered a physical collapse.
While she was in hospital in Middlesex, north London, it
was discovered that Weil had tuberculosis. She died some
months later at a sanatorium in Ashford in Kent.

Weil maintained voluminous notebooks that show the
extraordinary range and eclecticism of her reading and the
development of a unique theological position: a heterodox
and gnostic Christianity where we are asked to await a nearly
absent God.

Considering her self-starvation, it is poignant that the last
notebook entry she wrote was about the spiritual dimension
of food, mentioning such delights as Christmas pudding and
Easter eggs. In what is quite possibly her last written
sentence, Weil writes, "The joy and spiritual signification of
the feast lies in the delicacy [*la friandise*] that is particular to
the feast."

Rowan Williams, Archbishop of Canterbury, writes in
"Simone Weil at Ashford:"

> . . . *and if I cannot walk like god,*
> *at least I can be light and hungry, hollowing my guts*
> *till I'm a bone the sentenced god can whistle through.*

## Alfred Jules Ayer
### (1910–89)

It might be argued that I am
doing a disservice to analytic
philosophy in this book, the style
of philosophy that dominates
the universities of the English-
speaking world. It is true that,
particularly in the latter stages of
this book, it is Continental thinkers who preponderate.

While, to some extent, this is due to my own intellectual·
fancies that I could adorn with the gown of an academic spe-

cialism, it also has a more interesting cause. When one considers influential analytic philosophers like Quine, Donald Davidson or John Rawls, it is clear that they led wonderfully successful and influential professional lives and died in an undramatic manner which has no absolutely bearing on their philosophical views.

By contrast, if one considers Continental philosophers like Arendt, Foucault or Derrida, it is not so much the case that they led more complex and interesting lives and had more dramatic deaths, but rather that the line between philosophy and life is much harder to draw. These are thinkers for whom philosophy had a transformative effect in their lives, an effect that survives in the lives of their readers. Furthermore, people are—perhaps for less than virtuous reasons—simply intrigued by the life and death of a Sartre or an Althusser.

The idea that philosophy is something transformative or disruptive of a self is, as we saw above, a commonplace in and after antiquity. To this extent, sentences of death, exile or punishment imposed on philosophers seem to respond to a deep need that philosophy and life should fit together, but that its transformative power can come at the cost of one's life. To this extent, Alasdair MacIntyre is surely justified when he writes,

> Imprisoning philosophy within the professionalizations and specializations of an institutionalized curriculum, after the manner of our contemporary European and North American culture, is arguably a good deal more effective in neutralizing its effects than either religious censorship or political terror.

The effect of the professionalization of philosophy is the sense that it does not and should not matter to the conduct of one's life. Philosophy should aspire to the impersonality of natural science. Nothing more. Philosophy is a technically complex academic discipline with its own internal criteria of excellence and it should be kept away from other humanistic disciplines and from the unseemly disorder of private and

public life. Needless to say, this is a view that I have sought
to challenge in this book.

In addition to Wittgenstein and Russell, the glorious
exception to what I have just said about the lives of analytical
philosophers is A. J. Ayer, "Freddie" to his friends. This is
paradoxical, for Ayer, more than anyone else, sought to separate philosophy from life. Ben Rogers tells the story of Ayer
walking with Isaiah Berlin in Oxford in the 1930s. They were
discussing the nature and scope of philosophy. Ayer said,

> There is philosophy, which is about conceptual analysis —
> about the meaning of what we say — and there is all of *this*
> [with an excited sweep of the hands], all of life.

Stories about Ayer are legion. Many people know the incident when Ayer confronted Mike Tyson, at the time heavyweight boxing champion of the world. It took place in
Manhattan at the party of Fernando Sanchez, a fashionable
underwear designer (not many philosophers get invited
to underwear designer parties). Ayer was talking to a group of
models when a woman rushed in saying that a friend was being
assaulted in the next room. Ayer went to the rescue and discovered Mike Tyson trying to force himself on a young British
model called Naomi Campbell. Ayer warned Tyson to takes
his hands off her, to which Tyson replied, "Do you know who
the fuck I am? I'm the heavyweight champion of the world."
Ayer replied, without missing a beat, "And I am the former
Wykeham Professor of Logic. We are both eminent in our
field; I suggest that we talk about this like rational men." By
which time, Naomi Campbell had escaped Tyson's clutches.

Fewer people know about Freddie Ayer's near-death
experience. It is difficult to think of a more resolutely atheistic
philosopher, or a more candid one. (When asked by Brian
Magee in the mid-1970s what he thought was the chief
defect of his hugely successful and widely read 1936 book,
*Language, Truth and Logic*, he calmly replied, "Well, I suppose
the most important defect was that nearly all of it was false.")

The year before he died, after recovering from pneumonia in University College Hospital in London, Ayer choked on a piece of salmon, lost consciousness and technically died. His heart stopped for four minutes until he was revived. A day later, he had recovered and was talking happily about what had taken place during his death. He saw a bright red light which was apparently in charge of the government of the universe. He met ministers who were in charge of space, but they had not done their job properly with the result that space, like time in *Hamlet*, "was slightly out of joint." The ministers for space were oddly absent, but Ayer could see the ministers in charge of time in the distance. Ayer then reports that he suddenly recalled Einstein's view that space and time were one and the same and tried to attract the attention of the ministers of time by walking up and down and waving his watch and chain. To no avail, however, and Ayer grew more and more desperate and then regained consciousness. Ayer was shaken by the experience and in an article for the *Sunday Telegraph* he suggested that it did provide "rather strong evidence that death does not put an end to consciousness."

It appears that Ayer experienced a period of resurrection after his death and was much more pleasant company than he had been previously. His wife, Dee, said to Jonathan Miller, "Freddie has got so much nicer since he died." He died a philosopher's death the following year, apparently as calm and cheerful as Hume until the end.

## Albert Camus
(1913–60)

He famously writes at the beginning of *The Myth of Sisyphus* that "there is but one truly serious philosophical problem and that is suicide." Camus appears to answer the question some fifty pages later by asserting, "But the point is to live."

Sadly, Camus was killed in a pointless car accident in 1960, three years after receiving the Nobel Prize for Literature at the age of forty-four. He once said that he couldn't imagine a death more meaningless than dying in a car accident. Such is perhaps the random force of the absurdity that Camus so eloquently describes.

## Paul Ricoeur
### (1913–2005)

The great and gentle hermeneutician died peacefully and without incident in his sleep at the age of ninety-two.

## Roland Barthes
### (1915–80)

The author of the famous essay "The Death of the Author" died like Camus, following a road accident. Barthes stepped off the pavement and was hit by a dry-cleaning van on a street outside the Collège de France in Paris, where he taught. He had just finished lunch with Jack Lang, the future minister for culture.

There is a troubling aspect to Barthes's death. In the last months prior to the accident, he was fond of citing the lines of Michelet, *"La vieillesse, ce lent suicide"* ("Ageing, this slow suicide"). Barthes had become increasingly morbid and depressed since the death of his mother in the summer prior to his accident. Throughout his life, Barthes was excessively closely attached to his mother and apparently the name "Roland" was constantly on her lips. Although Roland had to conceal his homosexuality from her, it seems that when she died something died in him and he had no desire to continue living. After the accident, he practically stopped communicating and, according to Hervé Algalarrondo, he simply let himself die.

## Donald Davidson
### (1917–2003)

A question that we have seen emerging in this book is whether the ineluctable rise of the scientific conception of the world leaves open a space for human freedom. Can we reconcile the idea of nature as governed by deterministic physical laws with the experience of human autonomy? Are our actions simply the effects of physical causes? We saw above that Kant sought to preserve the authority of science while insisting on the primacy of human autonomy.

Davidson gives a powerful and updated defence of Kant's position with the idea of what he calls "anomalous monism." This view argues for a thoroughgoing materialistic conception of that which is, where events are nothing more than Hobbes's "matter and motion" governed by physical laws. However, this does not explain away what Davidson calls "the anomalism of the mental," what Kant more elegantly called "the thought of freedom." Davidson writes,

> Even if someone knew the entire physical history of the world, and every mental event were identical with a physical one, it would not follow that he could predict or explain a single mental event.

Mental events cannot be explained away by physical science in the manner of a reductive materialism. On the contrary, human freedom is anomalous with respect to matter and motion. This means that freedom and determinism are not pulling in opposite directions but are, in Kant's words, "necessarily united in the same subject." It follows from this view that although death is an event with an undeniable physical cause, our attitude towards it is not reducible to that cause or explained away by it. It is evidence of the anomalism of the mental that we can both know that death has a physical cause and that its meaning depends upon our freely chosen attitude towards it.

Davidson died from heart failure following knee surgery at the age of eighty-six. He led an active—indeed vital—life. He risked his life as a young man when he served in the U.S. navy for three and a half years as an expert teacher of gunners and pilots, helping them to identify enemy planes. He also participated in the invasions of Sicily, Salerno and Anzio.

When asked by Ernie Lepore for his impressions of the fog of war, he said,

> I didn't like risking my life and what I was doing was very dangerous. More than half the ships in the flotilla were sunk with everyone aboard. I was lucky. I hated the idea of being killed. I wasn't fighting so much; I so much disliked the concept. On these ships, almost everyone was confused and everything confusing.

Lepore also relates that the first time he met Davidson in the mid-seventies, he was asked to accompany him to give a paper on a branch campus of the University of Minnesota. Once airborne Davidson asked if he could take over the controls of the small passenger plane. He flew there and back.

## Louis Althusser
(1918–90)

From 1938 onwards, Althusser suffered from severe attacks of melancholy that apparently recurred every February. He was hospitalized during his four years in a prisoner-of-war camp during the Second World War. Althusser's life was a long struggle with mental illness that ended not in the suicide he sometimes threatened, but with lamentation for the murder of his wife, Hélène Rytman, a Jew who had been active in the French Resistance.

In his autobiography, *The Future Lasts Forever. The Facts*, he gives a quite chilling recollection of the murder. On a grey November morning in 1980, Althusser and his wife were sleeping in their apartment at the École Normale Supérieure in Paris. Althusser awoke and recalls kneeling beside his wife and massaging her neck in silence. Apparently, he would often massage his wife's body, using a technique that he had learnt in captivity from someone called Clerc, a professional footballer. Althusser recalls,

I placed my two thumbs in the hollow of her neck . . . a thumb to the left, a thumb to the right . . . I massaged in a V shape. I felt a great muscular fatigue in my forearms. Giving a massage always causes me pain in my forearms. Hélène's face was immobile and serene, her open eyes staring at the ceiling. Suddenly, I was struck with terror. Her eyes were staring interminably and I noticed that the end of her tongue was sticking out between her teeth and lips, in an unusual and yet peaceful way. I have seen corpses, but never the face of someone who has been strangled. And yet I knew that this was someone who had been strangled. But how? I straightened up and screamed, "I've strangled Hélène!"

But how, indeed. Should we believe Althusser's testimony? It was clear that he and Hélène were living in what Althusser describes as "our hell," no longer answering the door or telephone and living on a diet of anti-depressants. A French medical journal describes the murder of Hélène as a case of "altruistic homicide." This seems more than a little generous. However, Althusser was judged incapable of standing trial and was committed to Ste.-Anne psychiatric hospital.

After his release in 1983, Althusser ceased writing apart from his autobiography. He died of heart failure seven years later.

## John Rawls
(1921–2002)

For some, Rawls is the most important political philosopher of the twentieth century. He slipped behind the veil of ignorance after heart failure, but had been unwell since a stroke in 1995.

The experience of war had a profound, transformative effect on many of the philosophers we have discussed. In his almost painfully understated manner, this is also true of Rawls. In 1990, he was asked by the photographer Stephen Pyke to summarize in fifty words his idea of what philosophy means. Rawls wrote,

From the beginning of my study in philosophy in my late teens I have been concerned with moral questions and the religious and philosophical basis on which they might be answered. Three years spent in the U.S. army in World War Two led me to be also concerned with political questions. Around 1950 I started to write a book on justice, which I eventually completed.

This is a fulsome sixty-five words. Rawls witnessed the bloody conflict between the United States and Japan in the South Pacific and the aftermath of the atomic bombing of Hiroshima, an event that he considered immoral. Of course, the book to which Rawls so modestly alludes is *The Theory of Justice*, from 1971. Rawls's conception of justice as fairness, and his vision of a legitimate society as an overlapping consensus of peoples with different conceptions of the good within a framework of basic rights and liberties, exerted a powerful effect on liberal and social democratic politicians in the 1980s and 1990s. This culminated in Rawls being awarded the Medal of Freedom by President Bill Clinton in 1999. It is somewhat unlikely that Rawls was bedtime reading for Clinton's successor.

## Jean-François Lyotard
### (1924–98)

In the *Confessions*, St. Augustine writes,

> But do you, O Lord my God, graciously hear me, and turn your gaze upon me, and see me, and have mercy upon me, and heal me. For in your sight I have become a question to myself and that is my languor.

Augustine's words are cited in Lyotard's final, unfinished and remarkable text, the posthumously published *The Confession of Augustine*, an extremely Christian text for such an avowed pagan. For Augustine, my languor is the question that I have become for myself in relation to the God who watches me, who may heal and have mercy upon me, but whom I cannot know and whose grace cannot be guaranteed. The questions I pose to God make me a question to myself. Lyotard adds, gnomically,

> *Lagaros*, languid, bespeaks in Greek a humour of limpness, a disposition to: what's the point? Gesture relaxes therein. My life, this is it: *distentio*, letting go, stretching out. Duration turns limp, it is its nature.

The experience of languor, for Lyotard, is both the body's limpness, its languid quality as it passes out of being, and time as distension, as stretching out, procrastination. In languor, I suffer from a delay with respect to myself, my suffering is experienced as what Lyotard calls "awaiting": "The *Confessions* are written under the temporal sign of waiting." The weight of the past makes me wait, and awaiting, I languish. I grow old; I shall wear the bottoms of my trousers rolled. I am filled with longing.

Lyotard, close to dying of leukaemia as he is writing, quotes the above passage from Augustine for a second time, and adds:

> . . . *ipse est languor meus*, that is my languor. Here lies the whole advantage of faith: to become an enigma to oneself, to grow old, hoping for the solution, the resolution from the Other. Have mercy upon me, Yahweh, for I am languishing. Heal me, for my bones are worn.

## Frantz Fanon
### (1925–61)

On 7 December 1961, the *New York Times* ran a very short eighty-word obituary for Fanon which begins,

> United Nations, N. Y. Dec. 6 — Dr. Frantz Omar Fanon, a leader of the Algerian National Front, died today of

leukemia at the National Institutes of Health in Bethesda, Maryland, it was learned here. He was 37 years old.

As well as revealing how little the *New York Times* knew about Fanon, this obituary does raise the obvious question: what on earth was Fanon—the hero of anti-colonial liberation struggles and severe critic of all forms of racism and imperialism—doing dying in a hospital just outside Washington DC?

Fanon had been diagnosed with leukaemia in Tunis at the end of 1960. Unable to find adequate medical treatment in North Africa, Fanon initially refused to travel to the United States, which he viewed as the land of lynch mobs and racism, preferring to travel to Moscow. When he was back in Tunis, he began to dictate his second major book, *The Wretched of the Earth*, to his wife, Josie. Although written in what Fanon described as "pitiful haste" by a dying man, this extraordinarily impassioned book became the so-called "Bible of Third Worldism."

Fanon suffered a severe relapse in October 1961. Exhausted, emaciated and speechless, Fanon initially went to Rome, where Sartre met him for the last time. Sartre wrote a controversial preface to *The Wretched of the Earth* that Fanon's wife successfully removed from some subsequent editions of the book.

With the help of one Ollie Iselin, a CIA agent in North Africa, Fanon was flown to the United States on 3 October 1961. Despite the efforts of his American doctors, Fanon's condition worsened. He received the first, favourable reviews of *The Wretched of the Earth*, commenting that "that won't give me my bone marrow back." There are some who insist that Fanon was executed by the CIA. Although there is little evidence to support this view, such details never seem to stand in the way of a good conspiracy theory.

Fanon's body was flown back to Tunis on a Lockheed Electra II. His last wish was to be buried on Algerian soil, in the country he had moved to in 1953 and whose struggle for liberation from France consumed the final years of his life. On 12 December a small column of comrades from the FLN (*Front de Libération Nationale*) bore his body across the Tunisian border into Algeria where he was buried with full honours a mere 600 metres inside Algerian territory.

On the day that news of Fanon's death reached Paris, all copies of *The Wretched of the Earth* were seized by the police because it was believed that the book was a threat to national security.

## Gilles Deleuze
(1925–95)

At the centre of Deleuze's work is a concept of life that is not simply organic. He writes that "It is organisms that die, not life." Deleuze is a vitalist thinker in the tradition of Bergson and Nietzsche, a tradition that, in Spinoza's words (Deleuze calls Spinoza "The Christ of Philosophers"), "thinks of nothing less than death." This life is felt affectively through the experience of affirmative creation, an intensity that produces the feeling of joy.

How, then, to understand Deleuze's death by defenestration from his Paris apartment? Apparently, defenestration is not uncommon in patients suffering from emphysema, as Deleuze was. They are smothering, drowning really, and become desperate for air. On a sudden impulse, a high-speed fall appears one way of forcing air into one's lungs, desperately gulping for a lungful of life. (Apparently, this is the reason why the respiratory wings in hospitals are typically located on the first floor or have bars at the windows.)

Deleuze accorded no privileged importance to his own autobiography and claimed, rightly, that the lives of academics were seldom interesting. His long-time colleague in Paris, Lyotard, struck exactly the right tone after his defenestration in a fax sent to *Le Monde*:

He was too tough to experience disappointments and resentments—negative affections. In this nihilist *fin-de-siècle*, he was affirmation. Right through to illness and death. Why did I speak of him in the past? He laughed. He is laughing. He is here. It's your sadness, idiot, he'd say.

## Michel Foucault
(1926–84)

Foucault predicted that "perhaps one day this century will be known as Deleuzian." Deleuze repaid the compliment by publishing a book about Foucault two years after the latter's death. Foucault was fond of the French poet René Char's remark "Develop your legitimate strangeness" and he was able to put this into effect theoretically and practically in a series of visits to the University of California in Berkeley in the late 1970s and early 1980s. Foucault delighted in the openness of gay culture in San Francisco. In an interview with a gay newspaper in Los Angeles, *The Advocate*, Foucault said,

> Sexuality is part of our behaviour. It's part of our world freedom. Sexuality is something that we ourselves create. It is our own creation, and much more than the discovery of a secret side of our desire. We have to understand that with our desires go new forms of relationships, new forms of love, new forms of creation. Sex is not a fatality; it's a possibility for creative life. It's not enough to affirm that we are gay but we must also create a gay life.

At the same time, Foucault was developing the ideas about the formation of the self and the uses of pleasure that found expression in the second and third volumes of *The History of Sexuality*. In particular, Foucault was greatly preoccupied by the Hellenistic and Roman idea of care of the self and the techniques of self-government that were found in the pagan world prior to the emergence of Christianity. Foucault carefully documented the dietary, economic, philosophical and sexual practices in relation to which selves were formed and their pleasures were used.

Arguably, the central concept in Foucault's work is freedom, but this is not some piece of philosophical abstraction or political rhetoric. What interested Foucault

was the care of the self as a
practice of freedom, as something formed and developed:
a legitimate strangeness.

It might be asked: what's the
difference between paganism
and Christianity? Foucault
makes a distinction between
what he calls the Christian
"hermeneutics of desire" and
the pagan "aesthetics of existence." In a seminar at New
York University in 1980, Foucault is reported to have said
that the difference between late antiquity and early Christianity might be reduced to the following questions: the
patrician pagan asks, "Given that I am who I am, whom can
I fuck?" That is, given my status in society, who would it be
appropriate for me to take as my lover, which girl or boy,
woman or man? By contrast, the Christian asks, "Given that
I can fuck no one, who am I?" That is, the question of what it
means to be human first arises for Christians in the sight of
God. For thinkers like Paul and Augustine, it is in relation to
God's perfection that I become aware of myself as imperfect
and sinful and begin to develop the acute self-consciousness
of bad conscience.

Foucault was first hospitalized in June 1984 with the
symptoms of a nasty and persistent flu, fatigue, terrible
coughing and migraine. "It's like being in a fog," he said. But
Foucault didn't let up his relentless pace of research and carried on working until the end on the second and third volumes of *The History of Sexuality*, which appeared shortly
before his death. Although he was a very early victim of the
virus, it seems that Foucault knew that he had AIDS. His
friend, the classical historian Paul Veyne, said,

> Foucault was unafraid of death, as he sometimes told his
> friends, when conversation turned to suicide, and events
> have proved, albeit in a different manner, that he was not

bragging. In yet another way, ancient wisdom became a personal matter for him. Throughout the last eight months of his life, writing his two books played the same part for him that philosophical writing and personal journals played in ancient philosophy—that of work performed by the self on the self, of self-stylization.

Foucault was fond of reading Seneca towards the end and died on 25 June like a classical philosopher. It is the ambition of Foucault's study of late pre-Christian antiquity to show how a life could become a work of art. It has been an ambition of this book to show that often the philosopher's greatest work of art is the manner of their death.

## Jean Baudrillard
(1929–2007)

With a nod towards his professional deformation as a professor of sociology and one of its founders, Emile Durkheim, Baudrillard writes, "Philosophy leads to death, sociology leads to suicide."

In his final book, *Cool Memories V*, written when diagnosed with the cancer that eventually killed him, Baudrillard claims that he has never had any imagining of death. For him, this is the best attitude as it means that death remains a surprise, something other and magical, a strange rival in a duel with life. He writes pithily,

Death orders matters well, since the very fact of your absence makes the world distinctly less worthy of being lived in.

## Jacques Derrida
(1930–2004)

In a long, fascinating and now rather saddening interview with *Le Monde* from 19 August 2004, republished after his death, Derrida describes his work in terms of an "ethos of

writing." For me, Derrida was the supreme reader of philosophical texts and his example consists in the lesson of
reading: patient, meticulous, open, questioning and endlessly
inventive. At its best, Derrida's writing is able to unsettle its
reader's expectations and completely transform his or her
understanding of the philosopher and philosophy under
examination. What confusedly got named "deconstruction," a
term that Derrida always viewed with suspicion, is better
viewed as an ethos of reading and writing. Derrida's work
exemplifies an uncompromising philosophical vigilance that
is constantly at war with the governing intellectual orthodoxy,
what he liked to call—in a Socratic spirit, I think—the *doxa*,
opinion or narcissistic self-image of the age.

Derrida's work is possessed of a curious restlessness, one
might even say an anxiety. A very famous American philosopher, sympathetic to Derrida, once said to me, "He never
knows when to stop or how to come to an end." In the interview with *Le Monde*, he describes himself as being at war with
himself. He was always on the move intellectually, always
hungry for new objects of analysis, accepting new invitations, confronting new contexts, addressing new audiences,
writing new books. His ability in discussion simply to listen
and produce long, detailed and fascinating analyses in
response was breathtaking. Like many others, I saw him do it
on many occasions and always with patience, politeness,
modesty and civility. The whole ethos of his work was the
very opposite of the stale professional complacency that
defines so much philosophy and so many philosophers.

Derrida found the Ciceronian wisdom that to philosophize
is to learn how to die quite repellent for its narcissism. He
insisted, "I remain uneducatable [*inéducable*] with respect to
the wisdom of learning to die." To philosophize, on the contrary, is to learn how to live. In the words that begin *Specters of
Marx* from 1993, Derrida ventriloquizes, as so often in his
work, in another voice, "I have finally learnt how to live."

However, learning how to live did not eradicate the terror
of death. In 2002, shortly after the release of a documentary
about him and his work, Derrida gave an interview to the *Los*

*Angeles Weekly* and had to face a particularly silly series of questions. The interviewer asked him, "Should a philosopher have a biography?" To which Derrida replied, "How could a philosopher not have a biography?" In response to the question, "What's important to you today?" Derrida replied in good faith and with extraordinary candour,

> A constant awareness that I'm aging, I'm going to die and life is short. I'm constantly attentive to the time left to me, and although I've been inclined this way since I was young, it becomes more serious when you reach 72. So far I haven't made my peace with the inevitability of death, and I doubt I ever will, and this awareness permeates everything I think. It's terrible what's going on in the world, and all these things are on my mind, but they exist alongside this terror of my own death.

Perhaps it was in order to assuage this terror that Derrida wrote repeatedly about the deaths of friends and philosophers with whom he was sometimes close (Maurice Blanchot, Levinas), sometimes not (Foucault, Deleuze), but with whom he felt an elective affinity.

The theme of mourning became a major theme of his work after the death of Barthes in 1980 and even more so with the unexpected death, in December 1983, of his friend and colleague Paul de Man. In *Mémoires for Paul de Man*, Derrida writes with great passion and incisiveness about the experience of bereaved memory. For Derrida, to be bereft of a friend is to bear their memory trace within one in a way that cannot simply be internalized. It is as if the dead friend continues to live on in a way that haunts the self like a spectre. The self is not healed or made good after the other's death, but wounded and divided against itself. This defies what Freud calls "normal mourning," where the ego is meant to recover its integrity and unity after it has "got over" the death of the beloved. By contrast, Derrida argues for what he calls "impossible mourning," where we precisely do not get over the other's death, but where they live on in our bereaved memory. To be clear, Derrida insists that impossible mourning is neither the resurrection of the other, nor their narcissistic possession by the self. Rather, the friend or beloved lives on within me like a ghost that troubles the line that divides the living from the dead. Particularly in the writing of his last decade, Derrida was much preoccupied with ghosts, spectres and revenants.

Although Derrida refuses the classical view that to philosophize is to learn how to die, Cicero makes an appearance in the epigraph to the important 1994 book *Politics of Friendship*. Derrida cites the words ". . . *et quod difficilius dictu est, mortui vivunt*" (". . . and what is more difficult to say, the dead live"). That is, the dead live on, they live on within us in a way that disturbs any self-satisfaction, but which troubles us and invites us to reflect on them further. We might say that wherever a philosopher is read, he or she is not dead. If you want to communicate with the dead, then read a book.

## Guy Debord
### (1931–94)

The author of *The Society of the Spectacle* and prime mover in the Situationist International shot himself in the heart in his remote country cottage in France. Although some have claimed that his death was the final Situationist statement, where Debord's death becomes a commodity in a world of capitalist exchange to be used to sell his books, it seems that he killed himself in order to end the suffering brought about by a form of polyneuritis caused by excessive drinking. In his autobiography, *Panegyric* (1989), Debord writes,

> Among the small number of things that I have liked and known how to do, what I have assuredly known how to do best is drink. Even though I have read a lot, I have drunk even more. I have written much less than most people who write; but I have drunk much more than most people who drink.

# Dominique Janicaud
(1937–2002)

On the morning of 18 August 2002 at Èze on the Côte d'Azur in France, Janicaud died from a cardiac arrest after a swim. He was close to the foot of what is now called *le chemin Nietzsche*, the rough path, ascending some 1000 metres from the Mediterranean to the old castle and village, where Nietzsche used to walk during his seven winters in Nice in the 1880s and where he composed passages of *Thus Spoke Zarathustra*. I was a student of Janicaud's and made this ascent with him on a couple of memorable occasions.

Èze is just along the coast from his beloved Nice, where Dominique had been teaching philosophy since 1966, refusing many invitations to leave for Paris and elsewhere. He lived and worked in a wonderful house high on the slopes of the *arrière-pays*, close to the valley of the Var. On the day before his death, he had finished the first draft of an introduction to philosophy written for his daughter, Claire, who was planning to begin studying philosophy in secondary school. Dominique was so dissatisfied with the academic abstruseness of the various introductions to philosophy that he decided to write his own.

For Janicaud, the basic question of philosophy is Hamlet's "To be or not to be?" That is to say, the many seemingly abstract questions of philosophy circle back and have their roots in the existential question of who we are and what there is. The experience of such questioning can provoke, in Janicaud's words,

Wonder in the face of being, in the face of the very fact that there is being, this astonishment could be hailed and held precious, since it may be the most philosophical act of all.

What is crucial here is that this wonder should be experienced in the face of the *questionability* of things. We do not know for certain who we are and what there is: these are questions for us. Of course, this is where we began this book, some 190 deaths and a few millennia ago. Philosophy is a constant return to beginnings. This is why the history of philosophy and philosophers is not a redundant record of past mistakes, but a series of irresistible intellectual temptations from which we might finally learn how to live.

### Simon Critchley
(1960–?)

Exit, pursued by a bear.

# LAST WORDS

## Creatureliness

Death is the last great taboo. We cannot look it in the face for fear of seeing the skull beneath the skin. Various surveys show that when it comes to attitudes towards death what most people want is to die quickly, painlessly and, as the saying goes, "without being a burden to anyone." What this last platitude conceals, I think, is the fact that people don't want to be a burden because they ultimately don't trust their children or their loved ones to care for them. Fear of death is a fear of feebleness in an infirm state, stuck in a degrading nursing home, ignored by embarrassed friends and busy, distant family members.

The fact of finitude unpicks many of the truisms by which we live. A detailed national survey by the "Opinion Dynamics Corporation" from 2003 claimed that fully 92 percent of Americans believe in God, 85 percent believe in heaven and 82 percent believe in miracles. But the deeper truth is that such religious belief, complete with a heavenly afterlife, brings believers little solace in relation to death. The only priesthood in which people *really* believe is the medical profession and the purpose of their sacramental drugs and technology is to support longevity, the sole unquestioned good of contemporary Western life.

If proof were needed that many religious believers actually do not practise what they preach, then it can be found in the ignorance of religious teachings on death, particularly Christian teaching, which is why I have emphasized this in some of the entries in this book.

Christianity is about nothing other than getting ready to die. It is a rigorous training for death, a kind of death in life that places little value on longevity. Christianity, in the hands of a Paul, an Augustine or a Luther, is a way of becoming reconciled to the brevity of human life and giving up the desire for wealth, worldly goods and temporal power. Nothing is more inimical to most people who call themselves Christians than true Christianity. This is because they are actually leading quietly desperate atheist lives bounded by a desire for longevity and a terror of annihilation.

This is where the ideal of the philosophical death has such persuasive power in undermining the death-denying shibboleths of our age. Mortality is that in relation to which we can be said to shape our selfhood. It is in relation to the reality of death, both my death and the deaths of others, that the self becomes most truly itself. It is only in relation to the acceptance of self-loss that there might be a self to gain. That is to say, and of course this is stupidly obvious, death is the limit in relation to which life is lived. Accepting one's mortality, then, means accepting one's limitation.

This is crucial in my view, for it also means accepting what we might call our *creatureliness*. To be a creature, in traditional theology, is to be in a position of dependence with respect to God. I want to propose a less theistic variant of this thought. Namely, that human existence is limited. It is shaped by evolutionary forces beyond our control and by the movement of a desire that threatens to suffocate us in the clutches of its family romance.

We cannot return the unasked-for gifts of nature and culture. Nor can we jump over the shadow of our mortality. But we can transform the manner in which we accept those gifts and we can stand more fully in the light that casts that shadow. It is my wager that if we can begin to accept our limitedness, then we might be able to give up certain of the fantasies of infantile omnipotence, worldly wealth and puffed-up power that culminate in both aggressive personal conflicts and bloody wars between opposed and exclusive gods. To be a creature is to accept our dependence and limitedness in a way that does not result in disaffection and despair. It is rather the condition for courage and endurance.

Returning to the quote from Montaigne with which I began my introduction, to philosophize is to learn the habit of having death continually present in one's mouth. In this way, we can begin to confront the terror of annihilation that enslaves us and leads us into either escape or evasion. In speaking of death and even laughing at our frailty and mortality, one accepts the creaturely limitation that is the very condition for human freedom. Such freedom is not a passive state of being or the simple absence of necessity or constraint. On the contrary, it is an ongoing activity that requires the acceptance of necessity and the affirmation of the moving constraint of our mortality. This is not easy, I know. To philosophize is to learn to love that difficulty.

# GEOGRAPHICAL DETAILS
# AND THANKS

*The Book of Dead Philosophers* was entirely conceived and written in its first draft between an apartment on West Sunset Boulevard and the Getty Research Institute in Los Angeles between November 2006 and June 2007. To my eyes, the writing is marked by the strange mood of that city and its inescapable clichés: the melancholic Santa Ana winds, broad deserted night-time streets flanked by high palm trees, and sunlight so bright that it becomes indistinguishable from darkness. For me, Los Angeles is the city of film noir, in particular Billy Wilder's *Sunset Boulevard* (1950). Death, darkness and desperation lurk behind the various screens that human beings use to block access to the outside world: vast wrap-around sunglasses, Venetian blinds at every window and tinted glass in the black, usually German, SUVs.

Just off the Santa Monica Boulevard, in the shadow of Paramount Studios, tourists are invited to visit "Hollywood Forever Cemetery." It advertises itself as the "Resting Place of Hollywood's Immortals," such as Rudolph Valentino, Douglas Fairbanks, Jayne Mansfield and Cecil B. De Mille, who makes a final cameo appearance in *Sunset Boulevard*. The cemetery prides itself on the latest technological innovations, such as worldwide webcasts of funeral services. Those who are curious to follow the weekly cemetery tour are asked to contact someone called Karie Bible on 323-769-0195. In its peculiar terror of annihilation, Los Angeles is surely a candidate city for the world capital of death.

I'd like to thank my friend George Miller for suggesting

that I write this book a few years back and editing the manuscript with precision and care. I'd also like to thank Bella Shand for her continued support and expert editorial advice. I'd like to thank Marty Asher for bringing this book to Vintage and Jeff Alexander for his expert editing and countless improvements to the U.S. edition of *The Book of Dead Philosophers*. At Vintage, I'd also like to thank Daniel Yanez, Sloane Crosley and Russell Perreault.

The writing of the book was made possible by the generosity of the Getty Research Institute who hosted me as a scholar during 2006–7. I'd especially like to thank my research assistant, Courtney Biggs, who was very helpful in tracking down obscure sources and dealing with my vague bibliographical requests. I'd also like to thank Jack Miles, Peter Goodrich and Christopher Tradowsky for reading through my first draft and making valuable suggestions. The library staff at Getty were very helpful, too, and some of my colleagues passed on precious information, especially Silvia Berti, Todd Cronan, Bertram Kaschek and Thomas Lentes.

Outside the walls of the Getty ghetto, I'd like to thank Giovanni Levi for extensive help with Chinese philosophy, Shehab Ismail for some helpful leads on Medieval Islamic thinkers, Lisabeth During for a quotation that got me started, Genevieve Lloyd for a couple of memorable conversations, and James Plath, Cecilia Sjöholm, Anne Deneys-Tunney, Niklaus Largier, David McNeill, John Millbank, Mark Wrathall and Andrew Thomas. In particular, I'd like to thank Raymond Geuss for some extremely helpful corrections to my scholarship at a crucial stage of writing which have been silently inserted into the text. I'd like to thank the brilliant and assiduous students and auditors of my seminar "To Philosophize Is to Learn How to Die" at the New School for Social Research in the fall of 2007. Finally, I'd like to thank Jamieson Webster for pointing out to me, "Of course, the male obsessional is concerned with one question, whether they are alive or dead." Thanks to her, I feel slightly closer to the former than the latter. For the time being, at least.

# BIBLIOGRAPHY

## General Reference Works

Frequent reference has been made to the online academic edition of *Encyclopaedia Britannica*, which is full of small wonders and rarely unable to resolve a factual query (http://www .search.eb.com). In addition, I have made constant use of Paul Edwards's *The Encyclopedia of Philosophy* (8 vols., Macmillan, New York, 1967). Although there are other more recent and admirable encyclopaedias and dictionaries of philosophy available, the overall quality of the writing in Edwards remains unsurpassed in my view, particularly when it comes to the history of philosophy. Use has also been made of the *Stanford Encyclopedia of Philosophy* (http://plato.stanford.edu). Certain volumes of the *Dictionary of Literary Biography* (The Gale Group, Farmington Hills, 1978 onwards) have been extremely useful, especially Volume 90 on *German Writers in the Age of Goethe*, Volume 115 on *Medieval Philosophers*, Volume 129 on *Nineteenth-century German Writers*, Volume 252 on *British Philosophers 1500–1799* and Volume 279 on *American Philosophers 1950–2000*. Readers might also be amused to look at Hugh Mellor's "Causes of Death of Philosophers," which contains some witty entries, and some rather less so. Here are some nice examples of speculative causes of philosophers' deaths: "Adorno: Bad frankfurter. Bergson: Élan mortel. Fichte: Non-ego takeover. Heidegger: Not being in time. Luther: Diet of worms. Wittgenstein: Became the late Wittgenstein" (http://people .pwf.cam.ac.uk/dhm11/deathindex.html).

I cannot deny that I have dipped my toes, and sometimes both feet up to the knees, into the unruly waters of Wikipedia. This is a vast and growing resource, which is very uneven, not always to be trusted, but full of many fascinating articles and leads (http://en.wikipedia.org/wiki/Main_Page).

## General Bibliography

Abelard, Peter and Héloïse, *The Letters of Abelard and Héloïse*, trans. Betty Radice (Penguin, London, 1974).

Adams, H. P., *The Life and Writings of Giambattista Vico* (George Allen & Unwin, London, 1935).

Adorno, Theodor, *Minima Moralia: Reflections from Damaged Life*, trans. E. F. N. Jephcott (Verso, London, 1974).

Aldrich, Virgil C., "Messrs. Schlick and Ayer on Immortality," *The Philosophical Review*, vol. 47, no. 2 (March 1938), pp. 209–13.

Alexiou, Margaret, *The Ritual Lament in Greek Tradition*, 2nd Edn. (Rowman & Littlefield, Lanham, 2002).

Algalarrondo, Hervé, *Les Derniers Jours de Roland B.* (Stock, Paris, 2006).

Althusser, Louis, *L'Avenir dure longtemps. Les faits* (Stock/IMEC, Paris, 1992).

*American Piety in the 21st Century: New Insights to the Depths and Complexity of Religion in the US. Selected Findings from the Baylor Religion Survey* (Baylor University Press, Waco, TX, 2006).

Andrews, Carol (ed.), *The Ancient Egyptian Book of the Dead*, trans. Raymond O. Faulkner (British Museum Press, London, 1985).

Annas, Julia, and Jonathan Barnes, *The Modes of Scepticism: Ancient Texts and Modern Interpretations* (Cambridge University Press, Cambridge, 1985).

Arendt, Hannah, *The Life of the Mind*, 2 vols. (Harcourt Brace Jovanovich, New York, 1978).

Aristophanes, *The Clouds*, trans. W. Arrowsmith (The New American Library, New York, 1962).

Armstrong, A. H. (ed.), *The Cambridge History of Later Greek and Early Medieval Philosophy* (Cambridge University Press, Cambridge, 1967).

August, Eugene, *John Stuart Mill. A Mind at Large* (Charles Scribner's Sons, New York, 1975).

Augustine, *The Confessions of Saint Augustine*, trans. John K. Ryan (Image Books, New York, 1960).

Bacon, Francis, *Of Empire* (Penguin, London, 2005).

Bartelink, G. J. M., "Die literarische Gattung der 'Vita Antonii.' Struktur und Motive," *Vigiliae Christianae*, vol. 36, no. 1 (March 1982), pp. 38–62.

Bartelink, G. J. M. (ed.), *Vie d'Antoine* (Éditions du Cérf, Paris, 1994).

Baudrillard, Jean, *Cool Memories V 2000–2004*, trans. Chris Turner (Polity, Cambridge, 2006).

Becker, Ernest, *The Denial of Death* (Free Press Paperbacks, New York, 1997).

Benjamin, Walter, *Illuminations*, ed. Hannah Arendt, trans. Harry Zohn (Fontana/Collins, London, 1982).

Berkeley, George, *The Works of George Berkeley D.D.; Formerly the Bishop of Cloyne. Including his Posthumous Works*, ed. Alexander Campbell Fraser (Clarendon Press, Oxford, 1901).

Bernhard, Thomas, *The Voice Imitator*, trans. Kenneth J. Northcott (University of Chicago Press, Chicago & London, 1997).

Berti, Silvia, "Radicali ai margini: materialismo, libero pensiero e diritto al suicidio in Radicati di Passerano," *Rivista storica italiana*, vol. 3 (2004), pp. 794–811.

Boethius, *The Consolation of Philosophy*, trans. V. E. Watts (Penguin, London, 1969).

Boswell, James, *The Life of Samuel Johnson*, ed. Roger Ingpen, 2 vols. (Sturgis & Walton, New York, 1909).

Bowlby, John, *Charles Darwin: A New Life* (Norton, New York, 1992).

Bradatan, Costica, *The Other Bishop Berkeley: An Exercise in Reenchantment* (Fordham University Press, New York, 2006).

Brandt, Reinhard, *Philosophie in Bildern: Von Giorgione bis Magritte* (Dumont, Köln, 2000).

Briggs, Ward W. (ed.), *Dictionary of Literary Biography*, vol. 211, *Ancient Roman Writers* (Gale, Detroit, 1999).

Brochard, Victor, *Les Sceptiques grecs* (Vrin, Paris, 1932).

Burlaei, Gualteri, *Vita et Moribus Philosophorum* (Bibliothek des litterarischen Vereins in Stuttgart, Tübingen, 1886).

Butler, Alban, *Butler's Lives of the Saints*, ed. Michael Walsch (Harper, San Francisco, 1991).

Camus, Albert, *The Myth of Sisyphus*, trans. Justin O'Brien (Penguin, London, 1979).

Capaldi, Nicholas, *John Stuart Mill: A Biography* (Cambridge University Press, Cambridge, 2004).

Cave, Terence, *How to Read Montaigne* (Granta, London, 2007).

Chesterton, G. K., *Saint Thomas Aquinas* (Image Books, New York, 1956).

Chickering, Howell D., Jr., "Some Contexts for Bede's Death-Song," *PMLA*, vol. 91, no. 1 (January 1976), pp. 91–100.

Choron, Jacques, *Death and Western Thought* (Macmillan, New York, 1963).

Chuang Tzu, *The Inner Chapters*, trans. A. C. Graham (Hackett, Indianapolis & Cambridge, 2001).

Cicero, *De Finibus Bonorum et Malorum*, trans. H. Rackham (Harvard University Press, Cambridge, MA, 1971).

Cicero, *On Duties*, eds. M. T. Griffin and E. M. Atkins (Cambridge University Press, Cambridge, 1991).

Cicero, *Selected Letters*, trans. D. R. Shackleton Bailey (Penguin, London, 1986).

Clark, Ronald W., *The Survival of Charles Darwin: A Biography of a Man and an Idea* (Random House, New York, 1984).

Clement of Alexandria, *Stromateis*, trans. John Ferguson (Catholic University Press of America, Washington DC, 1991).

Cohen-Solal, Annie, *Sartre: A Life* (Heinemann, London, 1987).

Confucius, *The Analects*, trans. D. C. Lau (Penguin, London, 1979).

Critchley, Simon, *Very Little . . . Almost Nothing: Death, Philosophy and Literature*, 2nd Edn. (Routledge, London & New York, 2004).

Critchley, Simon, and Robert Bernasconi (eds.), *The Cambridge Companion to Levinas* (Cambridge University Press, Cambridge, 2002).

Critchley, Simon, and William R. Schroeder (eds.), *A Companion to Continental Philosophy* (Blackwell, Oxford, 1998).

Cronan, Todd, "Biological Poetry: Santayana's Aesthetics," *Qui Parle*, vol. 15, no. 1 (Fall/Winter 2004), pp. 115–45.

Crow, Carl, *Master Kung: The Story of Confucius* (Hamish Hamilton, London, 1937).

Cua, Antonio S., *Encyclopedia of Chinese Philosophy* (Routledge, New York & London, 2002).

Damrosch, Leo, *Jean-Jacques Rousseau: Restless Genius* (Houghton Mifflin, Boston & New York, 2005).

Davidson, Donald, *The Essential Davidson* (Clarendon Press, Oxford, 2006).

Deferrari, Roy J. (ed.), *Early Christian Biographies. Lives of St. Cyprian, by Pontius; St. Ambrose, by Paulinus; St. Augustine, by Possidius; St. Anthony, by St. Athanasius; St. Paul the First Hermit, St. Hilarion, and Malchus, by St. Jerome; St. Epiphanius, by Ennodius; with a Sermon on the Life of St. Honoratus, by St. Hilary*, trans. Roy J. Deferrari et al. (Catholic University of America Press, Washington DC, 1952).

Dematteis, Philip B., and Leemon B. McHenry (eds.), *Dictionary of Literary Biography*, vol. 279, *American Philosophers, 1950–2000* (Thomson Gale, Detroit, 2003).

Dematteis, Philip B., and Peter S. Fosl (eds.), *Dictionary of Literary Biography*, vol. 252, *British Philosophers, 1500–1799* (Gale, Detroit, 2002).

Deniker, P., and J.-P. Olié, "La Mort d'Hélène Althusser: un cas d'homicide altruiste rapporté par le mélancolique," *Annales Médico-Psychologiques*, vol. 152, no. 6 (1994), pp. 389–92.

Derrida, Jacques, *Mémoires: for Paul de Man*, trans. Cecile Lindsay, Jonathan Culler and Eduardo Cadava (Columbia University Press, New York, 1986).

Diels, Hermann, *I Dossographi Greci*, trans. L. Torraca (Cedam, Padua, 1961).

Diogenes Laertius, *The Lives of Eminent Philosophers*, trans. R. D. Hicks, 2 vols. (Harvard University Press, Cambridge, MA, 2005–6).

Döll, Helmit, "Hegels Tod," *Zeitschrift für ärztliche Fortbildung*, vol. 79, no. 5 (1985), pp. 217–19.

Edwards, Paul (ed.), *The Encyclopedia of Philosophy*, 8 vols. (Macmillan, New York, 1967).

Emerson, Ralph Waldo, *Selected Essays*, ed. Larzer Ziff (Penguin, London, 1982).

Enfield, William, *The History of Philosophy from the Earliest Times to the Beginning of the Present Century. Drawn up from Brucker's Historia Critica Philosophiæ*, 2 vols. (J. F. Dove, London, 1819).

Engels, Friedrich, "Funeral Oration for Marx," *Der Sozialdemokrat*, no. 13 (22 March, 1883).

Enright, D. J. (ed.), *The Oxford Book of Death* (Oxford University Press, Oxford & New York, 1983).

Epictetus, *Discourses and Enchiridion*, trans. T. Wentworth Higginson (Walter J. Black, New York, 1944).

Epicurus, *The Epicurus Reader: Selected Writings and Testimonia*, trans. B. Inwood and L. P. Gerson (Hackett, Indianapolis & Cambridge, 1994).

Erasmus of Rotterdam, *Praise of Folly and Letter to Martin Dorp*, trans. Betty Radice (Penguin, London, 1971).

Eribon, Didier, *Michel Foucault*, trans. Betsy Wing (Harvard University Press, Cambridge, MA, 1991).

Eusebius, *The History of the Church*, trans. G. A. Williamson and A. Louth (Penguin, London, 1989).

Evans-Wentz, W. Y. (ed.), *The Tibetan Book of the Dead* (Oxford University Press, Oxford & New York, 2000).

Feigl, Herbert, et al., "Homage to Rudolf Carnap," *PSA: Proceedings of the Biennial Meeting of the Philosophy of Science Association* (1970), pp. XI–LXVI.

Feuerbach, Ludwig, *The Fiery Brook: Selected Writings of Ludwig Feuerbach*, trans. Zawar Hanfi (Anchor Books, Garden City, NY, 1972).

Ficino, Marsilio, *The Letters of Marsilio Ficino*, vol. 3, trans. Language Department of the School of Economic Science, London (Shepheard-Walwyn, London, 1981).

Filodemo, *Storia dei Filosofi: La Stoà da Zenone a Panezio (Pherc. 1018)*, ed. Tiziano Dorandi (E. J. Brill, Leiden, 1994).

Fontenay, Elisabeth de, *Diderot: Reason and Resonance* (George Braziller, New York, 1982).

Freeman, Kathleen, *Ancilla to the Pre-Socratic Philosophers. A Complete Translation of the Fragments in Diels, Fragmente der Vorsokratiker* (Harvard University Press, Cambridge, MA, 1948).

Fung, Yu-Lan, *A History of Chinese Philosophy*, vol. 1 (Princeton University Press, Princeton, NJ, 1983).

Garrett, Don, *The Cambridge Companion to Spinoza* (Cambridge University Press, Cambridge & New York, 1996).

Gejrot, Tomas, "Descartes" sjukdom och död i Stockholm 1650," *Läkartidgningen*, vol. 63, no. 51 (1966), pp. 4917–21.

Géraud, M., and M. Bourgeois, "Friedrich Hölderlin (1770–1843). Réévaluation psychiatrique à l'occasion du cent cinquantenaire de sa mort," *Annales Médico-Psychologiques*, vol. 152, no. 3 (March 1994), pp. 173–8.

Gohlman, William E., *The Life of Ibn Sina* (State University of New York Press, Albany, 1974).

Goodman, Lenn E., *Avicenna* (Routledge, London, 1992).

Gouhier, Henri, *Blaise Pascal: Commentaires* (Vrin, Paris, 1966).

Graham, A. C., *Disputers of the Tao* (Open Court, Chicago, 1989).

Gramsci, Antonio, *A Gramsci Reader: Selected Writings 1916–1935*, ed. David Forgacs (Lawrence and Wishart, London, 1988).

Gregory of Nyssa, *The Life of St. Macrina*, trans. W. K. Lowther Clarke (The Society for Promoting Christian Knowledge, London, 1916).

Grondin, Jean, *Hans-Georg Gadamer: A Biography*, trans. Joel Weinsheimer (Yale University Press, New Haven & London, 2003).

Guthrie, W. K. C., *A History of Greek Philosophy*, 6 vols. (Cambridge University Press, Cambridge, 1977).

Hackett, Jeremiah (ed.), *Dictionary of Literary Biography*, vol. 115, *Medieval Philosophers* (Gale, Detroit & London, 1992).

Hägg, Thomas, and Philip Rousseau, *Greek Biography and Panegyric in Late Antiquity* (University of California Press, Berkeley & London, 2000).

Han, Feizi, *Basic Writings*, trans. B. Watson (Columbia University Press, New York, 2003).

Hannay, Alastair, *Kierkegaard: A Biography* (Cambridge University Press, Cambridge, 2003).

Hardin, James, and Christoph E. Schweitzer (eds.), *Dictionary of Literary Biography*, vol. 90, *German Writers in the Age of Goethe, 1789–1832* (Gale, Detroit, 1989).

Hardin, James, and Christoph E. Schweitzer (eds.), *Dictionary of Literary Biography*, vol. 94, *German Writers in the Age of Goethe: Sturm und Drang to Classicism* (Gale, Detroit, 1990).

Hardin, James, and Siegfried Mews (eds.), *Dictionary of Literary Biography*, vol. 129, *Nineteenth-Century German Writers, 1841–1900* (Gale, Detroit & London, 1993).

Hardin, James, and Siegfried Mews (eds.), *Dictionary of Literary Biography*, vol. 133, *Nineteenth-Century German Writers to 1840* (Gale, Detroit, 1993).

Hartman, Geoffrey, *The Fateful Question of Culture* (Columbia University Press, New York, 1997).

Havens, George R., "The Dates of Diderot's Birth and Death," *Modern Language Notes*, vol. 55, no. 1 (January 1940), pp. 31–5.

Heidegger, Martin, *Being and Time*, trans. John Macquarrie and Edward Robinson (Blackwell, Oxford, 1980).

Hippolytus, *Philosophumena or the Refutation of all Heresies*, 2 vols. (Society for Promoting Christian Knowledge, London, 1921).

Hoffmann, Yoel, *Japanese Death Poems* (Charles E.·Tuttle & Co., Rutland & Tokyo, 1986).

Hölderlin, Friedrich, *Der Tod des Empedokles*, ed. M. B. Benn (Oxford University Press, Oxford, 1968).

Hölderlin, Friedrich, *Essays and Letters on Theory*, trans. T. Pfau (SUNY Press, Albany, NY, 1988).

Hume, David, *Essays Moral, Political, and Literary*, ed. Eugene F. Miller (Liberty Fund, Indianapolis, 1987).

Hume, David, *On Suicide* (Penguin, London, 2005).

Israel, Jonathan I., *Radical Enlightenment. Philosophy and the Making of Modernity: 1650–1750* (Oxford University Press, Oxford, 2001).

Jacquette, Dale, "Schopenhauer on Death," *The Cambridge Companion to Schopenhauer*, ed. Chris Janaway, pp. 293–317 (Cambridge University Press, Cambridge, 1999).

Jäger, Lorenz, *Adorno: A Political Biography*, trans. Stewart Spencer (Yale University Press, New Haven & London, 2004).

James, William, *Some Problems of Philosophy: A Beginning of an Introduction to Philosophy* (University of Nebraska Press, Lincoln & London, 1996).

Janicaud, Dominique, *Philosophy in 30 Days*, trans. L. During (Granta, London, 2005).

Jankélévitch, Vladimir, *Penser la Mort* (Liana Levi, Paris, 1995).

Jansen, H. H., "Krankheit und Tod Friedrich Schillers," *Pneumologie*, vol. 55, Supplement 1 (March 2001), pp. S1–S5.

Jones, Ernest, *The Life and Work of Sigmund Freud*, vol. III, *The Last Phase 1919–1939* (Basic Books, New York, 1957).

Kapleau, Philip, *The Zen of Living and Dying* (Shambhala, Boston & London, 1998).

Kierkegaard, Søren, *The Sickness Unto Death: A Christian Psychological Exposition for Upbuilding and Awakening*, ed. and trans. Howard V. Hong and Edna H. Hong (Princeton University Press, Princeton, 1980).

Kübler-Ross, Elisabeth, *On Death and Dying: What the Dying Have to Teach Doctors, Nurses, Clergy, and Their Own Families* (Scribner, New York, 2003).

Kübler-Ross, Elisabeth, *Death: The Final Stage of Growth* (Scribner, New York, 1986).

Kühn, Rudolf A., "Schillers Tod," *Zeitschrift für ärztliche Fortbildung*, vol. 87, no. 12 (1993), pp. 1005–7.

Lanczik, M. H., "Die Psychose Friedrich Hölderlins aus der

Sicht Karl Leonhards," *Fortschritte der Neurologie Psychiatrie*, vol. 63, no. 5 (May 1995), pp. 206–8.

La Rochefoucauld, François de, *Maxims*, trans. Stuart D. Warner and Stéphane Douard (St. Augustine's Press, South Bend, IN, 2001).

Lavi, Shai J., *The Modern Art of Dying* (Princeton University Press, Princeton, NJ, 2005).

Leaman, Oliver, *Moses Maimonides* (Routledge, London & New York, 1990).

Lee, R. Warden, "Grotius: The Last Phase, 1635–45," *Transactions of the Grotius Society*, vol. 31 (1945), pp. 193–215.

*Leibniz 1646–1716. Aspects de l'homme et de l'oeuvre* (Éditions Aubier-Montaigne, Paris, 1968).

Leibniz, Gottfried Wilhelm, *Protogaea*, trans. Claudine Cohen and Andre Wakefield (University of Chicago Press, Chicago, 2007).

Liddell, Henry George, and Robert Scott (eds.), *A Greek-English Lexicon* (Clarendon Press, Oxford, 1968).

Locke, John, *An Essay Concerning Human Understanding*, ed. A. S. Pringle-Pattison (Clarendon Press, Oxford, 1934).

Long, A. A. (ed.), *The Cambridge Companion to Early Greek Philosophy* (Cambridge University Press, Cambridge, 1999).

Long, A. A., and D. N. Sedley, *The Hellenistic Philosophers*, 2 vols. (Cambridge University Press, Cambridge, 1987).

Lucian, "Dialogues of the Dead," in *Lucian*, vol. 7, trans. M. D. MacLeod (Harvard University Press, Cambridge, MA, 1961).

Lucretius, *On the Nature of the Universe*, trans. R. E. Latham (Penguin, London, 1994).

Lyotard, Jean-François, *The Confession of Augustine*, trans. Richard Beardsworth (Stanford University Press, Stanford, CA, 2000).

Macey, David, *Frantz Fanon. A Life* (Granta, London, 2000).

Machiavelli, Niccolò, *The Prince*, trans. George Bull (Penguin, London, 1981).

MacIntyre, Alasdair, *Edith Stein: A Philosophical Prologue* (Continuum, London, 2006).

Maimonides (Moses ben Maimon), *Ethical Writings of Maimonides*, ed. Raymond L. Weiss and Charles E. Butterworth (Dover Publications, New York, 1975).

Mansfeld, J., and D. T. Runia, *Aëtiana: The Method and Intellectual Context of a Doxographer* (Brill, Leiden, 1997).

Marcel, Le Chanoine, *La Mort de Diderot d'après des documents inédits* (Libraire ancienne Honoré Champion, Paris, 1925).

Marcus Aurelius, *Meditations*, trans. Maxwell Staniforth (Penguin, London, 2004).

McAlister, Linda Lopez, *Hypatia's Daughters: Fifteen Hundred Years of Women Philosophers* (Indiana University Press, Bloomington & Indianapolis, 1996).

McCormick, John, *George Santayana: A Biography* (Knopf, New York, 1987).

McDermott, Timothy, *How to Read Aquinas* (Granta Books, London, 2007).

McKenna, Kristine, and Jacques Derrida, "The Three Ages of Jacques Derrida. An interview with the father of Deconstruction," *L.A. Weekly*, 8–14 November, 2002.

Mei, Yi-Pao, *Motse, The Neglected Rival of Confucius* (Arthur Probsthain, London, 1934).

Ménage, Gilles, *The History of Women Philosophers*, trans. Beatrice H. Zedler (Lanham, New York & London, 1984).

Merleau-Ponty, Maurice, *Signs*, trans. Richard C. McCleary (Northwestern University Press, Evanston, IL, 1964).

Mettrie, Julien Offray de La, *Textes Choisis*, ed. Marcelle Tisserand (Éditions Sociales, Paris, 1954).

Metzger, Bruce M., and Roland E. Murphy (eds.), *The New Oxford Annotated Bible with Apocryphal/Deuterocanonical Books* (Oxford University Press, New York, 1994).

Mill, John Stuart, *Autobiography of John Stuart Mill* (Columbia University Press, New York, 1924).

Monk, Ray, *Bertrand Russell: The Spirit of Solitude, 1872–1921* (The Free Press, New York, 1996).

Monk, Ray, *Bertrand Russell: The Ghost of Madness, 1921–1970* (The Free Press, New York, 2001).

Monk, Ray, *Ludwig Wittgenstein: The Duty of Genius* (Penguin, London, 1991).

Montaigne, Michel de, *Essays*, vol. 1, trans. John Florio (J. M. Dent, London, 1965).

Montaigne, Michel de, *The Complete Essays of Montaigne*, trans. Donald M. Frame (Stanford University Press, Stanford, CA, 1976).

Moody, Raymond, *Life after Life* (Bantam, New York, 1976).

Muldoon, Paul, *Madoc: A Mystery* (Farrar, Straus and Giroux, New York, 1991).

Müller-Doohm, Stefan, *Adorno: A Biography*, trans. Rodney Livingstone (Polity, Cambridge, 2005).

Nagel, Thomas, "Death," *Nous*, vol. 4, no. 1 (February 1970), pp. 73–80.

Netton, Ian Richard, *Al-Farabi and His School* (Routledge, London & New York, 1992).

Nietzsche, Friedrich, *Ecce Homo: How One Becomes What One Is*, trans. R. J. Hollingdale (Penguin, London, 1980).

Pascal, *Pensées*, trans. A. J. Krailsheimer (Penguin, London, 1966).

Pascal, Gilbert, *The Life of Mr. Paschal* (J. Bettenham, London, 1744).

Paul, *The Writings of St. Paul*, ed. Wayne A. Meeks (W. W. Norton & Company, New York, 1972).

Petronius, *Satyricon*, ed. & trans R. Bracht Branham (Everyman, London, 1996), p. 66.

Phillips, Adam, *Darwin's Worms* (Basic Books, New York, 2000).

Philostratus, and Eunapius, *Lives of the Sophists. Lives of Philosophers*, trans. Wilmer Cave Wright (Harvard University Press, Cambridge, MA, 2005).

Plato, *Euthyphro, Apology, Crito, Phaedo, Phaedrus*, trans. Harold North Fowler (Harvard University Press, Cambridge, MA, 1914).

Plato, *The Last Days of Socrates*, trans. Hugh Tredennick (Penguin, London, 1954).

Plotinus, *Porphyry on Plotinus. Ennead I*, trans. A. H. Armstrong (Harvard University Press, Cambridge, MA, 1966).

Plutarch, *Moralia: Index* (Harvard University Press, Cambridge, MA, 2004).

Plutarch, *The Lives of the Noble Grecians and Romans*, trans. John Dryden, rev. Arthur Hugh Clough (Modern Library, New York, 1992).

Pollock, Frederick, *Spinoza: His Life and Philosophy* (Duckworth, London, 1899).

Quincey, Thomas de, *On Murder*, ed. Robert Morrison (Oxford University Press, Oxford, 2006).

Quincey, Thomas de, *The English Mail-Coach and Other Essays* (J. M. Dent & Sons, London, 1961).

Ricoeur, Paul, *On Translation*, trans. Eileen Brennan (Routledge, London & New York, 2006).

Rogers, Ben, *A. J. Ayer: A Life* (Vintage, London, 2000).

Rogow, Arnold A., *Thomas Hobbes. Radical in the Service of Reaction* (W. W. Norton & Company, New York & London, 1986).

Rosenzweig, Franz, *The Star of Redemption*, trans. William W. Hallo (Notre Dame Press, Notre Dame, IN, 1985).

Roudinesco, Elisabeth, *Jacques Lacan* (Columbia University Press, New York, 1997).

Rousseau, Jean-Jacques, *Reveries of the Solitary Walker*, trans. Peter France (Penguin, London, 2004).

Rowley, Hazel, *Tête-à-Tête: The Tumultuous Lives and Loves of Simone de Beauvoir & Jean-Paul Sartre* (HarperCollins, New York, 2005).

Russell, Bertrand, *Why I Am Not a Christian and Other Essays on Religion and Related Subjects*, ed. Paul Edwards (George Allen & Unwin, London, 1957).

Rzepka, Charles J., "De Quincey and Kant," *PMLA*, vol. 115, no. 1 (January 2000), pp. 93–4.

Safranski, Rüdiger, *Martin Heidegger: Between Good and Evil*, trans. Ewald Osers (Harvard University Press, Cambridge, MA, 1999).

Sandford, Stella, *How to Read Beauvoir* (Granta Books, London, 2006).

Scala, Spencer M. di, "Giovanni Gentile: Una Biografia," *The Journal of Modern History*, vol. 70, no. 1 (March 1998), pp. 210–11.

Schilpp, Paul Arthur (ed.), *The Philosophy of Rudolf Carnap* (Open Court, La Salle, IL, 1887).

Schopenhauer, Arthur, *On the Suffering of the World*, trans. R. J. Hollingdale (Penguin, London, 2004).

Seneca, *On the Shortness of Life*, trans. C. D. N. Costa (Penguin, London, 1997).

Shapiro, Herman (ed.), *Medieval Philosophy. Selected Readings from Augustine to Buridan* (Modern Library, New York, 1964).

Spinoza, Benedict de, *Ethics*, trans. E. Curley (Penguin, London, 1996).

Stanley, Thomas, *The History of Philosophy*, 3 vols. (Garland, New York & London, 1978).

Stevens, Wallace, *The Palm at the End of the Mind* (Vintage, New York, 1967).

Stone, I. F., *The Trial of Socrates* (Picador, London, 1989).

Stratton, George Malcolm, *Theophrastus and the Greek Physiological Psychology before Aristotle* (George Allen & Unwin, London, 1917).

Taylor, M., and D. Lammerts, *Grave Matters* (Reaktion, London, 2002).

Tenneman, Gottlieb, *Geschichte der Philosophie*, 11 vols. (Leipzig, 1789–1819).

*The Three Impostors*, trans. Alcofribas Nasier, http://www.infidels .org/library/historical/unknown/three_impostors.html.

Tiedemann, Dietrich, *Geist der spekulativen Philosophie von Thales bis Berkeley*, 6 vols. (Marburg, 1791–7).

Urvoy, Dominique, *Ibn Rushd (Averroes)* (Routledge, London, 1991).

Voltaire, *Miracles and Idolatry*, trans. Theodore Besterman (Penguin, London, 2005).

Ward, Benedicta, *The Sayings of the Desert Fathers* (Mowbray, London & Oxford, 1975).

Weil, Simone, *Cahiers, Volume 3, Février 1942–Juin 1942, La porte du transcendant*, établis et présentés par Alyette Degrâces, Marie-Annette Fourneyron, Florence de Lussy et al. (Gallimard, Paris, 2002).

Weinberger, Eliot, "Empedocles and Valmiki," *Fulcrum*, no. 5 (2006), pp. 33–8.

White, Caroline (trans.), *Early Christian Lives* (Penguin, London, 1998).

Wilkes, Johannes, "Friedrich Nietzsche: Die Geschichte seiner Krankengeschichte," *Psychiatrische Praxis*, vol. 27, no. 3 (April 2000), pp. 147–50.

Williams, Rowan, *The Poems of Rowan Williams* (William B. Eerdmans, Grand Rapids, MI, & Cambridge, 2002).

Wolf, A. (ed.), *The Oldest Biography of Spinoza* (Kennikat Press, Port Washington, NY, & London, 1927).

Xenophon, *Memorabilia & Oeconomicus*, trans. E. C. Marchant, *Symposium & Apology*, trans. O. J. Todd (Harvard University Press, Cambridge, MA, 1979).

Yates, Frances A., *The Art of Memory* (Ark, London, 1984).

Young-Bruehl, Elisabeth, *Hannah Arendt: For Love of the World* (Yale University Press, New Haven & London, 1982).

Zourabichvili, François, *Le vocabulaire de Deleuze* (Ellipses, Paris, 2003).

ILLUSTRATION CREDITS

Courtesy of Smithsonian Institution Libraries, Washington, D.C.: 7, 109, 127, 158.

Photograph © Erik Anderson: 37.

Photographs © Bettmann/CORBIS: 197, 207, 239.

Photographs © Hulton-Deutsch/CORBIS: 219, 226.